THE NEXT AMERICAN ECONOMY

Nation, State, and Markets
in an Uncertain World

SAMUEL GREGG

THE

NEXT

AMERICAN ECONOMY

Nation, State, and Markets
in an Uncertain World

SAMUEL GREGG

New York · London

First American edition published in 2022 by Encounter Books,
an activity of Encounter for Culture and Education, Inc.,
a nonprofit, tax-exempt corporation.
Encounter Books website address: www.encounterbooks.com

Manufactured in the United States and printed on
acid-free paper. The paper used in this publication meets
the minimum requirements of ANSI/NISO Z39.48-1992
(R 1997) (*Permanence of Paper*).

FIRST AMERICAN EDITION

LIBRARY OF CONGRESS CATALOGING-IN-PUBLICATION DATA

Names: Gregg, Samuel, 1969- author.
Title: The next American economy: nation, state, and markets in an
   uncertain world / Samuel Gregg.
Description: First American edition. | New York, New York: Encounter
   Books, 2022. | Includes bibliographical references and index. | Identifiers: LCCN 2022000078 (print) |
LCCN 2022000079 (ebook) | ISBN
   9781641772761 (hardcover) | ISBN 9781641772778 (ebook)
Subjects: LCSH: United States--Economic conditions--2009- | United
   States--Economic policy--2009- | United States--Commerce. | Economic
   stabilization--United States.
Classification: LCC HC106.84 .G75 2022 (print) | LCC HC106.84 (ebook) |
   DDC 330.973--dc23/eng/20220114
LC record available at https://lccn.loc.gov/2022000078
LC ebook record available at https://lccn.loc.gov/2022000079

1 2 3 4 5 6 7 8 9 20 22

The greatness of America lies not in being more enlightened than any other nation, but rather in her ability to repair her faults.

ALEXIS DE TOCQUEVILLE

CONTENTS

PROLOGUE

In December 2016, I was speaking at a conference in London and the discussion inevitably gravitated towards the topic of Donald Trump's election as forty-fifth president of the United States of America. It meant, I commented, that a free trade skeptic would be in the White House. At that point, a young French economist turned to me and said, "*Mon ami*, I thought that free trade was a done-deal.... Apparently, it isn't. We took far too much for granted."

As it turns out, it wasn't just free trade with which many Americans were expressing frustration. A systematic questioning of the emphasis placed upon free markets in the American economy since the 1980s was underway, and not simply from progressives who looked to the New Deal or European social democracy for inspiration. Some of the market economy's most articulate critics were to be found on the American right. In some instances, positions being advocated by some conservatives—implementation of industrial policy, mandating seats for employees on company boards, expanding the use of tariffs, etc.—bore more than a passing resemblance to stances adopted by progressives like Senators Bernie Sanders and Elizabeth Warren.

This corrosion of a pro-market consensus once shared by many American politicians, opinion-shapers, and citizens meant that the U.S. economy's future was now up for discussion to an extent that had not been evident since the 1970s. That future forms the subject matter of this book.

For good reason, the words "America" and "Capitalism" are synonymous in many people's minds. Yet some Americans today plainly doubt that the market economy—economic arrangements characterized by entrepreneurship, free exchange, competition at home, free trade abroad, strong property rights, robust rule of law, and a constitutional order that defines and limits the government's economic responsibilities—is the optimal way forward for the U.S. economy. Other Americans say that they want less government in their lives and that markets should be allowed to work their magic, but then insist in the next breath that their particular community, business, town, or state merits federal assistance.

Since the mid-2010s, I have found myself embroiled in debates with people across the political spectrum who hold that America's economy requires even more regulation and intervention beyond the already extensive role played by government in that economy. Sometimes the conversation has been with younger Americans who think that some type of socialism must be America's economic future. But I have also had Wall Street executives tell me that "stakeholder capitalism"—an idea that draws upon an older economic model known as "corporatism"—should replace what they regard as an economy too fixated on profits.

In other instances, some conservatives have informed me that the time has come for interventionist measures, often labelled "populist" or "economic nationalist," to be used to deliver specific economic outcomes. Such goals range from helping specific groups who, such conservatives claim, have been left behind by economic globalization, to bolstering America's place as a sovereign nation in a world in which great power competition is magnifying. They and others are especially troubled by the rise of a China governed by a nationalist-communist authoritarian regime intent on displacing America on the international stage. This alone, many Americans aver, necessitates a serious rethink of economic policy in general and trade policy in particular.

This skepticism about free markets could not be more removed from the atmosphere which prevailed in America following Communism's fall in Eastern Europe and the Soviet Union. The great rival to capitalism had failed comprehensively, and the subsequent rhetoric of many American thinkers and policymakers of the time suggested belief in a certain irresistibility to the advance of free markets. Many were also convinced that the case for mixed economies associated with the British economist John Maynard Keynes was faltering, perhaps in a decisive fashion.

That world seems very far away today. Instead advocates of market economies find their ideas subject to fierce critique on economic, political, and moral grounds, and they are derided by some of their opponents as "market fundamentalists." Many defenders of markets have indeed couched their responses primarily in economic terms. Much of the debate, after all, pivots arounds questions of economic cause-and-effect and disputed facts about what is happening in the American economy and society more generally. But for all its force, the economic case for free markets

cannot resolve all the apprehensions that many Americans have
about their country's future—one which cannot and should not be
reduced to economics. Alas, when some free marketers do attempt
to inject more explicitly normative and political dimensions into
their defense of free economies, many of them seem unable to
move beyond frameworks which absolutize individual autonomy
and see no common values beyond utility or ever-expanding rights
grounded in self-expression.

Yet however insufficient such answers may be to the criticisms
expressed by assorted progressives, economic nationalists, and
other advocates of greater state intervention, I regard the diagnoses of the economic problems facing America and the proposals for
change offered by market skeptics as flawed—often deeply so. In
some instances, implementation of their preferred policies would
worsen some of the problems they seek to address. Considerable
space is given in this book to explaining why.

That said, today's critics of markets have performed an important service. They have forced those like myself who regard free
markets as the most optimal set of economic arrangements for
America to restate, once again, the case for markets but in a manner which recognizes that we are not living in the 1980s, 1990s,
2000s, or 2010s anymore. Over the past two decades, some of the
most noteworthy changes in America's political landscape have
been associated with economic traumas like the 2008 financial crisis and Great Recession. Remaking the case for markets in America cannot disregard such realities. Nor can major developments
in the geopolitical sphere be ignored. As nation-state competition
intensifies across the globe, issues of *national* sovereignty, *national*

cohesion, and, above all, *national* identity have become key reference points around which international politics flow. To pretend
otherwise is quixotic.

It's one thing to outline compelling policy positions. Market
liberals are highly skilled at that. But such arguments are insufficient in an age in which questions like "Who are my people?"
or "Where do I belong?" have become omnipresent in Western
countries. People voted for Brexit for many reasons, but a desire
to reassert national sovereignty and therefore a sense of belonging
to one group rather than another was one strand uniting people
who otherwise disagreed about many other issues. So too, Donald
Trump's 2016 electoral victory signified many Americans' desire
to prioritize what they saw as America's needs over the globalist
concerns that they believed had preoccupied their political leaders
for far too long.

Recognizing this underscores the need to persuade Americans
that markets aren't just about economic growth. They can also help
express and bolster an understanding of America as a *commercial
republic*. This is an ideal of a republican form of political community that integrates a strong case for economic liberty into a vision
of America as a free and commercially orientated sovereign nation
in a world in which other sovereign nations are pursuing what they
regard as their national interests.

It is also the ideal which, I believe, represents that the surest
political underpinning for an American economy that takes free
markets and their institutional supports seriously. As readers will
discover, it brings together an understanding of the strong *empirical* case for free markets and limited government, a commitment

to the *moral* habits associated with commercial society, the conviction that these are *good* for Americans as a sovereign *nation*, and the argument that this is ultimately faithful to the *principles* which were given powerful expression in America during the Founding period.

Before beginning our journey, I want to make two points about this book's primary audiences and its approach to the topic.

First, this book is not written for specialists. Since the first great economic debates that occupied Americans' attention in the lead-up to the Constitutional Convention of 1787, American public opinion has mattered as much as that of politicians and intellectuals in the determination of economic policy. Weighty thinkers anxious to effect significant economic change in America, such as Alexander Hamilton or Milton Friedman, have always understood the need to communicate their ideas to broader audiences. Hence, I have minimized the use of economic jargon and entered into the particulars of economic policy only as far as necessary.

The devil is indeed in the details. Yet the reshaping of economic policy in Western nations from the 1930s onwards in the direction of greater government intervention would not have occurred without the broad direction in which economics was taken by John Maynard Keynes and the subsequent popularization of his theories. The same can be said of the broad shift towards market liberalization in the 1980s. The precise details of the 1981 budgets implemented by the Reagan administration in America and the Thatcher Government in Britain were important. But these measures would not have transpired without some intellectuals challenging the postwar Keynesian consensus over preceding decades, reframing free market ideas to meet twentieth-century needs, and, most importantly, disseminating the conclusions of that rethinking to wider audiences. Similarly, the U.S. economy's future will depend heavily upon ideas expounded in intellectual settings but then communicated in the wider public square: one which includes books and magazines but now extends to the even more easily accessed locales provided, for better or worse, by social media.

My second point concerns the focus of this book. It is about political economy rather than politics or economics. *L'économie politique* is a term which acquired traction in the eighteenth century and was used to describe three things. One was the new social science which related subjects that we regard as belonging to economics, like wealth and poverty, to law, government, and culture—and vice-versa. The phrase also denoted an integration of moral and political philosophy with the powerful analytical tools provided by the emerging economic way of thinking so singularly expressed in Adam Smith's *Wealth of Nations*. It thus brought together normative and political concerns with attention to information that is, to varying degrees, empirically verifiable. Lastly, political economy was understood by Smith and his friend David Hume to be what they called "the science of the legislator." In short, the knowledge furnished by this integration of moral, political, and economic inquiry needed to be brought to bear upon society by statesmen and governments in the interests of its improvement. That was the ultimate point of the exercise.

Political economy in all three senses drives the approach to the topics explored in these pages. Choices about America's economic future involve reflection on empirically verifiable economic logic and information. But this same reasoning and knowledge is not a sufficient basis for American citizens and policymakers to make economic decisions. Such economic choices also have a normative and political dimension. We do "truck and barter," as Smith noted. We remain, however, moral and political animals, and morality and politics extend, as Smith affirmed, beyond utility and efficiency issues. Humans exist within numerous associations and communities—families, schools, religious groups, businesses, towns, and nations—many of which are not economic in their nature or ends. Judgments about the direction of America's economy inevitably touch on issues like freedom, justice, and the common good. The last of these is understood throughout these pages not as an aggregated total of particular interests in American society but rather as those conditions that help Americans as individuals and communities realize important goods in all spheres of human endeavor.

Such is the lens through which we will engage our topic. It may therefore disappoint not only those who regard economics as providing, at best, supplemental information that statesmen need to consider, but also those reluctant to think beyond the contours of economics. It is a lens, however, that bears more than a passing resemblance to that through which many key American Founders viewed the world. And for Americans, that should surely matter.

CHAPTER 1

IT ALL
FALLS DOWN

The persons who now govern the resolutions of what they call their Continental Congress, feel in themselves at this moment a degree of importance which, perhaps, the greatest subjects in Europe scarce feel. From shopkeepers, tradesmen, and attorneys, they are become statesmen and legislators, and are employed in contriving a new form of government for an extensive empire, which, they flatter themselves, will become, and which, indeed, seems very likely to become, one of the greatest and most formidable that ever was in the world.

—ADAM SMITH

More than one person has remarked upon the providential character of one of the most important books ever written, *The Wealth of Nations*, being published the same year as that most consequential of modern political statements: the Declaration of Independence. The book's author, Adam Smith, widely regarded as the father of modern economics and the first great theorist of how a modern capitalist economy and commercial society should work, paid attention to what was transpiring in Britain's North American colonies. He even ventured that giving the colonies their independence might ensure that the tensions between them and Britain around the issues of taxation, trade, and sovereignty did not spill over into outright war.[1]

Smith believed that a great future lay before the colonies. He also recognized the ambition of America's Founders to create a new type of polity. So it was that, following the American Revolution and the Constitution's eventual drafting and ratification, the new country quickly emerged in the 1790s as a republic committed to constitutional government and in which social life as well as domestic and foreign policy was heavily influenced by business and trade. A century later, America surpassed Britain to become the world's biggest economy.

Few countries have been as defined by the character of their economy as the United States. To the world, America has come to mean capitalism. There have been occasions in America's history, however, when that economy came asunder. The Great Depression, for example, brought America to its economic knees and resulted in one of the federal government's greatest peacetime extensions into the economy in the form of the New Deal.

Cataclysmic events like the Depression leave an impression. Rightly or wrongly, narratives develop which become difficult to displace. This was certainly the case with the 2008 financial crisis and the subsequent global economic downturn known today as the Great Recession. The images of Alan Greenspan, the retired Chair of the Federal Reserve famed for his confidence in the power of markets, testifying before Congress that those same markets had broken down in the wake of a crisis emanating from the financial sector, shocked Americans. The reputational damage done to free markets proceeding from the freezing-up of credit markets, the plunging of stock and housing prices, and a sharp uptick in unemployment was incalculable. It also induced a great deal of soul-searching among Americans about the future character of the U.S. economy. The sight of the federal government and the Federal Reserve bailing out major banks and businesses and thereby (or so many believed) saving American capitalism from collapse created space for many to argue that this latest expansion of the state into the economy vindicated the need for government to take on more expansive roles in American economic life on a more permanent basis.

Doubts and debates about the future of American capitalism were not confined to the United States' shores. The Chinese political philosopher Jiwei Ci suggests that the financial crisis and America's struggle to get it under control left an impression upon many senior Chinese government officials.[2] Questions were raised in their minds about whether America would remain the world's economic superpower, what that meant for China's limited opening to commercial freedom,[3] and how China should deal with America and the world in general. Former paramount leader Deng Xiaoping's insistence that "hiding strengths, biding time"[4] was necessary to ensure that China's rise did not alarm other nations now seemed dated. For many Chinese leaders, the biding of time was over. It was time for assertion.

Viewed from this perspective, domestic economic problems in America helped spark new challenges from abroad. But they have also led to a sustained and often polemical debate about America's economic future that shattered assumptions which had been in place since the 1980s about *who* stood *where* on matters of economic policy, and *why* they did so. The political landscape that will eventually emerge from the sharpening of these disputes in our time is by no means certain.

To my mind, the future for the American economy amounts to a choice between two general systems. The first is what I will call a form of "state capitalism."

State capitalism has been used to describe systems ranging from command economies in which the government controls most businesses, to situations in which the government dominates the allocation of credit throughout the economy. Broadly speaking, the state capitalism that I have in mind is an economy in which the government, often with the aid of experts and technocrats and sometimes in partnership with different interest groups, engages in extensive interventions into the economy from the top down. The goal is not to extinguish private property and free exchange. Rather it is to shape and even direct many activities within the economy through state action to realize very specific economic and political objectives.

This type of state capitalism as it manifests itself in America is particularly focused on achieving greater economic security for specific groups. A certain degree of such security provided by the state, it is held, is something that any self-respecting nation morally owes to all its citizens, whether as a matter of solidarity between fellow Americans or by reference to a social compact. Markets, we are told, do not adequately meet some communities' economic needs and, in some instances, are undermining their well-being. That emphasis on security also extends to foreign affairs. The U.S. government, it is held, must act to ensure that our economy enhances rather than undermines national security. The means for realizing these domestic and geopolitical ends include protectionist measures, the use of industrial policy, and mandating particular ways in which businesses, other social groups, and the state should interact.

The alternative choice to this form of state capitalism in America today is a free market economy. By this, however, I have something quite specific in mind, which includes but extends beyond the classic economic arguments for markets. My thesis is that making the case for free markets in twenty-first-century America must involve rooting such an economy in what some of its most influential Founders thought should be America's political destiny: that is, a modern commercial republic. Politically, this ideal embodies the idea of a self-governing sovereign state in which the governed are regularly consulted; in which the use of state power is limited by strong commitments to constitutionalism, the rule of law, and private property rights; and whose citizens consciously embrace the specific habits and disciplines needed to sustain such a republic. These settings complement and support an economy characterized by powerful bottom-up entrepreneurial drives and in which businesses are constantly exposed to the discipline of consumer preferences expressed through open and free competition. The citizens of this republic also trade freely with each other and the rest of the world while being fully cognizant that there are no utopias in this life, particularly in the realm of foreign affairs. Like the state capitalism option, this set of political and economic arrangements is underpinned by particular normative commitments. One is to freedom and an emphasis on the idea that justice involves limiting arbitrary power. Another is the conviction that the spread of dynamic commerce is central (though insufficient) to the advancement of important virtues and civilization more generally.

Granted, there are varying ways in which each of these two alternatives can be expressed. Nonetheless I believe that America faces a basic choice between a form of state capitalism and the type of market economy outlined in these pages. This need for Americans to make such a decision about its economic future did not emerge from a void. To grasp the "hows" and "whys" underlying these circumstances, we need to go back to a different time: one in which America and the world rediscovered free markets.

HOW THE
PENDULUM SWUNG

Just as the Great Depression's causes remain disputed among economic historians, the same lack of resolution seems forever likely to characterize debates about the events of 2008. Some insist that bankers behaving badly and insufficient regulation were the prime culprits. Others blame serious monetary policy errors by the Federal Reserve as well as federal housing policies enacted in the late 1990s with cross-party support. What's not debatable is that the financial crisis and subsequent recession marked the end of an almost forty-year stretch in which the pendulum in economic rhetoric, ideas, and policy had swung towards liberalization of the American economy and global markets more generally.

That shift began in the 1970s, an unhappy time for the United States. The despair had an economic face. Increasing unemployment, low growth, and high inflation seemed intractable. President Richard Nixon's response to this crisis was textbook interventionist. His Executive Order 11615, issued on August 15, 1971, imposed a prices and wages freeze for ninety days. This was the first time that such measures had been adopted in America since World War II. The same order applied an import surcharge of 10 percent to try to prevent American products being hurt by expected exchange-rate fluctuations, and it terminated the U.S. dollar's last remaining link with the gold standard. Such measures suggested a nation and leadership unsure that a prosperous future lay ahead of it. Accentuated by a significant recession between 1973 and 1975, the torpor of declinism was captured by President Jimmy Carter's reference to "growing doubt about the meaning of our own lives and in the loss of a unity of purpose for our nation" in what came to be called his "malaise speech" of 1979.[5]

These unpromising circumstances did nevertheless create an opening. Throughout the 1970s, the consensus which had dominated economic policy throughout the Western world since the late 1940s came under serious pressure for the first time in decades. There had always been intellectuals, journalists, and business leaders opposed to the type of mixed and managed economies associated with British economist John Maynard Keynes and the brand of economic thinking that became an orthodoxy in the economics profession and the world's finance ministries and central banks after World War II. Critics of that orthodoxy were treated as outliers whose views had been discredited by the Great Depression. In the 1970s, however, economic dissidents like F.A. Hayek and Milton Friedman—neither of whom were young men—suddenly found themselves in demand both in America and in countries as distant as Chile and Australia. A counter-revolution in ideas had begun.

This sea-change achieved political expression with the Conservative Party's electoral victory in Britain in 1979 and Ronald Reagan's defeat of Jimmy Carter in the 1980 presidential election. The subsequent shift away from dirigiste policies in Britain and America became global in its scope and crossed ideological lines. Some of the most far-reaching economic liberalizations involving the dismantling of tariffs, curtailment of industrial policies, labor market reform, and privatization of state assets were implemented by center-left governments in Australia and New Zealand.

It would be an error to claim that these events meant that America and other Western countries somehow abandoned, holus-bolus, the Keynesian legacy. Governments still referred to their ability to "manage" multi-trillion-dollar economies. The state continued to control directly or indirectly large percentages of Gross Domestic Product (GDP). Major features of postwar economic life, like nationalized healthcare in Britain, remained largely untouched. But the momentum of ideas—"the climate of opinion"—was *with* market liberalism. Supporters of widespread intervention found themselves playing defense. Nothing symbolized this more than a Democrat president, Bill Clinton—heir to the party of Franklin Delano Roosevelt's New Deal and Lyndon Baines Johnson's Great Society—stating in his 1996 State of the Union address that "the era of big government is over"[6] and subsequently signing a bill passed by a Republican-led Congress to enact welfare reforms considered unthinkable only twenty years before.

In retrospect, the early-1990s represented the high-water mark of post-1970s market liberalism in America. From this point onwards, a decline in its influence began, including among that segment of the population where it had gained considerable traction: conservative Americans. Fissures started emerging between many of the American Right's generals and some of the armies which they thought they led. These differences burst into the open in 1992 and gravitated around issues that touched upon America's relationship with the rest of the world that in turn had important implications for domestic policy. The figure who brought these questions to the forefront of debate was the conservative thinker, journalist, and politician Patrick J. Buchanan.

The two matters on which Buchanan focused his attention during his primary challenge to a sitting president of his own party were immigration and trade policy. The latter issue garnered attention as a consequence of the negotiations for the North American Free Trade Agreement (NAFTA) which concluded that year. Buchanan insisted that NAFTA would undermine the well-being of blue-collar Americans and destabilize the middle-class. That same drum was beat by the Texas billionaire Ross Perot, who memorably claimed that liberalizing trade between Canada, Mexico, and America meant that "you are going to hear a giant sucking sound of jobs being pulled out of this country." Many Americans came to embrace that motif, despite the fact that unemployment stayed low throughout the 1990s and 2000s until the Great Recession. In 1998, Buchanan even claimed that "the hidden cost of free trade" included "broken homes, uprooted families, vanished dreams, delinquency, vandalism, [and] crime."[7]

NAFTA was eventually approved by Congress in 1993 with Republican and Democrat support. But a fuse had been lit. The fire flared up again in 1999 when the Seattle meeting of the World Trade Organization (WTO) was overshadowed by the presence of thousands of protesters, many of whom were Americans, ranging from environmentalists to trade unionists. Whatever their differences, these groups were as one in their negative assessment of economic globalization's impact on Americans.

Underlying the trade debate, however, were even more fundamental disagreements about what type of country America should be—and even if it had a future as a nation-state. In 1984, the *Wall Street Journal* editorial page, then led by Robert L. Bartley, editorialized in favor of a constitutional amendment stating, "There shall be open borders." In 2001, Bartley reminded readers of this in an article advocating discussion of open borders between NAFTA nations.[8] Pondering those claims in 2018, Buchanan insisted that they meant that "Bartley accepted what the erasure of America's borders and an endless influx of foreign peoples and goods would mean for his country." For Buchanan, it implied America's extinction as a sovereign nation. Many Americans' refusal to accept this as inevitable indicated, Buchanan believed, that the implications of Bartley's alleged claim—"I think the nation-state is

finished"—were by no means a certainty, and that a fierce struggle between "nationalists" and "globalists" which crisscrossed
party-lines was only just beginning.[9]

DISILLUSION, FOREIGN
AND DOMESTIC

Differing views about trade liberalization's implications for America were not confined to intellectuals and policymakers. According
to Gallup polling, Americans' views of foreign trade have oscil-
lated significantly since 1991. At the beginnings of the 1990s, most
Americans did not regard it as a net-positive for their country. This
was followed by a steady, albeit uneven growth in favorable views
of free trade. No doubt, economic growth and low unemployment
helped to bolster these inclinations throughout the 1990s and,
after the blip of the 2001 recession, into the 2000s. By the early
2020s, a majority still saw trade as an opportunity, though sharply
more negative views had started to prevail, especially among inde-
pendents and Republicans.[10]

One factor undoubtedly affecting American views of trade concerned its emergence as a flashpoint in America's relationship with
the rising power in the Asia-Pacific. In 1978, the Chinese Communist Party's leadership decided to embark on substantive reform
of China's economy by reducing the scale of central planning and
allowing wider scope for market exchanges. By 1992, China's leaders were referring to their country as possessing "a socialist market economy."[11] The economic results were impressive. In 1995,

China became one of the world's top ten trading nations. Throughout the 1990s, it emerged as the world's second largest destination
recipient after America for foreign direct investment. [12] By 2000,
China's progress had raised the question of whether the world's
most populous nation, which continued to be ruled by a Communist regime, should be admitted to the WTO. For China, it would
mean international recognition of its economic power and wider
access to global markets. For America, it raised other questions.
China's admission into the WTO would further open its markets
to American businesses, but it would also generate more competition for particular sectors of the U.S. economy. How would America navigate these changes? Another question was political. Would
accession to the WTO help facilitate a wider liberalization of Chinese society?

Much of the received wisdom of the time held that it was difficult to have substantive increases in economic freedom without
the taste for liberty seeping into other sectors of life. In the late
1990s, there was considerable confidence that integration into glo-
balizing markets would reduce poverty but also weaken the grip
of authoritarian regimes. That seemed to be the lesson offered by
Asia-Pacific states like Taiwan and South Korea. These countries
had economically liberalized before gradually adopting liberal constitutionalism in the 1980s and 1990s. Giving China wider access
to global markets, many believed, would allow *doux commerce*, a
phrase associated with the eighteenth-century French philosopher
Montesquieu, to achieve what political protests in Tiananmen
Square in 1989 could not.

That calculation turned out to be mistaken. China's wider access to global markets helped millions of people escape severe poverty, significantly reduced the costs of many products for American consumers (something which disproportionately benefited poorer Americans), and opened up new export markets for American companies. But neither the Chinese Communist Party nor the man who became its leader in 2012, President Xi Jinping, substantially loosened the regime's grip on political and social life. By the mid-2010s, the momentum inside China was visibly in the opposite direction. This "de-liberalization" extended to China's economy as Beijing began diminishing space for economic freedom in the mid-2010s. Under Xi the ruling party-state apparatus placed tighter constraints upon the economic freedom of entrepreneurs and investors, brought more and more Chinese businesses under direct state control, placed more party officials on company boards, demanded that CEOs inscribe China's national goals directly into their business plans, and required state-run banks to shift more credit towards state-run enterprises and away from more-or-less private companies. [13]

These developments, combined with many Americans' belief that China's accession to the WTO had cost many American jobs in the manufacturing sector, resulted in more and more Americans wondering if people like Buchanan and Perot had been onto something back in the early 1990s. These doubters included conservatives, many of whom were aware that while a Democrat administration negotiated China's entry into the WTO, it was a Republican administration which assented to this outcome in December 2001.

Another source of growing disillusionment with free markets among many Americans concerned the responses of a Republican administration and then a Democrat administration to the 2008 financial crisis: the point where, according to the Heritage Foundation's 2022 *Index of Economic Freedom*, overall economic freedom in America began its present trajectory of ongoing decline. [14] While the effectiveness of the subsequent bailouts and deep interventions into the economy continues to be debated, these actions clearly clashed with some important free market orthodoxies. Many were left wondering to what extent the post-1970s shift to markets had been more rhetorical than real.

Two basic axioms of free market thought are that failed or failing businesses should not be propped up by the government, and that it's generally a mistake to socialize the losses of business during economic downturns. Bailouts send the message that companies can take huge risks with the confidence that they will be rescued if they are big enough and fail badly enough. That mindset simply encourages more irresponsible choices and thus further failures down the line.

Perhaps there are cases in which the effects of major corporations or banks failing would be so socially, economically, or politically destructive that direct state intervention is unavoidable, if only to provide psychological support to a panicking populace. But the sight of an ostensibly fiscally conservative Republican administration and Federal Reserve rescuing large banks and other businesses was hard for many Americans to swallow. This was especially the case when many small and medium-sized businesses were facing bankruptcy or having to make sharp cutbacks through no fault of their own. That underscored in many Americans' minds the sense that many political leaders were all too quick to abandon free market ideas when times got tough for big business. They consequently asked themselves this question: if supposedly pro-market politicians and CEOs wouldn't abide by free market principles when the going got tough, why should ordinary Americans?

The gap between reality and free market rhetoric has been further accentuated by greater awareness of the degree to which much of the American economy reflects "crony capitalist" or otherwise "crony" arrangements. Cronyism involves dislodging the workings of free exchange and competition within a context of property rights and the rule of law, and replacing those processes with "political markets." This results in individuals and companies focusing less on creating and offering the best products to consumers at the best prices. Instead, economic success becomes premised on the capacity to harness government power to rig the game in one's favor. The market's outward form is preserved, but its protocols and institutions are subverted by businesses seeking preferential treatment from regulators, legislators, and governments via means like tariffs (a tax imposed by a government of a country on imports or exports of goods), subsidies, access to "no-bid" contracts, or government-provided credit at below-market interest rates.

Some businesses enter the market for cronyism to protect themselves against competitors already trying to use government power to limit other people's access to "their" markets. But the temptation to go from defense to offense is hard to resist. The potential profits associated with rent-seeking (someone's effort to augment his share of existing wealth without creating any new wealth) are considerable. Lobbying politicians for favors is often easier than trying to out-compete your rivals through innovation and cost reduction. On the other end of crony transactions, those in a position to dispense preferential treatment are not doing so for altruistic reasons. A 2015 report by the Committee for Economic Development pointed out that one common payback for legislators comes in the form of campaign donations and other electoral assistance.[15] As for regulators, the incredible number of government employees who secure positions in industries they once regulated is well documented.[16]

The injustice involved with politicians and government officials using state power to confer legal privileges on specific groups in return for their political and financial support should be obvious. The Nobel economist Joseph Stiglitz—no one's idea of a fiscal conservative—pointed out in his 2012 book *The Price of Inequality* that cronyism facilitates an unjustifiable form of income inequality based on well-connected people's ability to extract larger shares of wealth from the economy, instead of creating new wealth through enterprise and work.[17] There is something fundamentally wrong with arrangements that help to explain why, as economist Luigi Zingales commented in 2012, "seven of the ten richest counties in the United States are in the suburbs of Washington, D.C., which produces little except rules and regulations."[18] Seven years later, it was reported that nine of America's twenty richest counties were suburbs of D.C.[19]

How could such facts not infuriate those who insist that the American Dream is out of their reach, or who argue that economic success is increasingly about political connections rather than hard work? To the extent that populist leaders—by which I mean those expressing a highly charged rhetoric that revolves around concern for those who are not mega-wealthy, not close to Washington D.C. policymakers, not living in new technology hubs, or who have fewer formal credentials and believe themselves to be working harder for less—are perceived to be outsiders to this process of mutual enrichment, it's hardly surprising that evidence of widespread cronyism fuels their political emergence. As readers will discover, I believe that many policies proposed by such politicians are likely to compromise the American economy's ability to deliver on the American Dream. But it is the failure to address deep political problems like cronyism that creates opportunities for people pushing for the adoption of measures— such as industrial policy—which, as we will see, only accentuate crony behavior.

There is, however, another dimension to the disparity between rhetoric and reality that presently characterizes American economic debates. This concerns some important facts about what was actually happening in the American economy prior to the Covid-19 pandemic's outbreak in early 2020. The increasingly heated conversation about American economic policy from the mid-2010s onwards was shaped by the assumption that many Americans simply weren't getting ahead as they used to: that opportunities for advancing one's social and economic well-being were narrowing for many Americans. But what if

some of these presumptions were incorrect or obscured important realities about the development of America's economy over
the past thirty years?

This question was posed by the economist Michael R. Strain
in his 2020 book *The American Dream is Not Dead (But Populism
Could Kill It)*. His inquiries suggested that the U.S. economy was
performing in ways that belied the pessimistic assertions made by
sections of the Left and Right. Strain wasn't denying that there
were major social and economic problems in America. Particular demographic groups like young blue-collar men, he stated,
were enduring a suicide crisis. Some manufacturing towns, Strain
added, had been left behind by economic globalization and, more
particularly, automation and associated technological change. So
too had males who did not finish high school. Their wages, Strain
noted, had stagnated.

Strain nevertheless also found that the pre-coronavirus American economy was generally working for most Americans. Careful analysis of relevant datasets provided by the Bureau of Labor
Statistics, the Bureau of Economic Analysis, and the Congressional Budget Office, Strain argued, indicated that: (1) wages and
incomes for typical workers had not been stagnant for thirty years;
(2) most American households had experienced broad quality of
life improvements for several decades; and (3) Americans still generally experienced upward economic mobility.

Strain's picture of the American workforce didn't ignore problems. Some middle-income occupations, he affirmed, had been
hollowed out by technology replacing jobs that were repetitive and
required precision and accuracy—i.e., functions that computers and

robots do well. Interestingly, Strain maintained, some of the occupations not disappearing included: (1) many of the lowest-skilled, least-paying jobs that required regular interactions with people and a certain degree of adaptability; and (2) high-skill occupations in which people had to exercise judgment, adjust to change, and be creative—i.e., jobs which computers cannot do well. But there was also, he contended, a "new middle" of the labor market emerging in occupations like education, healthcare support, personal care, etc.—jobs requiring more education than, say, clerical work or being a factory line-worker but also the situational flexibility and social intelligence which technology can't replicate.[20]

If Strain's analysis of the relevant data and his subsequent conclusions were broadly correct—and I believe that they were—they indicate considerable distance between many Americans' perceptions of what was going on in the pre-coronavirus economy, and important measurable facts. The persistence of that fissure creates enormous challenges for American policymakers. When particular ideas, however mistaken or half-true, become set in people's minds, they are hard to dislodge, especially in political atmospheres in which people seeking public office are incentivized to tell voters what they want to hear.

ECONOMIC FIGHTS, POLITICAL BATTLES

All these developments—arguments about trade's effects on America and the rise of China, the impact of the 2008 financial crisis and

Great Recession, the gap between free market rhetoric and actual policy choices, growing fury about cronyism, the distance between perceptions and economic realities—provided openings for those convinced that America must pursue economic paths which differ significantly from those on which it embarked in 1980. In the mid 2010s, many politicians, policy thinkers, and intellectuals began developing political and economic alternatives that sought to relegate much of the pro-market agenda to obscurity.

Figures like President Donald Trump and Senator Bernie Sanders had always held economic views that departed significantly from certain free market positions. Trump's skepticism about free trade in a world where countries like China regularly broke the rules without real consequences (as he argued correctly) [21] was matched by Sanders's insistence that free trade had undermined American workers' economic well-being. Sanders would have resisted the economic nationalist label, yet like Trump he opposed America's entry into the Trans Pacific Partnership Agreement, viewed NAFTA as a mistake, and insisted that trade deals had devastated America's manufacturing industries. Both men's prominence in the 2016 and 2020 presidential campaigns, and the fact that many of their economic ideas resonated with significant segments of American opinion, was a sign that alternatives to free market economics were back in fashion.

Another theme linking some of these figures was their belief that America's well-being as a nation, often expressed via the invocation of common good language, required the government to assume more activist roles in the economy. On the right, proposals for action included the use of tariffs and greater deployments of industrial policy. On the left, calls for similar policies were accompanied by considerable openness to adopting explicitly social democratic agendas, especially on the part of younger Americans. Through the 2010s, opinion survey after opinion survey indicated that substantial numbers—and occasionally slight majorities—of younger Americans (between the ages of eighteen and thirty-five) favored socialism over capitalism.[22] For these Americans, socialism implied various things. These included using the tax system to engage in greater wealth redistributions, more welfare programs, higher taxes on the wealthy and corporate America, and a general move toward economic arrangements characteristic of 1970s European social democracy. This was associated with a general emphasis upon the need for greater equality in economic starting points and outcomes. In these conditions, Clinton Democrats found themselves on the endangered species list.

Compounding this uptick in interventionist sentiments among many policymakers and some significant demographic groups was the fact that, beginning in the first quarter of 2020, the United States witnessed what was arguably the biggest surge of the state into the American economy more broadly since Franklin Roosevelt's first one hundred days in 1933 and since the months following Japan's attack on Pearl Harbor in December 1941. In times of emergency—war, famine, insurrection, pandemic—we allow governments to do things that we would never otherwise tolerate. But never before had government officials shuttered major segments of the American economy so quickly and on such a scale. Similar choices by governments around the world as they reacted to the pandemic compromised global supply chains and brought home to Americans how much they relied on people in faraway lands for the supply of products, including some vital ones. They acquired knowledge of hitherto obscure facts, such as where most of the world's microchips were manufactured and the degree to which much of the American economy depended on this technology. Some of the risks associated with economic globalization and liberalized international markets loomed fully into view, and some Americans did not like them. Perhaps, they concluded, the state simply needed to do more.

The same interventions into the economy resulted in unemployment levels not seen since the Great Depression, the temporary closure or liquidation of thousands of businesses, and shortages of goods as supply chains struggled to adjust. But they also underscored to some Americans that many of their fellow citizens seemed quite at ease with the government dispersing billions of dollars to individuals and companies and assuming an even more central economic place in people's lives. Was this, they wondered, going to become a new normal in America?

Though arguments about the American economy's future grew tenser in Covid-19's wake, this was hardly the first time that Americans had become polarized around economic policy. Founders like James Madison had even suspected that such divisions would be inevitable. Writing in *The Federalist Papers*, Madison predicted that different interests would take opposing stances on trade issues. "Shall domestic manufactures be encouraged," he commented, "and in what degree, by restrictions on foreign manufactures? are questions which would be differently decided by the landed and the manufacturing classes, and probably by neither with a sole regard to justice and the public good."[23]

Preeminent scholars of American trade policy, like Harvard economist Frank William Taussig writing at the end of the nineteenth century and economic historian Douglas A. Irwin in more recent decades, have shown how deeply fights about trade policy are interwoven into America's political clashes. Many key political debates in the antebellum and postbellum republic revolved around tariffs. This reflected the interests of competing economic sectors as well as regional differences. Southern states long maintained a free trade disposition because of their desire to ensure that their cotton didn't encounter difficulties entering European markets. Conversely, considerable portions of Northern opinion held that industrial development through America required tariffs to be applied to foreign imports, especially those from British manufacturers.

Many of these debates were intertwined with disagreements about what type of nation America should be. In the Revolution's aftermath, some wanted America to have an economy and society largely focused on agriculture and small farms. Others envisaged America as a country in which the spirit of enterprise and the intensification of free-flowing domestic and external trade would become the engines of economic growth in a nation committed to rapid industrialization. These varied hopes contributed to spectacular conflicts between Thomas Jefferson and Alexander Hamilton. The former was suspicious of banks and had a strong distaste for cities. The latter wanted America to embrace commercial modernization and thus usher in a new type of nation ready to meet the challenges of the time.

Economic arguments in America have also long revolved around the role of government, especially the federal government, in the U.S. economy. It is the government that raises (or lowers) tariffs, gives (or withdraws) subsidies to particular industries, and imposes (or reduces) regulations. The impact of such decisions is not limited to domestic policy. The resolution to protect an industry in America from foreign competition via protectionism involves taxing imports of products created by businesses based in other countries. Not surprisingly, those nations in which these companies are located will be unhappy about this. They often retaliate by imposing their own tariffs on American-made goods. Conversely, when a government seeks to enhance a nation's competitiveness by reducing the regulatory burden on one or more sectors of its economy, this creates pressures upon other governments to follow suit if they want companies based in their own country to remain competitive. Few political leaders will relish taking such action. It often entails confronting powerful interest groups, including some of their supporters.

Nor can the conduct of economic policy be separated from political disputes about which value-commitments are to be given priority. The more interventionist policies proposed by market skeptics are often directed at protecting different regions and groups within a nation from economic stresses. If that means less growth, they say, then so be it: social cohesion and stability must be accorded as much if not more importance than liberty and wealth creation. Conversely, the decision to liberalize domestic markets and to open one's economy to the world means according preeminence to freedom in economic life over the desire to have more equal economic outcomes. Market liberalization also implies accepting the tough disciplines that are part-and-parcel of allowing people more space to be entrepreneurial and competitive in domestic and foreign markets. These disciplines exact a price as companies which struggle to compete go out of business. This brings social churn in its wake. The calculus is that, over the long term, a dynamic competitive market characterized by private enterprise and trade openness will always outperform the alternatives in enhancing a nation's capacity to provide products efficiently to its inhabitants. That matters because this capacity is what constitutes wealth. As Adam Smith stated long ago, wealth isn't about how much gold or money you possess. Wealth is your relative ability to satisfy your needs and desires.

These differences in priorities should not be oversimplified. Economic debates in America are sometimes portrayed as "economic nationalists versus libertarian globalists" cage-fights, but there's something misleading about that narrative. Not all American free marketers, for example, can be caricatured as Silicon Valley bubble-dwellers who consider the very idea of nations as *passé*. Many in fact regard national sovereignty as good and necessary, and are as proud of being American as any economic nationalist. Insofar as sovereignty means the independence of a state, combined with the right and power of regulating its internal affairs without foreign interference, they do not believe this translates into an American economy with limited engagement with the rest of the world. They even view exposure to competition, including foreign competition, as benefiting America and Americans. Such free marketers may also insist that their opposition to protection-ism owes something to their belief that tariffs actually hurt the U.S. economy and undermine many ordinary Americans' job prospects in the short, medium, and long terms.

Likewise, an economic nationalist may contend that failure by the government to smooth the economic ups and downs which are part of life in a market economy risks opening the door to politi-cal movements that have no particular regard for human freedom. This was one of the arguments made by Keynes in the 1930s as he witnessed the rise of Communism and Fascism throughout inter-war Europe and the subsequent faltering of constitutional democ-racy. Absent substantial state intervention into the economy, Keynes and others believed, political and civil liberties might find themselves being severely curtailed.[24]

CHOICES MATTER

Since 1788, the American economy has changed enormously in its sectoral composition, consumption patterns, employment con-figurations, and, most obviously, size. This is the result of factors ranging from innovation to technological change and immigra-tion. But it is also a product of choices made in light of the ascen-dency of particular ideas and a widespread sense that some type of major change was necessary.

In his book *Ages of American Capitalism* (2021), economic histo-rian Jonathan Levy maintains that the United States economy has experienced four different eras. He calls these "The Age of Commerce" (1660–1860), "The Age of Capital" (1860–1932), "The Age of Control" (1932–1980), and finally "The Age of Chaos" (1980–present). The end of each age, Levy argues, involved major shifts in political and economic ideas that reflected dissatisfaction with the status quo. "The Age of Control," for instance, emerged as a reaction to the Depression, with the federal government becoming the economic manager writ large. Other factors driving this change were the triumph of ideas, often associated with the Progressive movement, which held that it was possible and right for governments to act in a managerial fashion, as well as the willingness of people to put such theories into practice. Circumstances, political will, and ideas consequently created the possibility for a defining choice to be made, the effects of which still mark today's U.S. economy.

Given the sheer complexity of economic life and the multiple factors shaping any economy, however, some may wonder whether choices made by policymakers and ideas coined by intellectuals are all that important compared to the significance of fundamental institutional settings. Some scholars maintain, for example, that different legal traditions brought from Europe by Spanish, French, British, and Portuguese colonizers explain a great deal about why America is more prosperous than Mexico.[25] Those countries influenced by Anglo-Saxon common law frameworks, it is held, have provided stronger security for investments and investors than Iberian traditions and have more consistent histories of contract enforcement, stronger rule of law, and higher levels of property rights protection. In short, countries like America and Canada were simply lucky to have been British rather than Spanish colonies. No one planned this.

That institutions are significant to economic development is not in doubt. But we should be careful about drawing too many inferences. Many African countries also inherited British legal arrangements and remain relatively poor today. There are also good reasons to assume that economic policy choices at different points of time, especially during crises, matter. The American Founding period is a prime example.

In the 1780s, pressures were growing to give Congress the power to regulate trade within America and between America and other countries. Some American merchants wanted to break into foreign markets. Others engaged in interstate commerce were tired of navigating the varying trade rules of the Confederation's different members. Many Americans simply wanted to strike back at Britain's mercantile system that, as Adam Smith had pointed out, actively inhibited "advanced or more refined manufactures" from being made in the American colonies. [26] There was thus widespread agreement on the need for a common trade policy and a political framework capable of giving effect to it. These concerns played a major role in Virginia's invitation to the other states to meet in 1786 to devise a Confederation-wide regulatory regime for trade, and the eventual calling of the Constitutional Convention in 1787. [27]

Trade questions consequently helped push the American Confederation of the mid 1780s towards different political arrangements. The most general economic effect of the Constitution which came into force in 1789 was to establish the United States as a common market. This facilitated a greater division of labor and specialization throughout America.[28] Indeed, a spirit of entrepreneurship swept the country after the Constitution's ratification, dwarfing that which existed in colonial America.[29] The Constitution in itself did not create an entrepreneurial, competitive economy. But it did confer powers upon the federal government which allowed it:

- To lay and collect Taxes, Duties, Imposts and Excises, to pay the Debts and provide for the common Defense and general Welfare of the United States.
- To establish . . . uniform Laws on the subject of Bankruptcies throughout the United States.
- To promote the Progress of Science and useful Arts, by securing for limited Times to Authors and Inventors the exclusive Right to their respective Writings and Discoveries.
- To borrow Money on the credit of the United States.
- To regulate Commerce with Foreign Nations, and among the several States.
- To coin Money, regulate the Value thereof.

These powers needed, however, to be executed. While Article I, Section 8, gave Congress the responsibility "To make all Laws which shall be necessary and proper for carrying into Execution the foregoing Powers," policymakers—most notably, President George Washington's administration—still had to decide how to exercise these powers in areas ranging from trade to taxation, public finance, capital markets, bankruptcy, and property rights.

Among the choices made by Congress, under the guiding hand of Treasury Secretary Alexander Hamilton beginning with his 1790 landmark *Report on Public Credit*, were decisions to institute a national currency and national Mint, create a national bank, and consolidate and fund a public debt. As a collective whole, those political choices provided an institutional framework for the development of financial markets, much of which occurred at the state level. Laws to protect intellectual property rights and establish clear bankruptcy procedures were also passed. This reduced the costs involved in closing down failed businesses and diminished the incentives for politicians to bail out such companies. [30]

Many of these decisions were actively disputed at the time. Their acceptance required persuasion of legislators and powerful social and economic groups via carefully drafted formal state papers as well as highly polemical newspapers and pamphlets. But they led to vital developments, most notably a financial revolution that took the United States from having a premodern financial system to one which rivaled those of financial superpowers like Britain and the Dutch Republic by 1800. [31] These choices and their translation into legislation were crucial in consolidating and extending what Douglas A. Irwin and Richard Sylla call "a large and open market area." They go on to argue that

> The economic policy choices of the founding era released
> a burst of energy that would persist for more than two cen-
> turies. In half a century, the land area of the United States
> would triple in size . . . In a century the American economy
> would be the largest of any of the world's nations, drawing

to it large numbers of immigrants from around the world. In two centuries, a nation that in 1790 had less than half a percent of the world's population would become the world's third most populous nation, one in which 5 percent of the world's people would produce some 20 to 25 percent of world economic output, and enjoy a standard of living unimaginable a century to two ago. [32]

GENERAL WELFARE OVER PRIVATE INTEREST

This background illustrates that while context is important, economies are in many respects politically and legally engineered. Much therefore depends on the vision that informs those who are doing the engineering. This brings us to America's present circumstances.

With the exception of extreme outliers, American advocates of some version of state capitalism are neither proposing measures like the formal collectivization of property, nor insisting that Americans should never trade with people from other nations, nor looking to abolish the stock market. Rather, they want to use the government, primarily the federal government, to intervene into the American economy from the top down to realize specific goals. Sometimes the objective is to reconfigure the economy, sector by sector, through different interventions on the basis that the economy's present workings are impeding the realization of important social ends or hurting particular groups. In other cases, it is about using state power to reorganize the priorities of business so that pursuing profit becomes one of many goals rather than the primary objective around which business enterprises are organized. For others, such actions involve shoring up America's capacity to address geopolitical challenges like Communist China.

Readers will soon discern that I readily acknowledge that substantial domestic problems confront the United States. Nor is it deniable that America faces substantial political tests stemming from abroad. Domestic economic policy cannot be blind to these international realities, not least because America's relationship with the rest of the world helps to determine whether the American experiment in ordered liberty will prove durable. But the proposals being advanced to address these issues by convinced protectionists, advocates of industrial policy, or adherents of stakeholder theories of business, I will argue, clash with some important realities that will render them ineffective and, in many instances, will also have negative economic, social, and political consequences for America.

The alternative vision advocated by this book is a market economy that places a premium on entrepreneurship, vigorous competition, and free trade and that, crucially, is also informed by attention to particular realities. That involves acknowledging, for example, that nation-state rivalry is real and is not going away, and that trade liberalization has not made China a more benign presence in the world. But some other facts include various economic realities which boosters of state capitalism are insufficiently attentive to or simply ignore: that, for instance, the state of U.S. manufacturing is more complex than they commonly portray it; or that tariffs imposed by America on other nations hurt Americans as much as they damage those countries against whom the tariffs are directed.

I have no illusions that the United States will move decisively towards the vision that I am advocating. The pressures working against such a choice are formidable. In his own time, Adam Smith commented that "To expect, indeed, that the freedom of trade should ever be entirely restored in Great Britain, is as absurd as to expect that an Oceana or Utopia should ever be established in it." What was especially "unconquerable," he said, were "the private interests of many individuals [who] irresistibility oppose it."[33] The same is true of America today. A plurality of Americans may, for example, indicate that they want less government in their lives or that they see foreign trade as an opportunity rather than a threat. That does not, however, mean that their views will prevail.

America's Founders recognized the power of factions and interests, and the pressures which they bring to bear upon legislators and others involved in the design and execution of policy. Many interests today remain firmly aligned against the type of market economy and associated political arrangements that I believe America should embrace. Here, some will immediately think of groups like labor unions. They, however, are far from being the most powerful interest group that is lukewarm about free markets. We should recognize that many American businesses are not enthusiastic about bolstering other people's entrepreneurship, let alone dynamic competition—foreign or domestic.

In a 1977 lecture entitled "The Future of Capitalism," Nobel economist Milton Friedman argued that "The two greatest enemies of free enterprise in the United States . . . have been, on the one hand, my fellow intellectuals and, on the other hand, the business corporations of this country." Few will be surprised by Friedman identifying the first group, but some may wonder why he singled out business leaders as unfriendly to free markets. Friedman explained his position in the following way:

> Every businessman and every business enterprise is in favor of freedom for everybody else, but when it comes to himself, that's a different question. We have to have that tariff to protect us against competition from abroad. We have to have that special provision in the tax code. We have to have that subsidy. Businessmen are in favor of freedom for everybody else but not for themselves.
>
> There are many notable exceptions. There are many business leaders who have been extremely farsighted in their understanding of the problem and will come to the defense of a free enterprise system. But for the business community in general, the tendency is to take out advertisements, such as the US Steel Company taking out full-page ads to advertise the virtues of free enterprise but then to plead before Congress for an import quota on steel from Japan. The only result of that is for everybody who is fair-minded to say, "What a bunch of hypocrites!" And they're right. [34]

This type of business executive has been around for a long time. Smith's *Wealth of Nations* noted the propensity of the merchants of his time to seek privileges from governments, invariably on the basis that their industry was somehow uniquely vital to the realm's well-being. But as Smith commented, "I have never known much good done by those who affected to trade for the public good."[35] The full meaning of this Smithian insight is well summarized by Richard J. Shinder when he writes:

> Many of the arguments advanced by market participants having the result of limiting competition, increasing regulation, stifling innovation, and otherwise restricting the workings of the market's "hidden hand" are ultimately meant to entrench incumbency. While such enterprises initially may have prevailed over the competition on a level playing field, once having succeeded they frequently seek to limit competition and engage in various behaviors designed to extract economic rents from their position at the top of the heap. While CEOs are customarily deft at framing such policies as working in service of some other more appealing objective, the practical impact and underlying agenda is to advantage the advocate and disfavor competitors, customers, suppliers, or the general public.[36]

Overcoming the power of sectoral interests is extremely difficult. It is a permanent battle. One might therefore ask: Why bother investing so much time and effort promoting an alternative vision? Why not settle for something like an updated New Deal or simply accept something like the corporatist economic framework that, we will see, lies in the background of the stake-holder model of capitalism?

The answer to such queries is simple. It is a matter of promoting the common good, or what the U.S. Constitution calls "the general welfare," over those individuals and groups which seek to use state-power to prioritize their sectional interests. Moving the pendulum of the climate of opinion back towards a dynamic market economy politically grounded in a commercial republic is one way of promoting that goal.

THE WAY AHEAD

Though economic policy reflects pressures bought to bear by interest groups, it is also about ideas, and their coherence or otherwise. If the foundational ideas underlying a given economic policy are deficient in major ways, no amount of tinkering with the policy's design will make it successful.

If, for example, your economic policies are based on the premises that (1) the government must and can direct the economy from the top-down; (2) the state must subsequently determine the price of goods and services; and (3) private ownership is at best a necessary evil, then at some point the policies will fail. The failure lies in (1) the impossibility of the government being able to possess all the information it would need to be able to direct the economy; (2) the ways in which price-controls undermine the conveying of accurate information about the status of the supply and demand of millions of goods and services at any one moment in time; and (3) the negative effects of collective ownership on incentives to work and be creative.

Forthcoming chapters will elaborate on the central ideas underlying the two broad choices—American state capitalism versus American free markets—which lie before Americans as they debate what will be the next stage in the U.S. economy's development. This will be supplemented by reference to studies conducted by economists, legal scholars, historians, and political scientists whose empirical research shows how these ideas play out in practice.

In the first half, we consider the core political and economic ideas underlying state capitalism: specifically, a willingness to use protectionism, an affinity for industrial policy, and the advancement of expansive stakeholder models of business. In each case we will see that these measures are based on flawed claims and that they will consequently have negative effects upon the American economy and society more generally. The second half of the book presents the case for what I regard as the most optimal future for American capitalism: an economy driven by bottom-up creative private entrepreneurship, which grows within the context of market competition, and which looks at the rest of the world without fear, asking for no favors and expecting none.

While some attention is given to policy, my focus is on the broad picture. Many specific economic issues are not subsequently addressed in detail. Topics like levels of taxes and spending, the size of America's public debt, the scope of the welfare state, and the conduct of monetary policy are important. For the most part, however, those questions are put to one side, partly because they are highly specialized subjects in themselves, but also because the question of whether America goes down the path of state capitalism or chooses to reinvigorate some of the market economy's basic foundations and root them in a particular political framework will predetermine the responses to these and other issues.

That broad picture also involves engaging some normative questions. The best economists have always understood that economic disagreements are shaped by and spill over into questions of political economy. The choice for a highly activist state invariably reflects desires to have economic life conform to the demands of particular conceptions of justice. But so too do many free market arguments for placing strong limits on state power. Free market thought invariably accords priority to the type of justice and equity associated with the rule of law rather than egalitarian economic outcomes. Likewise, arguments about corporate law are also driven by differences about what should be the specific *telos*—the term employed by Aristotle to describe the inherent purpose or objective of a person or thing—of business that makes it different from a family or religious organization.

This reminds us that the battle for the future of the American economy goes far beyond issues of efficiency and economic growth. In our time, such questions touch especially on matters of identity. Many economic quarrels are often proxies for political questions, and debates about America's identity as a nation are clearly central to our present disputes about the economy. Perhaps it is because I am an immigrant to America, but it is apparent to me that what gives the United States its distinct character as a nation and makes America different from other countries is its rootedness in certain ideas. Historian Gordon Wood sums this up when he states that the principles embodied in the Founding documents and debates "seem to have a quality that transcends time and space. Americans look back to the eighteenth-century revolutionaries and the constitutions and documents they wrote with a special awe and respect. . . . no other major nation invokes its two hundred-year-old documents and their authors and in quite the way that America does."[37] Such is their importance for interpreting the Constitution or judging the actions of contemporary politicians, legislators, judges, and policymakers that they have become, Wood writes, "our source of identity":

> The identities of other nations, say, being French or German, have become lost in the mists of time, and their nationhood, their sense of having a common ancestor, has usually been taken for granted. . . . But Americans have never been a nation in any traditional or ethnic meaning of the terms. . . . Lacking any semblance of a common ancestry, Americans have had to create their sense of nationhood out of the documents—the declarations and constitutions and bills of right—and the principles embodied in them that accompanied their eighteenth-century Revolution.[38]

If this remains true for a substantive plurality of Americans, the case for the market economy in today's America must in some way be associated with the ideals and principles expressed and articulated in the American Founding era if it is to have *legitimacy*: that which leads us to accept something as consistent with America's history and identity as a country. Ironically, this is well understood by those proposing radically different ideas for America's economic future. Those associated with the 1619 Project understand that advancing their view of America and an economic agenda deeply hostile to free markets involves delegitimizing that Founding.[39] How else can they overcome the fact that phrases like "American Socialism" ring hollow for so many Americans?

For these reasons, the last chapter of this book argues for integrating the market economy into an understanding of America which emerged, after considerable opposition, out of the Founding in the 1790s. The idea of America as a commercial republic is, I will suggest, an especially apt political framework for a market economy in twentieth-first century America, both from a domestic standpoint and for shaping how America interacts with other nations. That relationship with the rest of the world remains central to today's arguments about America's economic future. Nowhere is this more evident in our time than in the call for America to embrace a major plank of state capitalism: the economics and politics of protectionism.

PART I

THE STATE CAPITALISM OPTION

CHAPTER 2

PROTECTIONISM DOESN'T PAY

As a rich man is likely to be a better customer to the industrious people in his neighborhood than a poor, so is likewise a rich nation. [Trade restrictions,] by aiming at the impoverishment of all our neighbors, tend to render that very commerce insignificant and contemptible.

—ADAM SMITH

Apart from slavery, few subjects divided Americans more consistently during the nineteenth century than tariffs. Disagreements about their scope, application, and effects pit regions of the country against each other, and even helped precipitate a major constitutional clash. The passage of the Tariff of 1828 and the Tariff of 1832 led to the Nullification Crisis, whereby South Carolina's claim that it could prohibit enforcement of these tariff acts within its boundaries led to President Andrew Jackson threatening to deploy federal troops to enforce federal law.

Americans as a whole have never been isolationists when it comes to trade. But ever since Adam Smith assailed what he called "the mercantile system" which dominated trade throughout the eighteenth-century world, those responsible for ordering trade relations between America and other countries had to consider whether they would levy duties on imports entering America and at what rate.

The first tariffs imposed by the federal government on imports into the United States via the Tariff Act of July 4, 1789, were primarily understood as a tax by which the government could raise revenue to cover its expenses and service the country's debts. Likewise, tariff increases throughout the 1790s were first and foremost directed to funding government operations and reducing the national debt rather than establishing an out-and-out protectionist trade regime.[1] Throughout the nineteenth century, however, the efficacy of protectionist policies became central to debates about the government's economic role. Divisions of opinion among Americans on this topic often reflected the industry prevailing in different parts of the country. The most notable was between much of the North and the South before and after the Civil War. Article I, Section 8 (1) of the Constitution of the Confederate States of America (1861) even specified: "nor shall any duties or taxes on importations from foreign nations be laid to promote or foster any branch of industry."[2]

This effort to constitutionally prohibit protectionist policies reflected the desire of many Southern states—and slave-owning Southern planters—to ensure that their cotton exports did not find themselves subject to retaliatory tariffs levied by European nations. By contrast, many Northern industrial interests viewed tariffs as a way to make the costs of buying imported goods from their foreign competitors more expensive for Americans than they would otherwise be. These Northern interests generally got their way after the Civil War. Many temporary duties on foreign imports to help pay for the war became permanent for decades afterwards.[3]

Postbellum America's embrace of protectionism achieved a type of apotheosis during the presidency of William McKinley (1897–1901). Donald Trump was not the first self-described "Tariff Man" to occupy the White House. While running for president in 1896, McKinley portrayed himself as "a tariff man standing on a tariff platform." McKinley was a firm advocate of tariffs from the beginning of his political career in 1877 as a young congressman from Ohio until his assassination on September 14, 1901. Significantly, he opposed tariffs imposed purely for revenue purposes. McKinley's commitment to protectionism reflected his views about the proper direction of the U.S. economy rather than taxation. Protectionism, he argued, was about giving American businesses, especially in manufacturing, a price advantage in American domestic markets when competing with goods produced by foreign companies. That, McKinley held, was the path to American prosperity.[4] Many legislators agreed and supported the McKinley Act of 1890. It raised the average tariff on imports from 38 percent to approximately 49.5 percent.[5]

McKinley was fully aware that tariffs meant that the federal government was actively choosing to favor some sectors of the economy over others and requiring millions of American consumers to absorb the costs. For that is what tariffs do. Protectionists who acknowledge this point maintain that the price is worth it. Most scholars and policymakers who promote protectionist policies today hold that such measures are needed to preserve *American* manufacturing, provide space and time for new industries to take off in *America*, inhibit the reduction of *American* wages, and help *American* businesses compete against foreign companies. Such things, they argue, are in America's national interest. By contrast, free trade is portrayed as subjecting American businesses and workers to unfair competition from abroad. Some further insist that the very idea of free trade is a myth insofar as no country will ever engage in unilateral free trade. Why then should not America deploy tariffs and import controls like everyone else?

My answer to that question is that America should avoid protectionist policies as much as possible because they do not serve the common good of Americans as consumers, as workers, or as a nation. Not only are protectionist arguments characterized by mistaken logic and a confusion of cause and effect; there is also a great deal of empirical research indicating how protectionism undermines America's long-term economic interests and international competitiveness, and how it breeds some of the worst and most lasting forms of cronyism. Such critiques of protectionism are not new. They were first outlined in detail in Book IV of Adam Smith's *Wealth of Nations*: a text which repays careful reading for anyone who wants to understand why protectionism is not good for America.

AGAINST THE MERCANTILISTS

Few books enjoy as good a claim to having decisively shaped human events as Smith's *Wealth of Nations*. Its impact owed much to the way in which Smith drew back the curtain on economic ideas and practices that had dominated the European world since the sixteenth century and showed how they were grounded on mistaken assumptions and faulty logic. Of all the blows dealt by Smith's *Wealth of Nations*, perhaps the most comprehensive was to mercantilism: an economic system which embodied various features characteristic of modern protectionism.

Perhaps the most important of these was the idea that any country's trade policy should focus on maximizing its exports and minimizing its imports. The more you minimized imports, it was argued, the more a country retained its wealth, especially in the form of gold and silver. Efforts were consequently made to discourage imports and boost exports via the government levying heavy duties upon foreign imports, trying to increase output and exports by subsidizing existing domestic industries, constraining laborers' ability to migrate in pursuit of new opportunities, and often outlawing technology transfers that might intensify competition from abroad.[6]

Smith found these arguments wanting. He pointed out that mercantilist efforts to protect domestic industries didn't increase a country's total output. No regulation, Smith stated, "can increase the quantity of industry in any country beyond what its capital can maintain." Instead, regulation diverted part of a country's capital "into a direction into which it might not otherwise have gone." But, Smith added, "it was by no means certain that this artificial direction is likely to be more advantageous to the society than that into which it would have gone of its own accord."[7] These words were echoed by James Madison speaking thirteen years later during the first

Congressional debates about tariffs: "it is also a truth," he observed, "that if industry and labor are left to take their own course, they will generally be directed to those objects which are the most productive, and this is a more certain and direct manner than the wisdom of the most enlightened legislature could point out."[8]

This insight, as we will see in Chapter Three, underscores a major problem with industrial policy. Smith's wider point, however, is that tariffs do *not* inherently increase production. Output is driven by factors such as efficiency, specialization, and the amount of capital invested in a given business or industry. The only thing that tariffs can do is encourage businesses to shift their investments elsewhere, and there is no way of knowing in advance if this will increase output.

Smith's more general problem with mercantilism's restricting or penalizing imports is that it reflected a mistaken apprehension of the purpose of economic production. The point of production was not to maintain production itself. Production was a means to an end. And the goal of production—of economic life as a whole—is *consumption*. We don't consume goods and services to promote production. Production is supposed to satisfy the needs and wants of consumers. "Consumption," Smith wrote, "is the sole end and purpose of production; and the interest of the producer ought to be attended to only so far as it may be necessary for promoting that of the consumer." The problem, he stressed, with "the mercantile system [is that] the interest of the consumer is almost constantly sacrificed to that of the producer; and it seems to consider production, and not consumption, as the ultimate end and object of all industry and commerce."[9]

PROTECTIONISM DOESN'T PAY

If, however, this point was so obvious, why did so many countries prioritize the interests of a minority (some producers) over
those of everyone else (consumers)? One answer, Smith said, lay
in the ability of such producers to exert disproportionate influence
over trade policy:

> It cannot be very difficult to determine who have been the
> contrivers of this whole mercantile system; not the con-
> sumers, we may believe, whose interest has been entirely
> neglected; but the producers, whose interests has been so
> carefully attended to; and among this latter class our mer-
> chants and manufacturers have been by far the principal
> architects. In the mercantile regulations . . . the interest of
> our manufacturers has been most peculiarly attended to;
> and the interest, not so much of the consumers, as that of
> some other sets of producers, has been sacrificed to it. [10]

In a letter written in 1783, Smith doubled down on this point:
"every extraordinary, either encouragement or discouragement
that is given to the trade of any country more than to that of another
may, I think, be demonstrated to be in every case a complete piece
of dupery, by which the interest of the state and the nation is constantly sacrificed to that of some particular class of traders." [11] The
injustice occasioned by what Smith called "the mean rapacity [and]
the monopolizing spirit of merchants and manufacturers" [12] didn't
end there. Smith recognized that mercantilism was premised upon
close collusion between particular merchants and government
officials. The losers from these arrangements included merchants

without political connections and consumers who had no choice but to pay higher prices for often lower quality goods and services. Without too much difficulty, the same criticisms are applicable to the arguments for increased protectionism in America today. To be a protectionist is, I submit, to prioritize sectional interests over the national interest.

AMERICA'S TARIFF STORY

In the second half of the nineteenth century, America caught up to and then eclipsed Britain as the world's biggest economy. This was a time in which protectionist measures were a major feature of American trade policy. Some consequently argue that these policies, especially after the Civil War, played a major role in America's emergence as an economic superpower between 1776 and 1890. [13]

There is, however, widespread evidence that protectionist policies actually impeded America's march to economic greatness. Douglas A. Irwin's extensive analysis of the late-nineteenth-century American economy indicates that growth during these decades was driven primarily by population growth, capital accumulation, and entrepreneurship, rather than the productivity improvements that come from nations pursuing something crucial for free trade: [14] i.e., comparative advantage.

Comparative advantage concerns the ability of an individual, business, or nation to produce a particular good or service at a lower opportunity cost (the potential benefits that we miss out on by choosing one alternative over another) than its competitors and trading partners. Exposure to the pressures of domestic and foreign competition plays a major role in helping nations discover and develop their comparative advantage. Nations learn what they do comparatively better and more efficiently than others. Protectionism, by contrast, gradually dulls our awareness of our comparative advantages and opportunities to pursue it. Tariffs, subsidies, and import quotas (the assignment of a maximum quantity of a given good allowed to enter America) seek to offset foreign competition's impact on a given industry—and may even succeed for a time. But such measures also discourage that industry from adapting and becoming more efficient. The more you protect an industry, the more inflexible and inefficient it will likely become.

Not coincidentally, Irwin points out, productivity growth was more rapid in those sectors of the nineteenth-century U.S. economy whose performance was not directly connected to the tariff. [15] Irwin's analysis is confirmed by economist J. Bradford Delong's major study of America's post-Civil War economy. Delong determined that protectionism weakened the gains made by America through technological innovation. The artificially high price of imported capital goods generated by protectionism made it harder and more expensive to build America's transportation and industrial infrastructure. [16] From this perspective, America's economic success throughout the nineteenth century occurred *despite* protectionist policies.

In 1945, American trade policy took a different turn. At the end of World War II, America and many other nations established the General Agreement on Tariffs and Trade (GATT). Its goal was to promote a multilateral liberalization of trade across the globe. That the GATT and its successor organization, the WTO, succeeded in reducing the scale of protectionism throughout the world and in America is clear. In 1947, average tariffs of industrial countries were about 40 percent.[17] By 2021, the trade-weighted average tariff rate applied by America was 2.4 percent.[18]

Compared to the post-Civil War period, this is a dramatically lower number. But it is not the whole story. The duty applied to almost 37 percent of tariff lines for imports in 2021, for example, was zero. Yet 5 percent of the lines in America's tariff schedule exceeded a 15 percent duty that same year.[19] Nor are tariffs the only form of protectionism. The United States imposes quotas upon many imported goods. Likewise, more than 2,300 non-tariff barriers (like product standards, health requirements, etc.) were applied to many products entering America in 2022.[20]

Further muddying the waters is the willingness of different Presidential administrations to deploy protectionist measures to respond (or be seen to be responding) to particular problems, such as downturns in particular industries or tariffs imposed by foreign governments upon U.S. exports to other countries. In March 2002, for instance, the Bush administration slapped tariffs ranging between 8–30 percent on steel imports.[21] These were designed to counter what the steel industry insisted was a surge of steel imports into America that were making it harder for American steel producers to compete. Seven years later, the Obama administration imposed new tariffs on truck and car tires imported from China for a three-year period. In 2018, the Trump administration levied higher tariffs on imports of particular goods (washing machines, aluminum, steel, solar panels, to name a few) but then moved to target imports specifically from China: 25 percent tariffs on $34 billion of imports in July, 25 percent tariffs on $16 billion of imports in August, and 10 percent tariffs on $200 billion worth of Chinese imports in September.[22]

The United States may have a low average tariff level, but this disguises the many ways in which protectionism still affects America's economy. That is all the more reason to understand why the arguments for protectionism are just as fallacious as those advanced by the eighteenth-century mercantilists confronted by Adam Smith.

TRADE DEFICITS DON'T MATTER

A common argument advanced by protectionists is that post-war trade liberalization has resulted in America importing more goods than it exports. Imports are seen as "costs" to the economy while exports are understood as "benefits." On this basis, Wilbur Ross, U.S. Secretary of Commerce from 2017 to 2021, argued that imports amount to a reduction of GDP. "It's Econ 101," he wrote, "that GDP equals the sum of domestic economic activity plus 'net exports,' i.e., exports minus imports." Ross subsequently concluded that when America runs trade deficits, its economy becomes weaker.[23] Trade policy should therefore, he held, focus on reducing imports so that America's GDP could grow.

This, however, is not Econ 101. It's bad economics. The reason why GDP calculations typically subtract imports is to ensure that we have a more accurate grasp of what is being produced domestically. It's no indication that America and Americans are becoming poorer. In fact, many goods and services made in America would not be produced in the first place (or would be created at a much higher price) without imports from abroad.

What's important to grasp here is that contemporary American protectionists are essentially expressing a modern version of the mercantilist assertion that you "win" by exporting more than you import. This is expressed through their treatment of what's called "the balance of trade." In simple terms, the balance of trade is the difference between a country's total exports and its total imports of goods and services. When a nation exports more than it imports, protectionists see this as positive and favorable because foreigners are buying American-produced goods and services. America thus "wins." The opposite—when imports exceed exports—is regarded as negative because America is taking in more than it sends abroad. To run a trade deficit therefore means that America is "losing."

This way of thinking is to understand trade precisely the wrong way around. The entire concept of a balance of trade is highly problematic. Adam Smith expressed himself forcibly on this point when he wrote:

> Nothing, however, can be more absurd than this whole doctrine of the balance of trade, upon which, not only these restraints, but almost all the other regulations of commerce are founded. When two places trade with one another, this doctrine supposes that, if the balance be even, neither of them either loses or gains; but if it leans in any degree to one side, that one of them loses and the

other gains in proportion to its declension from the exact equilibrium. Both suppositions are false. A trade which is forced by means of bounties and monopolies may be and commonly is disadvantageous to the country in whose favor it is meant to be established . . . . But that trade which, without force or constraint, is naturally and regularly carried on between any two places is always advantageous, though not always equally so, to both. [24]

Smith's insight is that when individuals and businesses enter into a free exchange within a country or between countries, they both "win" to varying degrees. Otherwise, neither would have agreed to the exchange in the first place. To the extent that protectionism makes it more costly for America to import goods and services from abroad, the benefits received from these exchanges are reduced.

HARMING AMERICANS

Placing extra costs on Americans' freedom to import goods and services is only the first of many problems with protectionist policies. At its most basic level, protectionism increases the price that Americans would otherwise pay for goods and services. From this, there are two sets of losers.

The first are everyday American consumers. It is they—not foreign companies—who pay for the costs of tariffs. [25] Wealthy Americans can easily absorb the increased costs. But the less-well off bear a proportionately larger burden as their increased costs are paid out of their much smaller resources. The second group of losers are American businesses forced to pay higher prices for various products than they otherwise would. That increases their production costs. Very large companies might be able to handle this without too much fuss. Smaller and medium-sized businesses are more likely to experience difficulty, especially when margins are tight. They often absorb the cost by raising prices for consumers or, sometimes, reducing their employee numbers.

This is precisely what occurred when the Trump administration increased tariffs on steel and aluminum imports in March 2018. A Federal Reserve analysis of the impact of these increases released in December 2019 estimated that, on balance, these tariffs resulted in a net *loss* of approximately 75,000 jobs,[26] the majority of which were blue-collar jobs located in mostly blue-collar towns. The reason, Douglas Irwin points out, is that "Many more workers are employed in steel-using industries than in the steel industry itself. Higher steel prices penalized domestic producers of steel-intensive products, such as farm equipment and machinery, harming their competitive position in domestic and foreign markets (by reducing their exports and increasing other imports)."[27] Such businesses were one or two removes from the steel-production industry, but they were certainly downstream from it. President Trump's tariffs may have helped preserve several thousand steel jobs,[28] but, as a 2020 Brookings Institution study illustrated, "any gains in importing-competing sectors appear to have been more than offset by losses in industries that use imported inputs and face retaliation on their foreign exports."[29] A similar turn of events occurred when

President Obama imposed tariffs on tire imports from China over a three-year period. The total cost for American consumers was an extra $1.112 billion each year because of the extra costs of tire imports and the higher price of domestically produced tires. While approximately 1,200 jobs were saved, almost 4,000 jobs—again, mostly blue-collar jobs—were lost in other industries.[30] These cases from the Obama and Trump years illustrate that tariffs really do involve choosing one industry over others and, in some instances, some blue-collar jobs in one sector over more blue-collar jobs in other sectors.

Though some protectionists may acknowledge that tariffs hurt American businesses and consumers, they maintain that the federal government can use them when trying to cajole other countries into opening their markets. Adam Smith, they note, agreed that tariffs might be justified as a way of pressuring other nations to reduce their tariffs. But those invoking Smith here are slower to acknowledge that he held that this was usually an unwise policy to follow. Not only, Smith maintained, was the legislator implementing such a policy likely to be an "insidious and crafty animal"[31] dominated by short-term considerations and thus unlikely to be truly interested in wanting to establish free trade; those who would suffer the high costs of retaliatory tariffs were seldom the same as those implementing the tariffs.

The ineffectiveness of retaliatory tariffs was on full display when the Obama administration imposed tariffs as high as 249 percent on a surge of Chinese solar panel imports into America. This import influx had been fueled by the Chinese government heavily subsidizing this industry. The Obama tariffs undoubtedly led many solar panel manufacturers to shift their operations out of China. But they did not move to the United States. Instead, they started assembling solar cells and modules throughout Southeast Asian countries, thereby avoiding America's tariff on solar panels made in China. Further complicating matters, China responded to the Obama tariffs by imposing its own tariffs of up to 57 percent on imports of United States–made polysilicon (a key material used in solar panels). These tariffs were aimed at hurting American solar panel producers by making American polysilicon too expensive for manufacturers in China. American businesses consequently declined from being manufacturers of 50 percent of the world's polysilicon in 2007 to less than 5 percent in 2021.[32] China, however, also paid a price for its actions. Beijing's willingness to subsidize the Chinese solar panel industry certainly reduced the world price of solar panels. But this meant that Chinese companies made far less profit than they otherwise would have, and that they have remained highly reliant on state subsidies.

Such is the bizarre world of mutual devastation into which trade wars take countries. It is as if, as the left-wing Keynesian economist Joan Robinson once wrote, we "dump rocks into our harbors because other nations have rocky coasts."[33] The Smoot-Hawley 1930 Tariff Act underscores the folly of going down this path. Initially Smoot-Hawley appeared to have a positive net-impact throughout America. Industrial production increased sharply, as did construction contracts and factory payrolls.[34] Irwin's study of Smoot-Hawley's effects, however, demonstrates that the raising of tariffs on more than 20,000 imports provoked significant retaliation against America from across the globe. This reduced U.S. exports and contributed to America's share of overall world trade dropping in the 1930s.[35] That eventually translated into businesses—and the jobs they provided—downsizing or disappearing altogether at a time when America could ill-afford such developments.

MANUFACTURING TRUTH AND FICTION

Given these problems with tariffs, why do such policies continue to attract support from considerable numbers of Americans? One reason concerns a subject that has garnered enormous attention over the past thirty years and featured in American presidential elections since the early 1990s. That concerns American manufacturing.

Many on the left and right have argued that American manufacturing is in decline, and that an associated reduction in manufacturing jobs has helped facilitate some of the social and economic problems facing American regions that have traditionally been major manufacturing hubs. This has, it is maintained, principally affected blue-collar communities who can no longer look to the local factory for jobs that, in the not-so-recent past, allowed people with relatively low educational levels to earn wages sufficient to marry and raise children in economically secure settings. As a result, the argument continues, entire communities have been devastated, with large numbers of people (especially young men) living in Rust Belt states turning to alcohol, illegal narcotics, and opioids to dull the pain. Many people living in these areas voted for Barack Obama twice but then voted for Donald Trump in 2016. Trump made a point of stating that he would do something to redress manufacturing's apparent decay, but he was also willing to speak about problems like opioid abuse in these communities. Trump likewise avoided the mistake of dismissing such concerns with throwaway "Go-And-Learn-To-Code" lines.

Trade liberalization is regularly blamed as contributing significantly to these economic and social challenges. American manufacturers, we are told, cannot compete with countries like China that pay lower wages. America should therefore raise tariffs and impose quotas on imports of manufacturing goods to stem the decline in American manufacturing jobs and manufacturing's share of the U.S. economy, thereby helping to promote social stability and more regular employment in parts of the country that need it. There is consequently a case, it is suggested, for using protectionist tools to stabilize or even increase American manufacturing jobs. An extra few dollars paid by American consumers to maintain such forms of employment is worth it, they say, in social terms.

There is no dispute that manufacturing has declined as a proportion of the postwar American economy, or that there has been an overall decline in the number of manufacturing jobs. Nor can it be denied that high levels of dysfunctionality have emerged in particular parts of America. But solutions to problems require accurate diagnoses of the sickness, followed by prescriptions likely to help rather than aggravate the situation. In both respects, those making the case for tariffs to protect and promote American manufacturing are seriously misdiagnosing the problem and proposing ineffective solutions.

First, we need to put some facts in front of us. The decline in American manufacturing jobs and this sector's declining share of U.S. GDP reflect long-term trends happening across the world, especially in developed nations—including those countries with manufacturing-intensive economies and which have used industrial policy to try to stem such trends.[36] But, we should note, the overall decline in manufacturing jobs in America has gone together with rising manufacturing sector output throughout developed countries, including the United States.[37]

Put another way, the number of people employed in an industry isn't a good indicator of productivity. Productivity concerns how much value is added—not how many people are employed in a factory. Indeed, while the number of Americans employed in manufacturing has declined, real manufacturing production in America grew by 180 percent between 1972 and 2007. By 2019, it was back to pre-Great Recession levels.[38] In his analysis of the state of American manufacturing compared to the world's other top manufacturing nations in 2018, Scott Lincicome illustrates that American manufacturing continued to be at or was "near the top of most categories, including output, exports, and investment."[39] In other words, America continues to be a major global manufacturer and a priority destination for manufacturing investment.[40]

To speak then of America undergoing deindustrialization is mistaken. So what is going on? This is where a second set of facts becomes extremely important. In his concise analysis of American manufacturing, economist Pierre Lemieux illustrates that American manufacturing jobs declined from 19 million in 1979 to about 12 million in 2016.[41] Throughout the same period, however, total employment in America grew from 99 million to 151 million, especially in the service sector. Not only did this dwarf the loss of manufacturing jobs. It also meant that millions of individuals who a few decades ago might otherwise have been employed in manufacturing were employed elsewhere.[42] Millions of jobs had been created in the American economy that offset the decline in manufacturing employment several times over.

Lemieux also demonstrates that the net manufacturing job decline in America has been driven by technological innovation as well as America embracing the shift in its comparative advantage towards high-skilled, high-end manufacturing—that is, in conceiving, designing, logistics, distribution, and engineering—while developing countries now have a comparative advantage in unskilled tasks like assembling the various components.[43] To walk inside an American factory today is to enter a world very different from that of the 1950s. Contemporary American factories employ far fewer unskilled or low-skilled laborers. Instead we find large numbers of highly trained technicians and engineers working together in a sophisticated high-tech environment. We also discover that many manufacturing jobs that existed from the 1950s to the 1980s have been replaced by machines and technology, rather than shipped abroad, as many advocates of protectionism regularly claim. Hence while "Physical things continue to be produced," Lemieux points out, "production occurs more efficiently" in America.[44] This is what happens when individuals and businesses are entrepreneurial, embrace new technology, adjust to domestic and foreign competitive pressures, and are not encouraged by tariffs to imagine that they can somehow ward off competitive pressures forever.

When I hear conservatives say that we cannot leave entire communities of Americans to rot, I can only agree. But solutions to problems, I repeat, require 1) accurate diagnosis of the sickness and 2) prescriptions likely to help rather than aggravate the situation.

Those advocating protectionist positions thus need to ask themselves some questions. Putting aside genuine national security concerns (a subject addressed in later chapters), why would we use tariffs to try to maintain forms of manufacturing where America does not enjoy a comparative advantage? Should we pretend that technology has not displaced certain types of manufacturing employment? And why should the United States seek to lock in the type of industrial structures and manufacturing jobs that existed seventy years ago but that are now obsolete?

When I have posed these questions to supporters of protectionism, the following type of response is often made: "For all the problems associated with protectionism, maybe we should use such measures to help distressed communities throughout Rust Belt towns and states. We cannot stand by and do nothing."

Americans should worry about the dysfunctionalities that mark particular demographic groups, towns, and regions throughout the United States. There is no denying the rise in social pathologies among particular demographic groups and in specific parts of America. Writing in the *Journal of the American Medical Association*, Steven H. Woolf and Heidi Schoomaker reported the following:

> Between 1959 and 2016, US life expectancy increased from 69.9 years to 78.9 years but declined for 3 consecutive years after 2014. The recent decrease in US life

expectancy culminated a period of increasing cause-spe-
cific mortality among adults aged 25 to 64 years that
began in the 1990s, ultimately producing an increase in
all-cause mortality that began in 2010. During 2010–
2017, midlife all-cause mortality rates increased from
328.5 deaths/100,000 to 348.2 deaths/100,000. By 2014,
midlife mortality was increasing across all racial groups,
caused by drug overdoses, alcohol abuse, suicides, and a
diverse list of organ system diseases. [45]

The biggest relative increases, Woolf and Schoomaker specified,
occurred in New England as well as the Ohio Valley: West Virginia, Ohio, Indiana, and Kentucky. [46] These states have long been
home to large manufacturing industries.

But these trends, however disturbing, should not inhibit us from
asking searching questions here about cause and effect. One such
question is how much can we attribute the rise in these pathologies
to America's gradual and overall diminishment of protectionist
policies since 1945? While a decline in employment opportunities
in particular forms of work may have contributed to such problems,
this would have likely happened anyway because of technological
change rendering particular types of jobs obsolete. Another question to ask is whether ascribing increases in these pathologies to
trade policy actually distracts us from some of the real causes? Are
we to believe, for example, that factors like the Sexual Revolution
of the 1960s, the breakdown of the family and marriage, and the
weakening of habits of civil association throughout America were
marginal contributors to these problems?

Even if, for the sake of argument, it was possible to attribute such social problems largely to economic changes, resorting to protectionism is unlikely to improve the situation. Certainly, changes in the economy associated with exposure to foreign competition can facilitate upheaval in job markets. What is often called the "China shock"—the growth of manufacturing imports from China, especially in the period from 1999 to 2011—exemplifies this. One estimate suggests that about 1 million of the 5.8 million manufacturing jobs that disappeared in this period were a result of some American manufacturers adjusting to compete with Chinese imports. The same study indicated that some who lost their jobs in this period struggled to find new employment or found themselves having to settle for lower wages. [47]

Before blaming the failure to protect American manufacturing from Chinese and other foreign competition for the apparent loss of one million manufacturing jobs, however, consider the following. First, many of those people *did* find jobs in other sectors of the economy. Second, we know that some of those who lost their jobs were reluctant to move to different parts of the country to find work. Surely, some such individuals felt connected to their community and were understandably unenthusiastic about moving. But in other cases, various government assistance and trade adjustment programs that were supposed to help workers manage the transition created what are called perverse incentives against adapting to change. The provision of unemployment benefits, healthcare, and disability assistance to aid these groups actually discouraged people from moving to find work. [48] Efforts to cushion the impact of foreign competition thus indirectly impeded the adjustment process. Third, we need to recall that of the 5.8 million manufacturing jobs that disappeared in these years, 4.8 million manufacturing jobs disappeared for reasons *other* than trade.

Other analyses of trade liberalization's effects on American manufacturing reveal a similar picture. One study by a team of economists estimated that about 20 percent of American manufacturing job losses between 2000 and 2010 could be reasonably attributed to increased foreign competition emanating from trade.[49] That is a bigger percentage than the previously cited study, but it still means that 80 percent resulted from other causes like technological enhancement. Yet another analysis of the same period indicates that just over 10 percent of the job losses were attributable to trade competition, while almost 90 percent flowed from technological advances and process improvement.[50] If these studies are accurate, blaming a dismantling of protectionism for reductions in manufacturing jobs is a serious mistake. Even if China had not entered the WTO in 2001, manufacturing jobs would *still* have undergone substantial decline because of technology.

Some may regard this as an excessively economic view of protectionism and its implications for manufacturing employment. Surely, they might add, we should at least consider using protectionist measures to maintain some jobs so that people in manufacturing towns can preserve a sense of being productive. Work is more than just a means for people to acquire what they need to consume. Work provides people with meaning beyond its economic significance. Through work, people can acquire important habits and even virtues which make them better, more rounded human beings.

Work does indeed have a significance beyond economics. Even so, that truth is not sufficient reason to deploy protectionist policies in invariably futile attempts to keep people working in particular jobs or industries. There is also something perverse about using the state to encourage people to produce goods and services that fewer and fewer people want or need, or to stay in jobs being rendered redundant by technology. It is the equivalent of a very wealthy person deciding to purchase secretly all the cars made by an American car manufacturer but insisting on anonymity because he doesn't want the producer and his employees to know that no one wants or needs their cars anymore. Should they discover that their products and their jobs are effectively supported by charity, it's reasonable to suppose that the satisfaction which they gained from producing unwanted and unneeded cars would be radically diminished.

POLITICAL GAMESMANSHIP

Despite all the advocacy in America today for some type of return to protectionism, surveys of American opinion suggest that protectionism has struggled to gain majority support among Americans since 1990.[51] Yet if Americans aren't especially enthusiastic about protectionism, why does it continue to influence trade policy?

Protectionism may make American consumers pay more for often lower-quality goods, but tariffs and import quotas directly benefit those American businesses who resent the disciplines of competition and want to make it harder for others to enter "their" markets. Unlike consumers, such businesses have the resources,

political contacts, and incentives to lobby legislators and governments for preferential treatment. Ergo, special interests tend to
prevail in trade policy debates, even if most people favor greater
trade liberalization. This insight was central to Smith's skepticism
of those proposing a particular regulation of commerce:

> The proposal of any new law or regulation of commerce
> . . . ought always to be listened to with great precaution,
> and ought never to be adopted till after having been long
> and carefully examined, not only with the most scrupu-
> lous, but with the most suspicious attention. It comes
> from an order of men, whose interest is never exactly
> the same with that of the public, who have generally an
> interest to deceive and even oppress the public, and who
> accordingly have, upon many occasions, both deceived
> and oppressed it. [52]

While these words sound cynical, analysis of protectionism's
history in America illustrates how much it has been about securing the interests of politically connected businesses at the expense
of American consumers and American companies lacking political connections. In the first systematic academic study of tariffs
in America, *The Tariff History of the United States* (1888), Frank
Taussig devoted considerable attention to exploring the political
background. One consistent finding of Taussig's study was that
lobbying to promote tariffs had little to do with a concern for
American consumers' well-being. Looking at the wool tariff act of
1867 and the copper tariff act of 1869, Taussig found no evidence

of direct bribery. He did, however, discover that "contributions to the party chest are the form in which money payments by the protected interests are likely to have been made."[53] Taussig also concluded that "some Congressmen thought it not improper to favor legislation that put money in their own pockets, and that many thought it quite proper to support legislation that put money into the pockets of influential constituents." More generally, Taussig established a consistent pattern of "manipulation of the tariff in the interest of private individuals."[54] The same interests, he notes, were successful in nullifying any significant effort to reduce tariffs significantly via the 1883 Tariff Act, despite growing opposition to tariffs in general throughout America.[55]

A similar picture of cronyism emerges from Irwin's study of Smoot-Hawley. The Act amounted, as its Congressional opponents noted at the time, to "a mass of private legislation carried out with little regard for national interest."[56] While Republican backers of the original bill insisted that it would be primarily focused upon agriculture, Smoot-Hawley quickly metastasized beyond that. The bill ended up increasing duties on manufactured goods more than on agricultural products.[57] For as soon as the prospect of tariff increases became politically real, numerous businesses began lobbying for protection, as did unions (especially after 1930) representing workers in these industries. In their 2020 study of Smoot-Hawley, Irwin and Anson Soderbery determined that about three quarters of tariff levels were determined by political lobbying.[58]

Smoot-Hawley's drafting was subsequently characterized, as Irwin puts it, by "logrolling, special interest politics, and [an] inability of members of Congress to think beyond their own district." [59] The possibility of higher tariffs encouraged legislators to put sectional interests before the country's overall well-being. Even worse, Irwin illustrates, many "politicians were more interested in the appearance than the reality of helping farmers cope with low prices and high indebtedness." [60] They wanted to be seen to be acting, whatever the actual consequences of raising tariffs. All this occurred despite a largely negative public reaction when the Smoot-Hawley Bill was first proposed. Though opinion polls were not used widely in America until the mid-1930s, the vast majority of newspaper editors in forty-three states opposed the Act. The opposition was also bipartisan. Even those supporting the bill were "tepid and even apologetic in doing so." [61] Nonetheless, the coalition of special interests and legislators triumphed.

POWERFUL MINORITIES BEAT PASSIVE MAJORITIES

These examples illustrate why those advancing protectionist positions are so adept at getting their way. Those who benefit from free trade are widely dispersed and unorganized. Those who want to secure protection are not only highly concentrated but also have strong incentives to get close to legislators. Lobbying for tariffs to be applied to one's industry or business is not a cost-free exercise, but the potential payoff is very big.

Industries which are regionally concentrated can also exercise disproportionate political influence, even if they constitute a relatively small portion of the overall economy. They can pressure their state's Congressional members and Senators to support tariffs; it is difficult (and rare) for legislators to vote in ways that directly conflict with some of their most economically influential constituents' interests. Legislators are also adroit at securing support from their colleagues for tariffs for particular industries within their state or Congressional seat by promising to support the tariffs desired by Congressmen and Senators in other districts and states. Nor it is unusual for those seeking to liberalize trade to secure the support of particular legislators by trading off support for tariffs that benefit those legislators' particular industries in return for legislators voting in favor of an overall trade liberalization package. Similar dynamics are in play when it comes to reducing tariffs once they have been legislated into place. No one likes to have a privilege taken away from them. Those who benefit from a tariff have every immediate incentive to resist. The same people are unlikely to be thinking about the ways in which tariffs will help render their industry uncompetitive in the long term. They will likely be retired by the time the un-competitiveness begins to bite.

Protectionists also enjoy some distinct advantages in the public relations battle. They can point to a particular product often produced in a specific place by well-known local companies, and thus can easily dramatize the immediacy of their situation. They can additionally claim that they are not asking for much, save a few more dollars from every American consumer. Those on the other side of the debate are stuck with having to point to protectionism's general and gradual negative effects over the long term, to which protectionists will invariably respond by refocusing the attention of the public and legislators on the immediate. Those seeking protection will often claim that the tariff increase is temporary and needed to get the industry over a bad hump, after which the tariff can be wound back. Such is the argument invariably made by American steel companies. "The management and unions of Big Steel," Irwin points out, "perpetually blame their problems on imports and are continually calling for import restraints to allow the industry to revitalize itself,"[62] despite the fact that "[t]he steel industry has received nearly continuous protection for over thirty years and is still seeking limits on imports."[63]

On the basis of the arguments and evidence assembled in this chapter, it is difficult to see why the extensive or selective deployment of protectionist measures should become part of America's economic way forward. Protectionist policies are not, however, the only interventionist option being suggested by those who want more state involvement in America's economy. While some may concede protectionism's ineffectiveness and recognize the damage that it inflicts, they insist that the U.S. economy requires specific sectoral interventions if it is to compete with China or if unemployment is to be reduced in certain regions of America. They have in mind a related form of government intervention which is just as unlikely to contribute to an optimal economic future for America.

CHAPTER 3

THE TROUBLE WITH INDUSTRIAL POLICY

The statesman who should attempt to direct private people in what manner they ought to employ their capitals, would not only load himself with a most unnecessary attention, but assume an authority which could safely be trusted, not only to no single person, but to no council or senate whatever, and which would nowhere be so dangerous as in the hands of a man who had folly and presumption enough to fancy himself fit to exercise it.

—ADAM SMITH

Through the 1980s and early 1990s, you didn't have to look far to find Americans convinced that America's place in the global economy was threatened by Japan. Popular films like *Black Rain* (1989) and *Rising Sun* (1993) portrayed Japan—a country levelled by the United States during World War II—as economically conquering America. Similarly, books such as *The Japan That Can Say No: Why Japan Will Be First Among Equals* (1989), *MITI and the Japanese Miracle: The Growth of Industrial Policy, 1925–1975* (1982), and *Blindside: Why Japan is Still on Track to Overtake the U.S. by the Year 2000* (1995) were penned by scholars and business executives who contended that the Japanese economic model was the future.

The tone of these publications often verged on the apocalyptic. In *Trading Places: How We Are Giving Our Future to Japan and How to Reclaim It* (1990), Clyde V. Prestowitz maintained that if America did not embrace Japanese ways, it might become an economic colony of Tokyo. [1] Likewise, American legislators and CEOs complained of the ubiquity of Japanese cars, computers, and technology, fretted about whether America could compete, and called for higher tariffs against Japanese imports. Above all, they insisted that what's commonly known as industrial policy had to be the centerpiece of the twenty-first-century American economy.

A quarter of a century later, similar arguments emerged with force across America with reference to another East Asian power. If government didn't take a far more proactive role in shaping the American economy's composition in ways that went far beyond what advocates of limited government would typically accept, America was destined to be left in the dust by Communist China. Alongside this went another argument: that extensive use of industrial policy was necessary if particular regions and demographic groups in America were to have meaningful futures.

Industrial policy is hardly foreign to the American economic experience. In the 1790s, Alexander Hamilton dabbled in proto-industrial policy, having been convinced by Assistant Treasury Secretary Tench Coxe to back the chartering of the Society for Establishing Useful Manufacturers and the associated effort to create a quasi-public manufacturing town. Today the federal government and state governments continue to deploy industrial policy in different sectors of the economy. Those who want America to make extensive use of industrial policy are not thus asking for a fundamental change in direction. They are asking for more of something that already exists.

The fact, however, that industrial policy is part of America's economic landscape also means that we can examine its track record and judge whether it should play a larger role in the U.S. economy. But before doing so, we must be clear about what is meant by industrial policy, because this is a precondition for assessing its impact.

NOT EVERYTHING IS INDUSTRIAL POLICY

The term "industrial policy" is fraught with ambiguity. In 1986, political scientist Aaron Wildavsky asserted that "Industrial policy is economic policy; its purpose is prosperity. It is more than that, however, for economic relationships vitally affect the distribution of political power. Broadly viewed, therefore, every country has an industrial policy roughly equivalent to its political economy."[2] Responding to this claim, economist Herbert Stein suggested that Wildavsky's definition of industrial policy was so broad as to be practically meaningless.[3]

These are not mere semantic questions. If industrial policy's definition is too vague, its critics and supporters will lack a common baseline for assessing particular endeavors as industrial policy successes or failures. The phrase is often used to describe an all-embracing economic alternative to free markets that avoids outright collectivization of the economy. But this would mean that industrial policy was simply be a synonym for social democracy. Debate about the pros and cons of industrial policy would consequently morph into broader arguments about the proper conduct of fiscal policy and monetary policy.

One way to determine what makes industrial policy distinct is to acknowledge that it is focused on using state intervention to shape specific sectors of a nation's economy from the top down. This point was central to the influential definition offered by economic historian Ellis W. Hawley. He described industrial policy as "a national policy aimed at developing or retrenching selected industries to achieve national economic goals."[4] Such goals might range from faster growth or helping parts of the country that are falling behind. A tighter economic variant of this definition was outlined in Howard Pack and Kamal Saggi's widely cited 2006 World Bank paper on the topic. They identified industrial policy "as any type of selective intervention or government policy that attempts to alter the sectoral structure of production toward sectors that are expected to offer better prospects for economic growth than would occur in the absence of such intervention, i.e., in the market equilibrium."[5]

These definitions help clarify certain points. First, the objective of industrial policy is not to comprehensively replace entrepreneurship, free prices, market-based allocations of production and investment, or private accumulations of capital in a given economy. Second, it rules out conflating industrial policy with defense policy. Industrial policy's purposes are commercial, not defense research and procurement. The direct goal of defense policy is national security, and the prime user of products produced for defense purposes is the military—not consumers in general. There may be commercial spillovers from defense research and production, but such side effects are not the object of defense policy. Third, industrial policy is generally targeted at specific economic sectors. This is why, for example, monetary policy or environmental policy do not qualify as industrial policy. Changes in monetary policy may have varying consequences for different economic sectors. But it is not immediately focused on influencing production in targeted industries or producing better results in particular economic sectors in specific parts of the country than would otherwise be produced by the market.

With these parameters in mind, we can say that industrial policy involves:

- Government efforts to address apparent failures on the market's part to produce particular commercial outcomes in terms of capital investments, goods and services, and employment levels.

- Microeconomic interventions into these areas through means such as subsidies, outright capital grants, special tax write-offs, joint public-private enterprises, etc.
- The targeting of such interventions at businesses and industries rather than whole-of-economy policies, often with a view to helping specific groups or regions.

This understanding of industrial policy has been embraced by some of its most prominent supporters. This includes figures from the right, like the historian Arthur Herman, [6] and from the left, like former Clinton administration Labor Secretary Robert Reich. [7] These individuals may disagree about what sectors and businesses should be targeted by industrial policy, or how that should occur. Nonetheless they agree upon what industrial policy is. They also recognize that adopting this position is to embrace one version of state capitalism insofar as the government effectively seeks to be entrepreneurial, even a major participant in parts of the market, and thereby shape the development of different economic sectors to try to realize predetermined goals.

FAULTY FOUNDATIONS

This definition of industrial policy makes it plain that there is scarcely a country which does not deploy it at some level. The differences are more about scale and form. But whatever these disparities, industrial policy is based on particular assumptions. One of the most important of these concerns knowledge.

Industrial policy involves trying to alter the allocation of resources and incentives in particular economic sectors that would otherwise transpire if entrepreneurs and businesses were left to themselves. The goal is to produce better results in that economic sector. Efficiently realizing such goals assumes, however, that political leaders, civil servants, and technocrats possess the knowledge to comprehend all the technical details, possible methods of production, the range of incentives, actual and future prices, unintended consequences, and alternative uses of resources (to name just a few sets of information) that they would need to decide accurately the most optimal allocation of resources and course of action.

Alas, no one can know all these things about a given economic sector, let alone an entire economy. Policymakers cannot know the optimal allocation of capital and labor in any given economy or industrial sector. Nor can they know the ever-changing preferences of millions of consumers and producers at any one moment in time. Even those attempting to implement industrial policy on a relatively small scale have to confront the fact that all the information they would need to achieve their goal efficiently is dispersed among thousands of people and is constantly changing. Some of the information that they require does not even exist yet. How does one know, for example, what technologies will be valuable in the future, and which won't? Moreover, the more knowledge we accumulate, the more we become aware of the importance of other data points that we did not previously know about. Nor can policymakers absorb all the ever-growing and ever-changing tacit knowledge possessed by humans which undoubtedly exists, even if it is difficult to explain, articulate, or measure.

In sum, humans lack not only all the data but also the ability to assimilate all the information they would need to be able to say with a considerable degree of confidence that a given industrial policy will realize a particular outcome efficiently or even effectively. Industrial policy advocates often respond by saying that this over-theorizes the problem. Of course, they agree, humans can't know everything. No entrepreneur or business, they point out, can know everything about their present and future market. And yet we allow them to embark upon thousands of endeavors, many of which fail—sometimes spectacularly. Why, it follows, should we not let technocrats and government officials engage in similar activity? A second argument of some industrial policy supporters is that while they recognize that realizing the goal is likely to be an inefficient and costly process, there are times when efficiency needs to be sacrificed if important economic and non-economic goals are to be achieved. Third, even if an industrial policy fails, some industrial policy boosters maintain that there is a significant possibility that it will have positive spillover effects. While these are unplanned, they end up indirectly benefiting many businesses and consumers. This, it is argued, helps compensate in the long run for any inefficiencies generated by such interventions by producing economic growth on a scale likely to outweigh any market inefficiencies caused by these same interventions.

There are no less than six major problems which, I'd suggest, should cause us to be skeptical about these claims. The first is called opportunity costs. If the state chooses to subsidize a particular company or inject capital into a particular economic sector, it cancels out the opportunity for those resources to be invested elsewhere. As economist Michelle Clark Neely explains:

> Each subsidy given to an industry or firm generates an opportunity cost: the cost of foregone alternatives. In other words, to correctly evaluate a policy, you need to know not only what you're getting, but also what you're giving up. Based on industrial policy experiments in several countries, most economists have little confidence in the government's ability to measure these benefits and costs properly.[8]

No government department—let alone a single technocrat—can know if the forgone alternatives might have been more profitable; or might have produced even more growth, innovation, or spillover effects for a greater number of businesses and consumers; or even have helped a region or social group overcome some of its economic challenges. No legislator or expert can consequently claim with any meaningful degree of certainty that a particular industrial policy will produce more such benefits than would have resulted if the state had not implemented the policy. They simply do not know what might have otherwise occurred.

The second problem is that there is a major difference between private sector initiatives and enterprises driven by industrial policy. Those involved in a private endeavor directly bear the costs of failure in economic and reputational terms. The same cannot be said of the government department or technocrat responsible for the design and implementation of a failed industrial policy. For one thing, their personal resources are not at stake: those costs are borne by and dispersed among millions of taxpayers. That diminishes the odds of government officials learning from their mistakes. It may even encourage them to take risks they would never take with their own assets, thereby increasing the chances that they will persist in promoting a failed industrial policy. Such individuals are also usually insulated to varying degrees from other costs of failure. Career government officials are notoriously hard to fire. They might find themselves transferred to another project or department. Rarely, however, are they let go.

Third, industrial policies are strongly political in their character and ends. They are created and overseen for the most part by elected officials, political appointees, and government employees. And because they are created through political processes, industrial policies are especially open to capture by rent-seeking individuals and groups who are forever looking for subsidies and skilled at explaining why they are uniquely equipped to implement the policy. That dramatically lowers the likelihood of industrial policy being characterized by a concern for economic efficiency while simultaneously raising the odds that the real goal will become the enrichment and perpetual privileging of those implementing the policy at everyone else's expense.

Fourth, government use of industrial policy undermines the market's ability to furnish the accurate information needed by entrepreneurs, investors, and businesses to identify the most optimal economic path for each of them to follow—a process which constantly allows millions of piecemeal improvements to be made across the overall economy. By contrast, if industrial policies become a central feature of economic life, inefficiencies will grow throughout the economy as people act on the basis of increasingly bad information.

Fifth, industrial policy supposes that if markets apparently fail to produce certain products, or to foster certain economic sectors deemed important for regional or national well-being, the government must intervene to rectify the problem. But what if the failure is not one of the private sector at all? What if the problem is pre-existing high taxes on profits generated by start-ups? Or regulatory barriers to entry for entrepreneurs? Or weak protections for intellectual property rights? Or preexisting subsidies that incentivize businesses to invest in established industries rather than new enterprises? Or some combination of these factors? In short, what if the problem is primarily government failure? Even relatively free economies contain numerous distortions that flow from government interventions that create perverse incentives for labor and capital to flow in less-than-optimal directions. The solution to such problems is less government intervention, not an industrial policy.

Sixth, industrial policy has difficulty proving its effectiveness in achieving both general and specific goals. Industrial policy is often touted as necessary to initiate or accelerate growth in a region or even country. But it is hard, for instance, to establish causality between a given industrial policy and economic growth. East Asian countries like Malaysia, South Korea, Taiwan, Thailand, and Japan are regularly posited as late-twentieth century examples of industrial policy being successfully used to transform these nations economically. Yet as a 1993 World Bank analysis of the East Asian economic miracle stated: "It is very difficult to establish statistical links between growth and a specific intervention and even more difficult to establish causality. Because we cannot know what would have happened in the absence of a specific [industrial] policy, it is very difficult to test whether interventions increased growth rates."[9]

The same critique can be made of the relationship between industrial policy and the realization of more specific ends. Industrial policy promoters, for example, often argue that it has significantly enhanced innovation in many countries. In her book *The Entrepreneurial State* (2015), Mariana Mazzucato maintains that government has played a major role in technological changes ranging from the iPhone to the Internet. On this basis, she argues for the state implementing industrial policies focused on fostering innovation within numerous economic sectors.

Again, the difficulty is one of establishing causality. Innovation is driven by many things. Spending on military technology and defense R&D may play a role. Levels and types of education have an effect. Security of intellectual property rights is likely important. So too are cultural mindsets. The Nobel economist Edmund S. Phelps has produced substantial evidence which indicates that varying attitudes towards liberty is one reason why entrepreneurship and innovation remains more present in America than in the European Union (EU).[10]

Even when it comes to the Internet, there is considerable doubt about whether industrial policy played a significant role. If the Internet has a precursor, it was the Advanced Research Projects

Agency Network (ARPANET). This was created by a U.S. Defense Department agency as a military-networking device to be used by government agencies and university researchers. But as economist Adam Thierer illustrated in his book *Permissionless Innovation*, it was not until the Clinton administration permitted open market commercialization of this technology that the modern Internet became possible. Indeed, the same administration consciously adopted an anti-industrial policy approach to this area. [11]

Thus, while ARPANET did have unintended spillover effects, it is a stretch to say that the decision to create it led directly to the Internet, let alone to claim the Internet as exemplifying successful industrial policy. There is no straight line between this government project's development of particular technologies and the Internet's emergence. Harvard economist Shane Greenstein's study of the Internet's development likewise demonstrates that the Internet as it exists today emerged largely from below, through innovation by private actors. [12] He underscores the "absence of any large, coordinating government planner" driving the Internet's development and notes that there was no government department overseeing its design, construction, and operation. [13] The same is true of the relationship between the iPhone's development and state-sponsored science projects. [14]

At a minimum, these six issues with industrial policy should make its advocates circumspect, and more humble, before they claim that particular interventions might facilitate greater overall growth, ignite a new economic sector, or produce thousands of manufacturing jobs in Western Pennsylvania. Nor can they rule out the possibility that a given industrial policy may undermine the economic and political well-being of a country, region, or industry, whether by generating massive inefficiencies that compromise the adaptability of part or all of the economy, or by creating tremendous incentives for businesses and politicians to engage in the cronyism which does such damage to the integrity of the political system. If all this is true, the burden of proof is on industrial policy advocates to demonstrate why a government should pursue an industrial policy.

None of these flaws associated with industrial policy mean that it is never able to realize pre-determined ends. If a government is willing to pour enough money and resources into any given industrial policy, it is bound to produce some wins. Yet the same is true of the gambler. If he stays in the casino long enough and spends enough money, he will win a few hands of cards. But the odds are that he will also lose a great deal of money, especially if he is as inept a gambler as the government is maladroit at identifying industry trends or entrepreneurial opportunities. Moreover, just as a compulsive gambler's behavior will have numerous negative effects on his family's well-being, so too does industrial policy risk inflicting wider damage upon a nation's economy and political system. In this sense, Thierer's description of industrial policy as "casino economics" is spot-on. [15]

LESSONS FROM JAPAN

Such are the intellectual arguments and important empirical data points that should make Americans cautious about intensifying the use of industrial policy to attempt to realize specific outcomes.

The same caution should arise from looking at other major economies which have used industrial policy on a fairly extensive scale
since World War II. In the instances of Japan and China, a similar
picture emerges.

From the 1950s onwards, Japan underwent a remarkable economic transformation that enabled it to overcome the devastation
of World War II. The reasons for this are manifold. The American
occupation helped, especially as the occupying authorities made a
point of breaking up the *Zaibatsu*: the industrial and financial con-
glomerates with strong links to the Japanese military, which had
dominated Japan's pre-1939 economy.[16] This opened the way for
more bottom-up entrepreneurship as well as much-needed competition in Japan's economy.[17]

Other factors contributing to Japan's success included an
increasingly educated workforce which maintained strong wage
discipline, high levels of investment in capital equipment, imports
and improvements of foreign technology, and patent purchases
from American companies.[18] Robust domestic competition also
played a role.[19] Tax rates remained moderate by international
standards. Another element driving Japanese growth was the
extremely high savings-rates that fueled capital and investment
accumulation. As economist Benjamin Powell points out: "Gross
private savings rose from 16.5 percent of GNP between 1952 and
1954 to 31.9 percent in 1970 and 1971. Average domestic savings
from 1960 through 1971 averaged 36.1 percent of national income.
The United States, by comparison, averaged only 15.8 percent
from 1961 to 1971." This contributed to high productivity growth
over a sustained period of time.[20]

Between the 1950s and 1980s, Japan's economy followed a similar trajectory to that of Western developed economies. It rode the wave of economic sectoral change: from agriculture to heavy manufacturing followed by a major shift to the service sector which began, like most other developed economies, in the 1970s. The Japanese workforce transitioned smoothly through all these phases, with most of the Japanese working population being located in finance, real estate, communications, retailing, insurance, and transportation by the 1980s. [21]

In the twentieth century's last quarter, many of those exploring the reasons for Japan's success claimed that industrial policy had played a central role. In 1983, for example, Robert Reich claimed that Japan's economic transformation owed much to the far-reaching use of industrial policy, especially as mediated and directed by experts and civil servants working in Japan's Ministry of International Trade and Industry (MITI). [22] Formed in 1949, MITI sought to spur growth by targeting particular industrial sectors. So powerful did MITI become that future Japanese prime ministers were expected to serve some time as its minister. MITI's attempts to outguess the market until its eventual absorption into Japan's economics ministry in 2001 were so widespread that the very phrase "industrial policy" became synonymous with "the Japanese model."

During the decades of MITI interventions, Japan's government discouraged foreign direct investment in sectors where Japanese businesses had some technological capacity to enter, while also funneling R&D subsidies to technology companies. The amounts, however, turn out to have been less than 5 percent of overall private sector R&D investment. This was lower than the same type of funding made available in America at the same time. Successive Japanese governments also directed capital to what were called preferred sectors through tax breaks, direct and indirect subsidies, and loans from state-owned or state-controlled banks. While some of this assistance was directed to technology R&D, most such subsides went to industries in decline, like agriculture, forestry, and fishing. [23]

The results of these interventions are best labelled mediocre. One of the most comprehensive studies of industrial policy's long-term impact in Japan concluded that it produced "little, if any positive impact on productivity, growth, or welfare." [24] Japan's two most successful industries in global markets—cars and consumer electronics—were not even recipients of extensive government support. [25] Nor could the same analysis uncover any clear indication "that industrial policy enhanced wealth or growth in the era immediately after postwar reconstruction. The evidence indicates that most resource flows went to large, politically influential 'backward' sectors:" [26] indeed, the greater the amount of government support to a given sector, the slower the rate of growth. [27]

MITI's efforts to engineer specific outcomes also turned out not to be especially effective. MITI tried, for instance, to force mergers of car companies and encouraged these businesses not to pursue export markets. MITI even attempted to impede the Sony Corporation from buying the manufacturing rights to the transistor from Western Electric. [28] This effort by MITI failed, much to the good fortune of Sony and Japan's economy. In the 1980s, MITI attempted to bolster major advances in artificial intelligence and supercomputers in what was called the Fifth Generation Project. This came asunder as a result of the sheer pace of change in the private sector's development of computer technology, with which MITI had diffi-culty keeping up. As reported in 1992 when the project was wound down, "After spending $400 million on its widely heralded Fifth Generation computer project, the Japanese Government said this week that it was willing to give away the software developed by the project to anyone who wanted it, even foreigners."[29]

Evidence also abounds of industrial policy's dysfunctional effects upon the Japanese political system. MITI's pursuit of industrial policy often conflicted with interventionist programs pursued by government departments like the Ministry of Posts and Telecom-munications in overlapping areas such as communications. That produced interdepartmental turf wars and bureaucratic empire build-ing: so much so that Japanese industrial policy has been described as becoming largely "the product of self-interested political actors."[30] Moreover, the proceeds of industrial policy became heavily tilted to businesses politically connected to the Liberal Democratic Party that dominated Japanese politics between 1955 until 1993. Loans from state banks to businesses were "systematically higher in prefectures represented by senior or electorally vulnerable Liberal Democratic Party incumbents."[31] This cronyism went together with the spread of outright corruption. It also crowded out, Adam Thierer notes, "not just private financing, but also the development of private-financing knowledge and capabilities for many important emerging sectors. It was one of the many reasons American venture capitalists were able to take such a commanding lead in funneling massive investment into digital-era computing and internet companies."[32]

In the early 1990s, Japan's economy began slipping into what are known as the "Lost Decades." The strong growth that had powered

Japan from the 1950s suddenly stopped. Between 1991 and 2003, Japan's GDP grew a mere 1.14% on an annual basis.[33] The reasons include an aging population, heavy private sector indebtedness, a sclerotic banking system, serious monetary policy errors, and asset bubbles.[34] But industrial policy played a role insofar as it had helped prop up large inefficient and bloated constituencies (like state-owned banks and joint private-public enterprises) that had no interest in being exposed to greater domestic and international competition. Likewise Japanese politicians and government officials had few incentives to end practices that helped them attain and keep political office. This created major obstacles to economic reform. The rigidity in the banking system, for example, owed much to the fact that so much lending had been directed by state officials from the top down. That may have benefited Liberal Democratic politicians wanting to exercise patronage and bolster their supporters, but it was not so good for a Japanese economy in desperate need of greater flexibility.

LESSONS FROM CHINA

By the beginning of the third millennium, some Japanese policy-makers were willing to affirm on the record that industrial policy had not served their country well. In 2002, the Japanese Ministry of Finance's Policy Research Institute stated: "The Japanese model was not the source of Japanese competitiveness but the cause of our failure."[35] Far from industrial policy positively contributing to Japan's economic reemergence after World War II, it had created economic and political dysfunctionalities that were impeding necessary changes. Thirty years later, similar patterns had become apparent with regard to the People's Republic of China.

In the mid-2010s, China's rise to the status of one of the world's three largest economies began setting off alarm bells throughout America. This was especially the case among American conservatives, many of whom demanded a more proactive response from the federal government. In late 2019, Florida Senator Marco Rubio called for "a twenty-first-century pro-American industrial policy." The Chinese, he maintained, were "picking winners and losers." America should do the same. He referred to the need to reverse "the depletion of America's manufacturing sector" and maintained that "from the internet to GPS, many of the innovations that have made America a technological superpower originated from national defense–oriented, public-private partnerships." [36]

Neither of these claims accord with the evidence detailed in this and the previous chapter. At different points, Rubio came close to arguing that America should effectively mimic some of the ways in which China deploys industrial policy. He spoke of using the Small Business Administration to "prioritize encouraging investment in high-potential firms in strategically important industries such as aerospace, rail, electronics, telecommunications, and agricultural machinery. In essence, in the same industries China is trying to dominate via their Made in China 2025 initiative." [37]

In 2021, similar sentiments were expressed by the congressionally authorized bipartisan National Security Commission on Artificial Intelligence (AI). In a major report on AI, the Commission stated that America needed to develop "an integrated national strategy to reorganize the government [and] reorient the nation" so that

America could "compete in the coming era of AI-accelerated competition and conflict."[38] The Commission further contended that
"The Federal Government must partner with U.S. companies to preserve American leadership and to support development of diverse
AI applications that advance the national interest in the broadest
sense."[39] It also claimed that "The government must make major
new investments in AI R&D and establish a national AI research
infrastructure," "build a resilient domestic base for designing and
fabricating microelectronics," and "develop a single, authoritative
list of the technologies that will underpin national competitiveness
in the twenty-first century."[40] China, the Commission stated, was
well down these paths. America should proactively respond.

The Commission's operating assumption was that a grand
industrial policy was absolutely necessary if America was to maintain its innovative edge in AI. Tellingly, its report averred that now
is "not a time for abstract criticism of industrial policy"[41]—as if its
authors knew that critiques of industrial policy are far more than
just theoretical. Yet there was no reason to suppose that any of the
criticisms of industrial policy listed above would not apply to this
particular scheme. Moreover, other entities, such as the EU, have
employed industrial policy in the technology sector for decades in
an effort to give member-states an edge in these types of technological innovation. But as outlined by Adam Thierer and Connor
Haaland in their study of industrial policy EU–style:

> the Europeans don't have much to show for their attempts
> to produce home-grown tech champions. Despite highly
> targeted and expensive efforts to foster a domestic tech

base, the EU has instead generated a string of industrial
policy failures that should serve as a cautionary tale for
U.S. pundits and policymakers, who seem increasingly
open to more government-steered innovation efforts. [42]

Hesitation about embracing widespread industrial policy in this
and other economic sectors should be further reinforced by a closer
look at the Chinese experience. As in Japan's case, there is strong reason to doubt its effectiveness in stimulating economic and technological development in China, and good grounds for believing that
it has often proved counterproductive. To understand this, a brief
excursion into recent Chinese economic history is highly instructive.

The Chinese road out of mass poverty began in 1978 when China's leadership concluded that the Maoist economic model had
not only failed to promote economic progress but severely dam-
aged the country. The new path forward was never about radically
extracting the Chinese Communist Party (CCP) and government
from China's economy, let alone the CCP giving up power. Rather,
it involved selectively embracing particular market mechanisms.
These included allowing some use of private contracts in specific economic sectors; authorizing people in certain industries in
parts of the country (especially rural areas) to keep some profits;
allowing more entrepreneurial initiative from below; providing
some limited security for ownership; decollectivizing much of the
agricultural sector; engaging in some partial privatizations; and
transforming many state enterprises into entities that resembled
some internal structures of Western corporations. "The reforms,"
stated a 1997 International Monetary Fund (IMF) report "raised

economic efficiency by introducing profit incentives to rural collective enterprises (which are owned by local government but are
guided by market principles), family farms, small private businesses, and foreign investors and traders. They also freed many
enterprises from constant intervention by state authorities."[43]

These and other changes were introduced incrementally. They
went together with gradually allowing the free price mechanism to
work, and slowly expanding openness to foreign trade and investment. The latter began attaining momentum in the 1980s. This
had the important effect of connecting China's cheap and plentiful
labor with global trade flows.[44] Throughout the 1990s and early
2000s, efforts to liberalize the Chinese economy were cautiously
extended. This resulted in considerable and ongoing productivity
gains.[45] While we should not exaggerate the extent to which China
embraced economic liberalization, economist Barry Naughton is
not alone in attributing China's success primarily to these policies, limited and haphazard as they were, which lasted from 1978
until 2007.[46] Liberalization was especially crucial in enabling
China to engage in "catch-up growth": the idea that poor or developing economies can grow faster compared to economies with a
higher per capita income by replicating what developed nations
have already done, especially by opening themselves to trade and
quickly embracing production methods and technologies that took
developed nations decades to acquire.

How much of this economic development can be attributed to
industrial policy? Naughton poses precisely that question in his
book *The Rise of China's Industrial Policy, 1978–2020*. "The answer,"
he states, "is simple: none."[47] Industrial policy is far more a feature

of post–2008 financial crisis China than the China which engaged in cautious and selective liberalizations until 2007. One reason for China's turn to extensive use of industrial policy in the late-2000s was an acute awareness of what is called "the middle-income trap," and consciousness that most developing countries that followed a trajectory similar to China get stuck in it.

The middle-income trap occurs when a developing nation loses its comparative advantage in exporting manufactured goods because of rising wages, and then struggles to shift from resource-driven development which relies on cheap labor and capital towards growth based on innovation and ever-increasing productivity. China has long been at risk of falling into this middle-income trap because the transition to innovation is very hard. After 2012, Xi Jinping took China down the path of direct state intervention to try to accelerate growth. This went together with efforts to restrict the scope of private enterprise and the workings of markets. [48] Xi's objective was not to eliminate markets altogether. But as the *Wall Street Journal*'s chief China correspondent, Lingling Wei, observed, Xi did view himself as creating a Chinese economic model to compete directly with American capitalism. [49]

Whatever Xi's ambitions, this state-driven approach to growth has resulted in the pursuit of useless infrastructure projects as well as the emergence of oddities like cities dominated by uncompleted high-rises, uninhabited apartment buildings, and streets empty of shops and people. It has produced severe misallocations of capital by state-controlled banks as they lend to inefficient state enterprises and zombie businesses that need constant propping-up, and the enlargement of market-access restrictions that discourage foreign investment.[50] In its 2021 Article IV Consultation report on China, the IMF estimated that state-owned enterprises were on average only eighty percent as productive as private firms across sectors in China, and were a major reason for China's ongoing fall in productivity and business dynamism since the early-2000s.[51] It subsequently urged Beijing to cease giving state enterprises preferential access to credit, remove any implicit guarantees that state enterprises will be perpetually underwritten by the government, and address the mismanagement problems that characterized these businesses.[52]

These problems bring us squarely to China's use of industrial policy. Not only did industrial policy emerge as a significant component of the regime's post-2008 economic agenda; there is also little doubt of the many failures that have gone along with this. From 2008 onwards, industrial policy CCP–style began to manifest itself through vehicles like new public-private industrial guidance funds (IGFs) that sought to promote innovation in strategic economic sectors like advanced manufacturing, technology, the service sector, infrastructure, and agriculture. Subsidies, direct state investments, and cheap loans featured prominently among the various other vehicles used.[53]

The Chinese regime has never been especially forthcoming about when, where, and why these policies have often gone awry. Perhaps not coincidentally, China's National Bureau of Statistics has restricted more and more information about the size and nature of China's economic growth from public scrutiny since the mid-2010s.[54] In the wake of the coronavirus pandemic, Beijing further intensified the ways in which it limited the release of information to foreigners. A data security law implemented in September

2021 subjected almost all data-related activities (including col-
lection, storage, use, and transmission) to government oversight.
Even the release of financial statements by Chinese companies to
foreign businesses is formally prohibited.[55]

But to the extent that Beijing's use of industrial policy can be studied, there is clear evidence of generally lackluster, if not counterproductive, results. Scott Lincicome and Huan Zhu's detailed analysis
of industrial policy in China illustrates that while it appears to have
aided the development of ultra-high-voltage transmission projects,
renewable energies, steelmaking, and machinery, it has also resulted
in colossal failures in areas like the production of semiconductors,
electric vehicles, domestic aircraft and automotive manufacturing
industries, and 3G mobile technologies.[56] Even in the critical area of
semiconductors, China has been estimated to be three to four generations behind what is considered to be leading technology.[57]

Lincicome and Zhu's conclusions line up with those other analyses of state intervention into particular sectors of the Chinese
economy. In the area of microchip technology, for example, Axel
He points out that

> Despite massive investment in chip manufacturing, China
> generally lags two to three generations behind the lead-
> ing economies. Indeed, China still lags behind in most
> of these core technologies and related advanced man-
> ufacturing, such as high-end chips; basic software and
> operating systems; high-end precision manufacturing
> equipment, for example, machine tools; key equipment
> and materials for chip making; and aircraft engines.[58]

Lincicome and Zhu also underscore some of industrial policy's more general effects on the Chinese economy that call the whole strategy into question. Such problems include: [59]

- Major misallocations of capital and human resources across the whole Chinese economy. This has even been conceded by regime officials who estimate that Beijing wasted at least $6 trillion on ineffective investments between 2009 and 2014 alone. [60]
- Widespread and growing corruption in major sectors of the economy like banking and infrastructure. Corruption is especially rampant in the highly subsidized R&D sector. [61]
- The growth of major investment bubbles in many targeted industries and an increasing number of non-performing commercial loans.
- The emergence of overcapacity in steel, cement, chemical fiber, aluminum, solar panels, and other industries. This means that they are creating too many goods that will most likely never be purchased, will probably be dumped on other markets, and thereby will generate tensions with other countries.

These difficulties are magnified by two other factors. One is the Chinese regime's nature. Reforms instituted by Deng Xiaoping to ensure internal political flexibility and regular personnel changeover have been undermined by Xi's re-centralization of power in the CCP's higher ranks. That has corroded something needed by any government: a willingness to entertain fresh thinking and the type of internal critique which encourages policy corrections. Instead, it has facilitated sycophancy among party officials towards their superiors and a reluctance to tell the unvarnished truth about things like industrial policy failures. To do so is to risk having one's career cut short by a regime that desperately wants these measures to be successful because they are closely linked with Xi's ambition to make China a superpower and provide an alternative economic prototype to American capitalism. The feedback mechanisms which allow Beijing to know what people are really thinking and what is really going on in the Chinese economy are consequently degrading.

Some might argue that this is what makes industrial policy in China different from America. The regime's authoritarian nature means that there is less scope for pushing back against failed policies by legislators and others. In America, by contrast, it is possible to name, shame, and critique industrial policies gone awry. Unfortunately, the American experience with industrial policy suggests a different picture. The core problem is not an absence of feedback mechanisms. It is the inherent flaws of industrial policy itself.

LESSONS FROM—AND FOR—AMERICA

Industrial policy has long been part of the story of America's economy. Hence, there are also numerous studies of its effectiveness. The evidence suggests that industrial policy in America reflects the same problems that manifests itself in other places where it has been tried.

In 1991, the Brookings Institution commissioned five industrial policy–sympathetic economists to undertake a study of the federal government's use of industrial policy in the 1970s and 1980s. They focused on efforts to support and promote sophisticated technological development in six major areas: supersonic transport, communications satellites, the space shuttle, the breeder reactor, photovoltaics, and synthetic fuels. It's important to note that the study did not set out to praise or condemn industrial policy. The objective was to examine why the private sector often fails to fund commercially applicable research adequately, and to propose how the government might concentrate its support for some industries and less on others. Three quarters of the study involved analysis of the results, costs, and management of the six areas mentioned above. It also examined the political aspect of these policies, such as the way they related to congressional votes.

The results of the Brookings study were not favorable to industrial policy. Though the authors proposed changes that they believed might help alleviate specific problems, their key conclusions were as follows:

- "The case studies . . . justify skepticism about the wisdom of government programs that seek to bring new technologies to commercial practice." [62]
- "American political institutions introduce predictable, systematic biases into R&D programs so that, on balance, government projects will be susceptible to performance underruns and cost overruns." [63]

- "In the public sector, the ultimate external test of an R&D program is its ability to generate more political support than opposition."[64]

Nor, despite their sympathy for industrial policy, were the authors optimistic that changes to how decisions about industrial policy were made would improve the government's ability to contribute to the commercialization of R&D.[65]

Have things improved since the 1990s? The evidence suggests not. Lincicome and Zhu found little success and plenty of failure in case after case of industrial policy in America. Their focus was on "how past U.S. attempts at industrial policy (properly defined) have fared [and] whether proposed industrial policies today can fix the economic problems they target." What they discovered were "numerous problems that argue strongly against the adoption of new U.S. industrial policies and establish a high bar for future government action."[66] Among Lincicome and Zhu's more prominent findings were the following:

- Efforts by the federal government to protect and promote manufacturing jobs via industrial policy in the form of tax preferences, direct subsidies, import restraints, and other federal programs have consistently failed.[67]
- Subsidized successes have performed no better than their un-subsidized competitors.[68]
- Industrial policy has encouraged individuals and companies inclined to take excessive risks to do so by incentivizing them to behave in such a way and protecting them from the consequences of failure.[69]

■ Industrial policies often contribute to trade disputes with other countries and generate retaliation from foreign trading partners. [70]

■ There are significant unintended negative consequences of industrial policies not foreseen by those responsible for their design and implementation, and which also undercut realization of the policies' own objectives. "Steel protectionism," for example, "has boosted less productive and innovative firms' lobbying efforts and financial returns, thus discouraging overall innovation (R&D spending and creative destruction) in the industry." [71]

■ Industrial policy has often discouraged private investment in industries that the government is trying to promote by crowding out private investment. [72]

Lincicome and Zhu additionally underscore a sobering fact that touches on an issue addressed in Chapter Two. They found few examples in which industrial policy reversed decline in communities which had been especially reliant upon particular forms of manufacturing. [73] Overwhelmingly, such efforts have failed, whether it is Massachusetts textile towns like Lawrence and Lowell or similar communities in the Midwest, most especially the steel town of Youngstown, Ohio.

The American political system's particularities have exacerbated these problems. Given the extent to which industrial policy is driven by politics, it tends to be characterized in America by great uncertainty in goals and direction because American politics is especially subject to political ups and downs. [74] Elections are frequent in America at the federal, state, and local level. Many elected officials thus gravitate towards looking for solutions that hold out the promise of fixing an immediate economic problem in, or a speedy economic boost to, their electoral district or state. Industrial policy consequently allows political leaders to claim that they are responsible for a tax-break, subsidy, or regulation that will somehow save (or promote) a particular business or industry. Furthermore, by the time the industrial policy's failures and dys-functionalities become hard to hide, many of the legislators who supported it are no longer in office.

In 2017, for example, the Taiwan-based Foxconn Technology Company was offered $3.6 billion worth of tax incentives and sub-sidies by the State of Wisconsin on the basis that Foxconn would build a 13,000-employee facility worth $10 billion that would produce liquid crystal display panels for TVs and similar technol-ogies. That $3.6 billion figure magnified to $4.5 billion once infra-structure expenses incurred by utilities and local municipalities were added. That amounted to the government effectively paying $346,000 for each job. [75]

As it happens, the project did not come anywhere near meet-ing its objectives. In 2021, the contract between the State of Wis-consin and Foxconn was consequently revised. Instead of 13,000 new jobs, the new number was 1,454 positions, and no TV screens were going to be manufactured. And yet, as Lawrence Tabak's detailed analysis of the entire saga revealed, Foxconn "now owned 1,000 acres of prime land already supplied with state-of-the-art infrastructure and virtually unlimited access to Lake Michigan water." [76] These are major corporate assets. But for our purposes, what's most important to note is that, by the time these changes were made to try to save this particular industry policy from complete failure, the state governor and many of the legislators who had initially promoted it were no longer in office.

More broadly, industrial policy in America has proved as prone to being captured by political lobbying and rent-seekers as it is everywhere else. This is exemplified by federal attempts to promote clean energy technology via the 2009 American Recovery and Reinvestment Act (ARRA). Much of the support ended up going to coal-related projects. Technologies like nuclear power, renewables, and gas-fired electricity plants were largely ignored. Why? Because the coal lobby was more powerful and connected than the others. [77]

Another prominent instance of politics coopting industrial policy is the Department of Energy's $535 million loan-guarantee to the Solyndra enterprise via the ARRA. The rationale for this failed industrial policy was America's apparent need to develop solar energy as a fossil-fuel alternative and the market's ostensible failure to deliver. That lobbying played a major role in Solyndra securing this loan-guarantee is not to be doubted. Solyndra spent $1.8 million on lobbyists and six firms with close links to the Obama administration and members of Congress while its application was being studied by the Department of Energy. [78] As investigative reporting by the *Washington Post* recounts:

> Meant to create jobs and cut reliance on foreign oil,
> Obama's green-technology program was infused with
> politics at every level, *The Washington Post* found in an
> analysis of thousands of memos, company records, and

internal e-mails. Political considerations were raised
repeatedly by company investors, Energy Department
bureaucrats and White House officials. . . . "Employees
acknowledged that they felt tremendous pressure, in general, to process loan guarantee applications," the report
said. "They suggested the pressure was based on the significant interest in the program from Department leadership, the Administration, Congress, and the applicants."[79]

Developing fossil-fuel alternatives may or may not be desirable
for America. Regardless, the Solyndra case illustrates how industrial policy means selecting some solar energy companies over
many other such businesses, not to mention the thousands of other
companies seeking to promote other energy renewables. Given the
sheer amount of ever-changing information to be absorbed and
processed by state officials if they are to make the optimal investment choice, it's hard to believe that governments could ever know
which solar energy companies are more worthy of investment than
others or, for that matter, which energy renewables will be more
profitable and sustainable than others. That makes it even more
likely that political influence will be the decisive factor in deciding
who will be the beneficiaries of a given industrial policy.

CORPORATIONS AND POLITICS

Industrial policy illustrates how the intersection of business and
politics is good for neither the economy nor politics. The dynamic

is similar to the one we noted in the previous chapter. Specific interest groups eager to secure privileges are more incentivized and organized to secure any number of favors for themselves. The consumers and taxpayers who pay the costs are dispersed and unorganized. Those businesses who advocate for industrial policy consequently often get their way.

The same logic manifests itself in another set of ideas being advocated as integral to a reshaping of America's economy and which, to my mind, is as much a manifestation of state capitalism as protectionism and industrial policy. It is called many things, but it is commonly known as "stakeholder capitalism."

CHAPTER 4

BUSINESS AGAINST THE MARKET

*People of the same trade seldom meet together, even for
merriment and diversion, but the conversation ends in a
conspiracy against the public, or in some contrivance to
raise prices.*

— ADAM SMITH

A common confusion that has long characterized American political debates is the assumption that supporting business and free
markets are the same thing. Neither Adam Smith nor Milton
Friedman made that error. Whenever I inform students of Smith
and Friedman's unflattering opinions of eighteenth-century
merchants and American business leaders respectively, they are
shocked. But their eyes start opening when I note that many established businesses don't like competition, aren't excited about other

people's new products threatening their bottom line, and are happy to work with complaisant legislators to use state power to make life difficult for their competitors. At this point, students begin realizing that being pro-market is frequently different from being pro-business. The two outlooks are often at odds.

Smith had drawn attention to how the mercantile system was predicated upon some merchants' close relationships with government ministers and civil servants in emerging state bureaucracies. These merchants had no immediate incentive to favor increased domestic or foreign competition. For competition meant that they needed to be entrepreneurial, work harder, refine their products, and cut costs. If unable to do so, their companies would fail. No wonder so many of them resisted economic liberalization.

Contrary to what is often supposed, many American CEOs like economically interventionist governments. There has never been a dearth of American businesses who support protectionism and industrial policy or who spend money to try to skew the economic playing field in their favor. In more recent years, however, many private-sector and publicly traded companies have started promoting a particular vision for business itself that would further extend state intervention into the economy.

In 2019, the Business Roundtable—a major association of CEOs of America's leading companies—issued a document, endorsed by 181 CEOs, in which the Roundtable committed itself to "modernizing its principles on the role of a corporation." Previous iterations of this document, according to the Roundtable, had "stated that corporations exist principally to serve their shareholders." But, the Roundtable added, "It has become clear that this language on corporate purpose does not accurately describe the ways in which we and our fellow CEOs endeavor every day to create value for all our stakeholders, whose long-term interests are inseparable." [1]

That phrase—"stakeholder"—is key to understanding a significant shift on the part of many businesses who are the face of twenty-first-century American capitalism. Whereas past Roundtable statements stressed the importance of delivering value for shareholders, the 2019 statement committed its signatories to leading "their companies for the benefit of all stakeholders—customers, employees, suppliers, communities, and shareholders." This view of business did not emerge *ex nihilo*. There is an entire historical and political apparatus underlying it that is decidedly unfriendly to free markets.

FROM STRATEGY TO POLITICAL AGENDA

The idea that a business has constituencies with a "stake" in the company with whom it must work if it is to achieve its objectives is hardly radical. Every day, CEOs pursuing profit must consider how "internal" stakeholders like their employees and company shareholders fit into their plans. They also have to think about "external" stakeholders: most notably, their actual and potential customers as well as the ever-changing networks of potentially friendly or hostile entities that surround any company. "Stakeholder modelling" is a way of describing how companies navigate the different priorities and agendas associated with these constituencies. Stakeholder modelling also involves consideration of "externalities:" those costs proceeding from a business's choices which affect third parties who didn't agree to incur that cost. Pretending that there are no side effects from a corporation's choice about where to locate an industrial plant makes little sense if you want to gain support from the communities in which the plant will be built.

For a CEO to ignore such stakeholders and their interests would be foolish. A corporation that disregarded changes in political sentiment in the city in which it is headquartered, or new cultural trends in its target markets, would weaken its capacity to create economic value and maximize profit. Milton Friedman made this point in his famous essay on the purpose of business:

> it may well be in the long-run interest of a corporation that is a major employer in a small community to devote resources to providing amenities to that community or to improving its government. That may make it easier to attract desirable employees, it may reduce the wage bill or lessen losses from pilferage and sabotage or have other worthwhile effects. [2]

Insofar as the concepts of stakeholder and stakeholder modelling help business to factor such realities into how they achieve their goal of realizing profit, it can be a useful strategic management tool. This is not, however, what some scholars and business executives have in mind by stakeholder theory.

Traceable in more recent history to the early 1980s,[3] advocates of expansive theories of stakeholderism[4] maintain that businesses are obliged to realize goals far beyond maximizing profit and shareholder value. That goes together with pressures to engineer major changes in the governance structures of business. Companies need, proponents of expansive stakeholderism argue, to engage stakeholders to address challenges that not only affect their ability to realize profit, but also their capacity to promote another objective: the democratization of businesses, especially large corporations.[5] "Democratization" includes: (1) building into business planning a commitment to the principle that stakeholders should be treated by businesses as ends in themselves; (2) recognition of the rights which flow from this commitment; and (3) establishing formal processes for involving different stakeholders in companies' governance structures.

Who are these stakeholders that are ends in themselves? The literature on this topic is rife with disagreement.[6] One scholar identified no fewer than 593 different interpretations of who qualifies as a stakeholder.[7] A prominent stakeholderism booster has argued that stakeholders include "any group or individual who can affect or is affected by the achievements of the firm's objectives."[8] Such all-embracing conceptions of stakeholders underpin what is called pluralistic stakeholderism: the theory that companies must consider the effects of their choices on potentially infinite numbers of stakeholders—even to the point of requiring businesses to consult with, if not receive approval from, numerous constituencies before making any significant decisions.

This theory of stakeholders, Harvard Law School scholars Lucian Bebchuk and Roberto Tallarita emphasize, "posits that the welfare of each stakeholder group has independent value, and consideration for stakeholders might entail providing them with some benefits at the expense of shareholders."[9] Shareholders and investors are effectively reduced to one of several entities to whom boards of directors and CEOs are accountable. This is to be realized through "pluralistic governance structures" which entail more than one center of authority. These structures might range from advisory boards to social councils endowed with governance teeth.

One way in which the logic driving the stakeholder model is being advanced through American business, especially publicly traded companies, is through efforts to mandate Environmental, Social, and Governance (ESG) disclosures. In brief, ESG involves integration of environmental, social, and governance concerns into a company's decision-making protocols. For individual and institutional investors especially concerned about, for instance, how the companies in which they invest treat the environment, ESG allows them to align their investment choices with their environmental commitment.

Many businesses have responded to investor demand for such alignments by setting up funds described as ESG-compliant. Other businesses have voluntarily embraced ESG disclosure principles put forward by nonprofit groups like the Sustainability Accounting Standards Board.[10] These companies freely disclose how their internal practices and investment choices align with principles that such nonprofits regard as important. Examples might include sufficient adherence to transparency requirements, or whether a business has embraced quotas based on race, gender, etc., in their hiring practices.

Should a business choose to embrace such approaches to investment, or submit themselves to assessment by various activist groups, or adopt hiring practices that actively discriminate in favor of particular individuals on grounds of race, gender etc., it is free to do so—though it might find itself liable to anti-discrimination lawsuits for possible violation of the equal protection principles of the Constitution and the Civil Rights Act of 1964. [11] There are, however, two broader problems associated with ESG.

The first is that ESG principles have become thoroughly incorporated into strategies for making businesses in some way accountable to large numbers of stakeholders. One group of experts, for instance, writing about executive compensation at a Harvard Law School Forum outlined the following possibility:

> If the stakeholder model represents an emerging model for the *strategic* vision of a company, ESG . . . metrics can be used to assess and measure company performance and its relative positioning on a range of topics relevant to the broader set of company stakeholders in the same way that financial metrics assess company performance for shareholders. [12]

Observe how ESG evaluation tools are deployed here to establish an equivalency between profits realized for shareholders and the achievement of goals relevant to stakeholders when assessing overall company performance. As noted, establishing accountability to very broad sets of constituencies is central to the goals of expansive stakeholder theories.

Some of the criteria identified for assessing stakeholder performance in the same article about executive compensation include human rights, employee engagement, fair wages, minority representation, gender equality, sensitivity training, corporate philanthropy, equal opportunity and participation, and alliances with key organizations, councils, and institutions. It does not take much imagination to see how some of these criteria could be interpreted as requiring companies to endorse or advance specific ends that go far beyond solid financial returns. Is, for example, "employee engagement" a question of requiring worker representatives to be given seats on the board? Or: consider the reference to alliances with "key" organizations. This criterion could be easily invoked by activist groups claiming the status of stakeholders as a basis for demanding that a business create social councils or environmental advisory groups and then integrate them into the company's governance structures.

This ties into the second problem with the association between ESG and broad conceptions of who qualifies as a stakeholder. This concerns efforts to mandate legally various ESG requirements as a way to force businesses to embrace expansive stakeholderism. Diversity requirements for boards of directors and composition of workers, for instance, feature prominently in ESG guidelines and have been embraced by such American institutions as the Nasdaq stock exchange.

In December 2020, Nasdaq announced that it had filed a proposal with the Securities and Exchange Commission (SEC) to embrace new listing rules related to board diversity and disclosure. These involved the requirement "to publicly disclose consistent, transparent diversity statistics regarding their board of directors" and to adhere to rules requiring "most Nasdaq-listed companies to have—or explain why they do not have—at least two diverse directors, including one who self-identifies as female and one who self-identifies as either an underrepresented minority or LGBTQ+."[13] The new rules required Nasdaq-listed firms to provide annual reports and aggregated statistical information about the self-identified gender and racial composition of their boards of directors using a Board Diversity Matrix.[14]

Nasdaq, it could be argued, is a privately owned financial services corporation and is therefore free to require its members to embrace particular disclosure requirements. It isn't, however, as simple as that. First, requiring companies to classify its employees on grounds of "race, color, religion, sex, or national origin" may well be a violation of the 1964 Civil Rights Act.[15] Second, Nasdaq is officially deemed a Self-Regulatory Organization, meaning that it has been delegated a high degree of regulatory authority by the SEC and Congress. Some courts have held that this indicates that Nasdaq is therefore a state actor and regulator and thus not purely a private entity.[16]

Whatever the legal debates, eight months after Nasdaq announced its new diversity requirements, the SEC formally approved these rules.[17] This provided them with legal teeth, but also sent a message to the rest of the financial sector about the SEC's priorities. This went together with the efforts of social and environment activists and particular institutional investors to persuade the SEC to mandate even wider ESG requirements across the entire investment industry.[18]

Legal scholars Paul G. Mahoney and Julia D. Mahoney point out that an SEC which went down this path would effectively be engaging in a substantial and unauthorized departure from the SEC's "stated mission of 'protecting Main Street investors' and 'maintaining fair, orderly, and efficient markets'." It would, they argue, effectively require the SEC to pursue public policy goals for which it "neither has expertise nor the political accountability to pursue." [19]

Should mandated ESG requirements become even more widespread and enforced by federal regulators, it will shift many companies' focus away from maximizing shareholder value and towards promoting the concerns of potentially endless numbers of self-identified stakeholders. Another effect would be to widen the opportunities for boards of directors and company executives to ignore shareholder expectations by claiming that their hands are legally tied. Indeed, in the 1980s and 1990s, many boards and CEOs lobbied for laws to be passed to allow them to appeal to stakeholder interests as a means of warding off investors demanding better performance or even to resist hostile takeovers. [20] After all, the more stakeholders there are for a company's management to answer to, the less accountable those executives can be to any one in particular. [21]

As these trends gain traction, they will negatively impact a fundamental way in which private sector companies contribute to the common good. Pursuing shareholder value and maximizing profit is how publicly traded businesses create economic value by facilitating choice in goods and services for consumers, providing wages and benefits to their employees, repaying their loans to banks, and paying just taxes. This helps increase the total material wealth in society, something that permits people who have never owned a share in their lives to realize goods ranging from health care to education. Capacious ideas of who and what is a stakeholder—especially when accompanied by social pressures from activist groups and backed up by regulations that seek to make ESG compliance a requirement of law—compromises the ability of business to make its unique contribution to the wider common good. Instead, they will find themselves tethered to the realization of political agendas more properly decided by legislatures. As Mahoney and Mahoney state, "In a democracy, climate policy should be determined at the ballot box, not on the corporate proxy card." [22]

FROM BUSINESS MODEL TO ECONOMIC SYSTEM

The goals of those seeking to entrench political agendas into the operations of businesses do not stop here. In some cases, advancing expansive understandings of stakeholders is seen as core to changing American capitalism's very nature. In July 2020, then–presidential candidate Joe Biden stated that "It's way past time we put an end to the era of shareholder capitalism." [23] That same year, a Harvard Business School professor contended that America needed to rethink capitalism along the lines of companies "embracing a pro-social purpose beyond profit maximization and taking responsibility for the health of the natural and social systems." [24]

Similar sentiments have been echoed by progressive senators such as Bernie Sanders and Elizabeth Warren, conservatives who want employees to be allocated seats on company boards,[25] and individuals like the Chairman of the World Economic Forum (WEF), Klaus Schwab.[26] Six months after the Business Roundtable issued its revised statement, a self-styed manifesto appeared on the website of the WEF: an organization often regarded as reflecting widespread sentiments prevailing within the world's leading corporations.

Entitled *Davos Manifesto 2020: The Universal Purpose of a Company in the Fourth Industrial Revolution*, this document—specifically Section A—underscored the importance of businesses understanding the political and social environment in which they operated. The manifesto also focused upon the importance of profit, creating goods and services for customers, and generating shareholder value over the short, medium, and long term. It also specified common sense guidelines for good business practice and showed how generating economic growth contributes to wider innovation and the development of knowledge.

The tone and emphases of Sections B and C of *Davos Manifesto 2020* were, however, decidedly different. Section B stated:

> A company is more than an economic unit generating wealth. It fulfils human and societal aspirations as part of the broader social system. Performance must be measured not only on the return to shareholders, but also on how it achieves its environmental, social, and good governance objectives. Executive remuneration should reflect stakeholder responsibility.

This goes beyond a business being attentive to the context in which it operates so as to better realize its core economic objectives. Instead a concern for profit and realization of shareholder value is put on the same level as undefined ESG goals in assessing overall company performance and executive remuneration. Section C of the manifesto went even further to re-envisage completely the place of business in wider society:

> A company that has a multinational scope of activities not only serves all those stakeholders who are directly engaged, but acts itself as a stakeholder—together with governments and civil society—of our global future. Corporate global citizenship requires a company to harness its core competencies, its entrepreneurship, skills, and relevant resources in collaborative efforts with other companies and stakeholders to improve the state of the world. [27]

These sentences give rise to numerous questions. What is meant by "our global future?" Who gets to decide that future? What is the content of a business's duty to "improve the state of the world"? What constitutes an improved "state of the world?" Note also the emphasis upon collaboration with government, civil society, and "other stakeholders" in the pursuit of goals that go beyond creating economic value for consumers. At this point we start to see that the *Davos Manifesto 2020* is effectively advocating a new economic system. The objective is to shift the business sector towards embracing "stakeholder capitalism."

Though the expression "stakeholder capitalism" was not mentioned in the statement, the phrase is used regularly by its author,
the WEF's Founder and Chairman, Klaus Schwab. Indeed, in
2021 Schwab authored a book titled *Stakeholder Capitalism: A
Global Economy that Works for Progress, People and Planet.* Schwab
has been arguing publicly for this revised conception of capitalism since 1971. In 1973, he wrote the first *Davos Manifesto* on the
WEF's behalf. It began by stating that "The purpose of professional management is to serve clients, shareholders, workers, and
employees, as well as societies, and to harmonize the different
interests of the stakeholders." [28]

What then is stakeholder capitalism? Schwab describes it as
"a form of capitalism in which companies do not only optimize
short-term profits for shareholders, but seek long-term value creation, by taking into account the needs of all their stakeholders,
and society at large." By value creation, Schwab has in mind "Prosperity" but also what he calls "People," "Planet," and "Peace." Precisely how these rather general concepts ought to be assessed and
prioritized in practical terms is left unspecified. But those four Ps
underscore how all-encompassing Schwab's stakeholder capitalism
aspires to be. He identifies the stakeholders responsible for these
four Ps as "companies," "governments," "civil society" (NGOs,
unions, universities, etc.), and "the international community." By
the last of these, Schwab does not have in mind the world's 7.8
billion people. He is thinking of international and supranational
organizations like the UN and the EU.

Schwab's vision isn't without its own pedigree. It goes back
much further than the stakeholder language and ideas which began

emerging in the late 1960s. Schwab effectively reveals what he has in mind while reminiscing about postwar Europe:

> This approach was common in the postwar decades in the West, when it became clear that one person or entity could only do well if the whole community and economy functioned. There was a strong linkage between companies and their community. In Germany, for example, where I was born, it led to the representation of employees on the board, a tradition that continues today. [29]

Here Schwab is alluding to "corporatism:" an approach to organizing society whose roots are traceable back at least to the Middle Ages. As a modern set of ideas, it has been given different expressions by people from the left and right. But whatever its precise form, corporatism comes with significant drawbacks which stakeholder capitalism has the potential to inflict upon the American economy.

WE'VE BEEN HERE BEFORE

As a modern political and economic program, corporatism emerged in the nineteenth century. It was shaped by thinkers like the French sociologist Emile Durkheim and the German Jesuit theologian Heinrich Pesch. Corporatism attracted support from socialists, nationalists, Christians, progressives, and fascists. Though there were many schools of corporatist thought, the following propositions featured prominently in statements of corporatist belief:

- Private enterprise and markets are useful. But they generate excessive wealth-disparities, weaken communities, diminish security, and undermine "solidarity" (a word frequently used in German corporatist circles from the nineteenth century onwards).

- Private property and free exchange must be imbedded in a legal and political framework that prioritizes building consensus around achieving specific social and economic goals.

- Every industry and profession should have organizations that embrace everyone who works in it. These corporate bodies have the prime responsibility for deciding wages and conditions. They also provide workers with a voice in management decisions.

- The principal place for resolving disputes within industries should be within these corporate groups assisted by special tribunals which issue binding resolutions.

- The activities of corporate bodies should be coordinated by the state which bestows legal recognition upon these organizations.

Different corporatists emphasized some of these ideas more than others. Many focused upon establishing worker co-determination structures whereby employees (invariably union officials) were allocated seats on company boards. Some corporatists were more concerned with creating corporate bodies to embrace entire industries, which would then be coordinated by the government to achieve particular national goals. [30]

That often included objectives of an authoritarian nature. In a 1935 article published in the journal *Economica*, the German economist Wilhelm Röpke demonstrated how Benito Mussolini was using corporatism to reinforce the Fascist regime's grip on the economy and society.[31] What might be called "hard corporatist" policies were also pursued in countries like Franco's Spain, Vichy France, Dollfuss's Austria, and, following World War II, Perón's Argentina. After 1945, corporatism took on softer forms. Christian Democrat–led governments sought to foster consensus among employers and workers within industries. They consequently established structures like work councils (whose leadership was dominated by union officials) that management was legally bound to consult as well as worker co-determination arrangements.

Soft corporatism achieved constitutional expression in some nations. Article 41 of Italy's 1947 Constitution states that "Private-sector economic initiative is freely exercised." One sentence later it adds, "The law shall provide for appropriate programs and controls so that public and private-sector economic activity may be oriented and coordinated for social purposes."[32] Other corporatist provisions appear in Article 46: "For the economic and social betterment of workers and in harmony with the needs of production, the Republic recognizes the rights of workers to collaborate in the management of enterprises, in the ways and within the limits established by law."[33] Corporatist aspirations have even been integrated into the EU's Charter of the Fundamental Rights. Article 27 refers to the right of workers "or their representatives" (union officials) to be consulted about an enterprise's operations.[34]

Some historians argue that soft corporatism helped Western Europe recover from World War II. Through neo-corporatist arrangements, they maintain, governments secured the buy-in of businesses and unions into policies that helped many European nations overcome their grave postwar challenges. Over time, however, the same corporatist arrangements have had, or are likely to have, seriously negative effects upon markets in general and business in particular, including through the medium of stakeholder capitalism.

GOODBYE FREEDOM AND ACCOUNTABILITY

Perhaps the most obvious problem with corporatist-influenced stakeholder models of capitalism is that they provide established companies with political and legal mechanisms to advance their interests over and against consumers, taxpayers, and new entrepreneurs. By definition, taxpayers, customers, and start-up businesses are less organized and more diffuse. They are subsequently less able to promote their concerns than companies who long ago hardwired themselves into policy-influencing structures. In a corporatist world, success depends less on innovation and much more on your institutional clout. That exacts a considerable economic cost. Edmund Phelps has detailed at length the clear linkages between the prevalence of corporatist mindsets and structures, and weakening overall economic performance in many European countries. [35]

Phelps's conclusions track closely with legal scholar Nadia E. Nedzel's research into this topic. She demonstrates that many European nations' mandating of seats for representatives of banks, governments, and company staff on boards of directors results in priority being given to continuity of employment and general stability, as well as pleasing many groups besides shareholders. [36] This undermines the ability of businesses to make necessary but often difficult changes. Without such adjustments and focus, the chances magnify of a business becoming complacent and uncompetitive. That means that it will likely disappear, along with all the jobs it provided. These factors, according to Nedzel, help explain the feebler economic performance of many large companies in European civil law jurisdictions compared to those businesses located primarily in the Anglo-American world. By contrast, the (present) shareholder focus of Anglo-American commercial law incentivizes the flexibility and innovation which is key to producing the wealth that benefits shareholders and, albeit unintentionally, millions of other people in the form of incomes, employment, and increased living standards.

Second, corporatism enables widespread cronyism. There is no shortage of empirical studies showing how client-patron relations between businesses and politicians facilitated by corporatist structures have helped companies to shut potential competitors out of entire economic sectors. [37] Nor can we discount how easily corporatist cronyism morphs into outright corruption. One notorious example was the scandal that engulfed the Volkswagen Corporation in 2008. Facing increased global competition and the subsequent need to reduce labor costs, VW executives created a slush fund to buy off employee representatives (i.e., union officials) on the VW works council to secure their consent for changes in labor conditions. [38] Among the inducements were paid-for shopping sprees for union officials' spouses, paid visits to prostitutes, and outright bribes. [39]

Third, corporatism doesn't place great emphasis on freedom. The focus is upon establishing and enforcing consensus on political, social, and economic policies. But what happens, for example, if the owner of a large business does not assent to stakeholder capitalism's four Ps because he thinks that three of the Ps are so broad as to mean whatever state officials want them to mean? Corporatism struggles to answer such questions and positively discourages people from asking them in the first place. For corporatism does not deal well with dissent. Whether the question is economic policy or defining "Progress," corporatism prioritizes the harmonization of views, however artificial the consensus.

Fourth, stakeholder capitalism undermines and distorts accountability. It helps entrench incompetent boards and executives by allowing them to excuse poor performance by telling shareholders that the company's legal obligations to help actualize various national and international objectives means that investors must settle for less profit. This goes together with the extension of state power over internal company governance. That becomes clearer when we pose this question: under Schwab-like stakeholder capitalist arrangements, who would represent the "Planet," "Peace," or "People"? Perhaps it might be environmental NGOs (many of which receive state funding) who claim to be "the" representative stakeholder by asserting that they represent trees and animals' interests? More probably, though, the most likely representative would end up being government officials. Governments do have particular responsibilities vis-à-vis protecting the planet from wanton destruction, preserving domestic peace at home, and promoting it abroad. They can also claim to represent the people. On these foundations, governments could insist that state officials should represent the "Planet," "Peace" and "People" on company boards, thereby further diminishing the influence of those who represent shareholders. The same logic could be deployed to extend the reach of regulation to further constrain companies' exercise of their legitimate commercial freedoms, whether it concerns hiring practices or the types of technology they use.

Another way in which stakeholder capitalism blurs accountability is by exacerbating what economists call the principal-agent problem within publicly traded companies. Such entities are somewhat unique business ventures. As the leading American corporate law scholar Stephen Bainbridge points out:

> Corporations differ from most other forms of business organizations in that ownership of the firm is formally separated from its control. Although shareholders nominally "own" the corporation, they have virtually no decision-making powers—just the right to elect the firm's directors and to vote on an exceedingly limited albeit not unimportant number of corporate actions. Rather, management of the firm is vested by statute in the hands of the board of directors, who in turn delegate the day-to-day running of the firm to its officers, who in turn delegate some responsibility to the company's employees. [40]

The individual and institutional shareholders of such companies are often dispersed. Their composition also changes as investors buy and sell shares in these firms. Nonetheless the shareholders are the "principals" insofar as they are the business's owners; it is by virtue of their ownership that they are entitled to receive the company's profits. "Agents" are those whom the principals have delegated to direct and manage the business to realize that profit. These agents—executives, managers, etc.—are usually more informed than the principals about the trials and opportunities facing the firm, and more deeply involved in the company's everyday workings.

One advantage of this arrangement is the division of labor. Investors focus on how best to allocate their capital throughout the economy; boards, executives, and management concentrate on organizing and managing capital, risk and labor in ways that they believe will most effectively realize a profit. The disadvantage is that it is hard for the principals to ensure that agents always act in the principals' best interests—or that agents will never pursue their own interests at the principals' expense. "Given human nature," Bainbridge observes, "it would surprising indeed if directors did not sometimes shirk or self-deal."[41] Some executives may delay making the hard decisions that are often the difference between profit and loss because they prefer a quiet life. Managers might decline to employ efficiency-enhancing technologies that reduce labor costs, because they are fearful of confronting unions. In such cases, agents are no longer fulfilling their responsibilities to the principals. But because ownership of a publicly held company is pooled among many shareholders, there are limits to how much pressure even major investors can bring to bear to make management address such problems.

Expansive stakeholderism and its corporatist underpinnings only exacerbate these difficulties. Publicly traded companies that consistently subordinate shareholder interests to every other moral claim (however real or dubious) advanced by other constituencies (however genuine or fictitious) will undermine the incentives and governance arrangements that help them create wealth and enable the wider flourishing of individuals and communities. Virtue-signaling would be prioritized over the market signals conveyed by profit and loss. On the basis of their claim to be stakeholders, any number of social actors could declare that publicly traded companies should pursue various political causes in addition to—or even prior to—profit and shareholder value. If such actors prevailed, the interests of those who risk investing their capital in the firm would be considered equal to those who bore no such risk. Not only will that undermine a major force for economic prosperity; it will strike many as essentially unjust.

ENTER THE WOKE

These problems should give Americans pause before seeing stakeholder capitalism as a path forward for the American economy. There is, however, something else that makes stakeholder capitalism even more problematic. This is its growing association with "woke" ideology.

Woke ideology's deeper roots are to be found in intellectual movements like critical studies and the Frankfurt School of
political theory as well as the work of thinkers such as the Italian
revisionist Marxist Antonio Gramsci (1891–1937) and the Ger-
man-American political theorist Herbert Marcuse (1898–1979).
They sought to shift Marxism's traditional focus away from class
as the engine of social change, and to direct attention to capturing
those institutions that shape culture: educational organizations,
newspapers, the law, religion, etc. [42] If you capture the commanding heights of culture, the Gramscian argument goes, everyone
will gradually come to recognize the systematic biases and forms
of oppression that permeate the entire social order—including the
economy—and act to redress these injustices.

Many people working in the private sector have attended col-
leges, universities, and even business schools where many of these
claims about systematic injustice are subtly, and sometimes not
so subtly, omnipresent. There is no reason why these individuals should be less influenced by such atmospherics than anyone
else. In his 2021 book, *Woke Inc.*, Vivek Ramaswamy illustrated
that many young people entering corporate America in the 2010s
sincerely believed that the promotion of social justice, invariably
understood in woke terms, must be part of what business does. [43]
Likewise, sociologist Jonathan Haidt and free speech advocate
Greg Lukianoff (neither of whom could be labelled "conservatives") argue that since 2017 corporate America has experienced
an "explosion of social justice movements, employee political
activism, and internal conflict about that activism . . . all playing
out on social media." [44]

From this standpoint, expressions like "woke capitalism" or "corporate wokeness" are a way of describing the extent to which many people working in the private sector, ranging from CEOs of publicly traded companies to employees of tech companies, want businesses to do more than focus upon the creation of products and services for consumers and delivering returns to their owners. They believe that business has a responsibility to support progressive positions on political and social issues. This helps explain events such as Nike recalling Betsy Ross flag–emblazoned shoes in 2019 after being counselled by activist advisors that the flag represented slavery,[45] or almost 200 CEOs of major firms signing a full-page *New York Times* advertisement that same year describing laws restricting abortion's availability as "bad for business."[46] In some cases, internal activism emanating from within these companies likely dovetailed with pressures from institutional shareholders who wanted their investments to cohere with progressive priorities.[47] There are, however, other factors influencing these trends.

One is that many companies recognize that many Americans want their buying choices to reflect their politics. One reputable consumer survey, for example, found in 2021 that 66 percent of respondents believed that it was important for companies to take political stands. The majority of such respondents were self-identified liberals.[48] Economic self-interest, the logic goes, compels many businesses to sound as progressive as possible and thereby preserve and magnify their customer base among particular demographic groups, especially millennials who are (at least according to Pew Research)[49] the only more-or-less consistently progressive generational demographic in America. For some companies, this matters because millennials are, or will be, one of their major consumer markets.

A second factor driving these trends in corporate America has been the rapid extension of anti-discrimination law since 1964 and the growth of federal and state agencies charged with responsibility for enforcing it. Reflecting on the 1964 Civil Rights Act's impact, Richard Hanania points out that "While most at the time thought this would simply remove explicit discrimination, and many of the proponents of the bill made that promise, courts and regulators stretched the concept of 'non-discrimination' to mean almost anything that advantages one group over another." [50] It has become, he says, "the legal basis for enforcing ideas, practices, and behaviors across American institutions that have now morphed into what we call 'wokeness'." [51] Going woke is one way for businesses, as Hanania states, "to make their way in a world where government and the courts [are] always on the lookout for 'discrimination,' a term whose definition [is] unclear and continually expanding," [52] especially in a country as litigious as America.

Hence, even if a board of directors has reservations about their company supporting a particular left-leaning cause, it may decide that it is simpler easier to go along to get along. But thinking that appeasement—to put it bluntly—will work in these cases betrays a serious lack of vision on the part of business leaders. This is not a new problem. Milton Friedman, for one, was scathing in his view of the tendency of business leaders to lose sight of the bigger picture:

> I have been impressed time and again by the schizo-
> phrenic character of many businessmen. They are capable

of being extremely far-sighted and clear-headed in matters that are internal to their businesses. They are incred-
ibly short-sighted and muddle-headed in matters that are
outside their businesses but affect the possible survival of
business in general.

Friedman highlighted the example of American CEOs backing
wage and price controls as an example of supporting policies that
do considerable damage to markets in general and the capacity of
businesses to adapt to changes in the economy. He underscored
the inclusion of various social causes by business leaders as part
of the *raison d'être* of commerce as another instance of business
undermining its own position:

> The short-sightedness is also exemplified in speeches
> by businessmen on social responsibility. This may gain
> them kudos in the short run. But it helps to strengthen
> the already too prevalent view that the pursuit of prof-
> its is wicked and immoral and must be curbed and con-
> trolled by external forces. Once this view is adopted,
> the external forces that curb the market will not be the
> social consciences, however highly developed, of the
> pontificating executives; it will be the iron fist of Gov-
> ernment bureaucrats. [53]

Many business leaders do not grasp that no matter how much
they buy into woke agendas or financially support these causes,
whether for expediency's sake or out of ideological conviction, it

will *never* be enough for proponents of woke ideology. They will always want more. There is every reason to expect that this "more," as we have witnessed with the growth of antidiscrimination law, will eventually translate into more state regulation of the workings of business: whether through mandating racial and gender quotas for a company's workforce, or requiring the formal representation of workers on boards, or forcing companies to consult and receive the approval of representatives of groups identified by woke ideologues as marginalized.

In 2021, the Biden administration stated its intention of imposing new ESG disclosure requirements on publicly traded companies. Upon examining the requirements in question, legal scholar Todd Zywicki found that "the disclosures advance left-wing causes such as environmentalism and race, sex, and sexuality 'diversity' initiatives, not issues such as the rule of law, economic development, or affordable energy policy."[54]

Here we see how the demands of woke ideology start to intersect with the logic of stakeholder capitalism. Both woke ideology and the corporatism underlying stakeholder capitalism seek to integrate—through external social pressures or through legislation and regulation—the demands of particular groups into businesses' internal functioning and decision-making processes. Indeed, like corporatism, embracing woke positions opens up new possibilities for cronyism. It is easy to envisage CEOs calculating that engaging in public displays of wokeness or contributing financially to various progressive organizations may enhance their chances of obtaining subsidies from a progressive legislature, or persuading legislators to implement regulations that place disproportionate burdens

BUSINESS AGAINST THE MARKET

upon their competitors. Corporate wokeness can thus help further a business's efforts to use the government to undermine the ability of other individuals and groups to compete in markets—all in the name of tolerance, diversity, and equality.

MERCANTILISM REDUX

Amidst these developments, it's telling that corporate America's dalliance with the language and priorities of stakeholderism often turns out to be largely rhetorical. In their analysis of the corporate documents of the over 130 U.S. public companies that signed onto the 2019 Business Roundtable (BRT) statement, Bebchuk and Tallarita discovered that of "the almost one hundred BRT Companies that updated their corporate governance guidelines in the sixteen-month period between the release of the BRT Statement and the end of 2020," none had added "any language that improves the status of stakeholders and, indeed, most of them chose to retain in their guidelines a commitment to shareholder primacy." Upon further reviewing all the corporate governance guidelines of BRT companies in place at the end of 2020, Bebchuk and Tallarita also found that "most of them reflected a shareholder primacy approach, and an even larger majority did not include any mention of stakeholders in their discussion of corporate purpose." Turning to the same businesses' corporate bylaws, they determined that these generally reflected "a shareholder-centered view," something that tracked with the fact that "the BRT Companies continued to pay directors compensation that strongly aligns their interests

with shareholder value." "Overall," Bebchuk and Tallarita concluded, "our findings support the view that the BRT Statement
was mostly for show and that BRT Companies joining it did not
intend or expect it to bring about any material changes in how they
treat stakeholders."[55]

Given these facts, why do CEOs sign documents like the BRT
Statement in the first place? Stephen Bainbridge suggests three
reasons. The first is that such business leaders are trying to attract
wealthy investors who see themselves as socially responsible. The
second is to fend off regulation from progressive politicians. A
third is that some CEOs want to insulate themselves from pressures from investors dissatisfied with their performance by suggesting that profit sometimes has to be sacrificed to promote
various causes, unvaryingly of a progressive or woke nature.[56]
Bebchuk and Tallarita agree with much of Bainbridge's analysis.
CEOs, they argue, often engage in these activities to help insulate themselves from investor oversight, as well as deflect political pressures for expansive stakeholder-promoting regulation that
would radically diminish their autonomy and undermine their
ability to pursue profit.[57]

The problem confronting American businesses is that those
prioritizing corporatist visions of stakeholder capitalism, or the
parallel political agendas often being pursued by ESG and woke
activists, have no difficulty in recognizing appeasement for what it
is. And the response of such groups will not be to back off and say
that they are satisfied. They will swear that the failure of American businesses to embrace stakeholder capitalism properly, or to
integrate woke priorities sufficiently into their internal company

operations, simply proves the need to use government regulation to corral businesses down these paths.

Such are the immense challenges posed by expansive stakeholder theories of business and stakeholder models of capitalism. Just as protectionism and industrial policy significantly compromise the workings of market exchange by using state power to privilege connected groups of businesses and political leaders, so too do would government enforcement of capacious visions of who are stakeholders. Expansive stakeholderism's blending of politics and business would gradually weaken the dynamics of competition and further shift the economy's focus away from meeting the economic needs and wants of 330 million American consumers and towards promoting the interests of politically connected businesses. And that is essentially mercantilism, whether it manifests itself in the garb of an eighteenth-century European merchant or a twenty-first-century CEO.

This is what makes the case for state capitalism in America so paradoxical. Advocates of protectionism, industrial policy, and stakeholder capitalism claim to be promoting the common good of Americans and America as a nation. In truth, the state capitalism of which I speak is really neo-mercantilism insofar as it promotes particular businesses over others, allows well-organized interest groups to engage in rent-seeking, makes American consumers pay more for often sub-standard products, and weakens America's long-term competitiveness in the global economy.

What then is the alternative? What type of economy is best suited for America going forward? What priorities, habits, and institutions should drive it?

In a way, the problems associated with state capitalism point to an answer. The opposite of top-down industrial policy is an economy driven from the bottom up by entrepreneurship. The alternative to stakeholder capitalism is the vigorous free competition of which corporatism is so wary. The critique of protectionism suggests its long-standing rival: free trade.

In Part Two, we look at these three central features of market economies, beginning from the bottom with entrepreneurship, and then working our way up—first to domestic competition and then, by extension, to free trade. Their importance for a growing and dynamic American economy is explained, as are some of the obstacles which they encounter today. But we will also see how they can be embedded in a polity faithful to America's particular origins and identity as a nation, and how this republic might interact with the rest of the world.

PART II

MARKETS
IN
AMERICA

CHAPTER 5

CREATIVE

NATION

The natural effort of every individual to better his own condition . . . is so powerful, that it is alone, and without any assistance, not only capable of carrying on the society to wealth and prosperity, but of surmounting a hundred impertinent obstructions with which the folly of human laws too often encumbers its operations.

—ADAM SMITH

American capitalism emerged as a global force in the nineteenth century. The development of a sophisticated financial sector, capital investment, ongoing immigration from Europe, and accelerating industrialization wrought many changes in a relatively short period of time. After the Civil War, there was an explosion of new inventions—typewriters, telephones, phonographs, and electric light—and discoveries of raw materials. The subsequent economic growth was powered by increased use of sophisticated mass production methods and the deployment of scientific management

strategies that encouraged ever-greater efficiencies. While vast
business empires were created in the "Gilded Age," millions of
ordinary Americans also prospered as wage growth in America
outpaced that of most European nations. So too did the millions
of immigrants to America who found opportunities that they were
unlikely to have enjoyed in their native lands.

Many of the foundations for this spectacular growth were
established in the first half of the nineteenth century. In 1800, the
American economy was dominated by agriculture and mineral
production, with about 85 percent of the workforce engaged in
farming. By the eve of the Civil War, America had the world's second largest GDP and its second largest industrial base. This transition was accompanied by new businesses springing up across the
country as people moved west by foot, wagon, boat, and rail. [1]

Who were the Americans who drove the U.S. economy's rapid
development throughout these years? One answer may be found
in a book of observations on America penned by a French visitor
in the early 1830s. The author of *Democracy in America*, still considered the quintessential study of the still young American republic, was primarily interested in understanding its experiment in
democracy. Alexis de Tocqueville's observations about American
economic life are nonetheless also informative.

Through Tocqueville's eyes, we catch a glimpse of the spirit of
Americans, their restlessness and vigor, as well as American society's fluid character and the sheer breadth of opportunity that the
native-born and immigrants alike sensed in America. Tocqueville
noted how Americans speedily moved to different parts of the country seeking new pursuits. He was also astonished at Americans'

willingness to take risks. Significantly, Tocqueville's most lasting impression of the American economy was its profoundly entrepreneurial character. "Almost all [Americans]," Tocqueville commented, are "entrepreneurs."[2] A "spirit of enterprise,"[3] he wrote in several places, dominated American culture, and was underpinned by a deep restlessness that permeated the republic. In the America witnessed by Tocqueville,

> a man carefully builds a dwelling in which to pass his declining years, and he sells it while the roof is being laid; he plants a garden and he rents it out just as he was going to taste its fruits; he clears a field and he leaves to others the care of harvesting its crops. He embraces a profession and quits it. He settles in a place from which he departs soon after so as to take his changing desires elsewhere. Should his private affairs give him some respite, he immediately plunges into the whirlwind of politics. And when toward the end of a year filled with work some leisure still remains to him, he carries his restive curiosity here and there within the vast limits of the United States. He will thus go five hundred leagues in a few days in order better to distract himself from his happiness.[4]

Tocqueville did not have access to the type of data sets used today by social scientists to support their hypotheses. But not all knowledge depends upon our ability to measure it. Tocqueville asked searching questions of people from all segments of American society in ways that elicited a great deal of information from them. This was the basis on which Tocqueville determined that Americans were "a commercial people"[5]—though he pointedly noted that slavery in the South had diminished many white Southerners' sense of the value of work, leaving many of them "without industry or the spirit of enterprise."[6]

Much has happened to the American economy since Tocqueville's time. The influence of the Progressive movement from the 1890s onwards, the colossal growth of the federal government occasioned by the New Deal in the 1930s and the Great Society programs of the 1960s, and the relentless increase in regulation since World War II means that America's economy is far from the laissez-faire stereotype which many imagine it to be. Yet entrepreneurship remains an important feature of American economic life and a major conduit for upward economic mobility.[7] Entrepreneurs also drive innovation[8] in important sectors of the U.S. economy and create many new jobs.[9] As far as the demographics of entrepreneurship are concerned, they broadly track changes in the American population, with overall trends since 1996 showing a fall in the share of new entrepreneurs who are white, and significant growth in those who are Latino, Asian, or Black. Migrants have more than doubled their share of new entrepreneurs since 1996, with over one in four new American entrepreneurs being foreign-born in 2020.[10]

This is good news. Opportunity is what many people crave and expect in America. According to the Archbridge Institute's *Survey on American Attitudes—2021*, sixty percent of Americans maintained a positive view of entrepreneurs.[11] The bad news is that there is evidence of ongoing deterioration in entrepreneurship throughout America.

In December 2020, the Congressional Budget Office (CBO) issued a report about long-term trends in entrepreneurship in the United States. The picture painted in the report was mixed. The CBO noted that there was a steady decline throughout America between 1982 and 2018 in the number of young firms ("young" meaning five years or less) as a percentage of all businesses (38 percent to 29 percent) as well as young firms' share of job creation and employment (14 percent to 9 percent).[12] This trend was observable across American industries ranging from services to construction. By the mid-1990s it had started manifesting itself in the high-tech sector.[13] A similar picture emerges from economist Chris Edwards's study of entrepreneurship in twenty-first-century America. His analysis found that young firms' share of employment dropped 60 percent in high-tech manufacturing, 56 percent in information, 53 percent in high-tech, 38 percent in services, 38 percent in manufacturing, 33 percent in construction, and 13 percent in retail between 2000 and 2018.[14]

These statistics are worrying because of entrepreneurship's role in keeping the American economy productive.[15] The CBO, for example, estimated that the decline in entrepreneurship was related to "a falloff in labor productivity of at least 3 percent to 4 percent by the mid-2010s."[16] In the early 1990s, the CBO stated, innovation sparked by new information and high-tech firms resulted in greater supply of "products that were useful to a wide range of industries," with the proliferation of those firms being "accompanied by greater productivity growth." But as the growth of new businesses in these sectors started declining towards the end of that decade, the CBO report noted, "so did the growth rate of productivity." [17] That wasn't the end of the matter. Declining entrepreneurship, the report stressed, negatively impacted innovation and diminished the intensity of the competition that new firms provide to incumbent businesses. [18]

Plainly, private entrepreneurship matters for a dynamic American economy. Before, however, we explore how to revitalize entrepreneurship throughout America, we need to understand its nature and wider significance for economic life.

ENTREPRENEURS AS DISCOVERERS

Until relatively recently, many economics textbooks said little about entrepreneurship's place in the economy. Much post-Keynesian economics looked at the economy from the top down, in terms of broad aggregates like total economic growth and overall employment. Entrepreneurship was obscured in that paradigm because it is a bottom-up phenomenon. It also didn't fit into the mathematically orientated modelling that dominated postwar economics. Writing in the mid 1970s, economist Harvey Leibenstein noted that one of the "curious aspects of the relationship of neo-classical theory to economic development" was that "in the conventional theory, entrepreneurs, as they are usually perceived, play almost no role." [19] Those who build economic models typically don't like loose ends. One way to address this is to ignore them. Consequently, as economist Israel Kirzner points out, "the entrepreneur receded more and more from theoretical view." [20] Much postwar research done on entrepreneurship tended to occur on the economics profession's fringes among thinkers like Kirzner or in business schools.

None of this boded well for greater understanding of entrepreneurship's economic role. Examining the state of economics in the mid-twentieth century, the Jesuit economist Oswald von Nell-Breuning noticed that most economists described businesses as made up of people who contributed labor or capital.[21] But this, he pointed out, ignored the fact that "[w]ithout question, *intellectus* comes first, that is. . . . initiative and enterprise."[22] Without people who look ahead and envisage new products and services, or use new combinations of property rights to create goods, or devise new cost-saving processes, or refine existing products and services, or discover better ways of providing existing products and services, the economy would less vibrant, if not stagnant. This was the basis on which Wilhelm Röpke insisted that the "free economy stands or falls with the free entrepreneur."[23]

Entrepreneurs function as bottom-up agents of change. Some degree of management is often part of their work, and they often possess technical skills and formal qualifications. But entrepreneurship relies far more upon sudden insights, creativity, and imagination, often backed up by tacit knowledge. They invariably possess, economist Ludwig von Mises perceived, "more initiative, more venturesomeness, and a quicker eye than the crowd."[24] These qualities are hard to teach. More often, they are innate. Taken together, however, they allow entrepreneurs to transcend the bounds of existing knowledge. Their subsequent discoveries often open up the desire to explore the next level.

So what motivates entrepreneurs to act? One cause, as Mises perceived, is that lack of contentment which causes people to want to change themselves, others, and the world so as to live and be better.[25] This facilitates an eagerness to "substitute a more satisfactory state of affairs for a less satisfactory one."[26] But this desire must be matched by some expectation that an action will bring about the envisaged better state of affairs for themselves and others. Hence the activation of entrepreneurship must offer the prospect—an incentive—of some direct gain for the potential discoverer. Such people, Mises explained, are "eager to profit from adjusting production to the expected changes in conditions."[27]

An element of speculation is involved insofar as no entrepreneur can be sure that his idea will interest consumers. Not every entrepreneurial initiative succeeds. Many fail, often within a few years.[28] Entrepreneurs have no crystal ball to tell them if a new idea or product will succeed. They may dramatically misjudge the marketplace. But even when an entrepreneur suffers a loss, this tells us that the innovation didn't interest consumers or they considered it too expensive.[29] Entrepreneurial failures can thus be of wider benefit to other innovators.

On a more general level, entrepreneurship challenges the status quo in the allocation of resources and opens up new possibilities for more efficient and ongoing redeployments of skills and capital. This brings competitive pressures to bear upon entire economic sectors, because new ventures are generally more productive than the businesses which predated them.[30] When the rate of establishment of new businesses slows down, overall productivity tends to decline,[31] partly because newly established businesses are typically more productive than pre-existing firms.

The processes fueled by dynamic entrepreneurship are enhanced by the development of new technologies. Though most start-ups do not engage in R&D, some do, and their work tends to be more R&D-intensive than that of existing firms. They are also more willing to engage new technologies. This is especially true of manufacturing. Those manufacturing firms which eventually become large businesses generally engaged in R&D from the beginning.[32]

The benefits flowing from entrepreneurship go far beyond entrepreneurs becoming rich. Leaving aside the provision of new and refined products, the competitive pressures unleashed by entrepreneurship often lower prices in different economic sectors. Existing businesses have to react to entrepreneurially driven changes by seeking new ways to maintain their market share and keep their competitive edge. Such companies often react by becoming more efficient. They take advantage of: (1) their economies of scale (their ability to produce more units of a product on a larger scale, yet with average fewer input costs) by vertically integrating their input supply, manufacturing, and distribution; and (2) their economies of scope (when producing a wider variety of products in tandem is more cost-effective for a firm than producing less of a variety or producing each good independently) to offer a wider range of services and products.[33] Competition from new entrepreneurs also causes large existing businesses to invest more in R&D. Indeed, such firms account for a much greater proportion of R&D[34] spending than smaller new businesses.[35]

In the end, however, the biggest winners from these entrepreneurially driven changes are consumers. Thanks to the changes and innovation which entrepreneurs generate throughout an economy, consumers pay less for many goods and gain access to new products and services. Entrepreneurship is thus more important for a dynamic and growing economy and those it serves than most of us realize—so much so that we can say that there are good reasons to worry about America's economic future if the negative trends in entrepreneurship persist. This being the case, we need to ask ourselves what stimulates entrepreneurship.

INSTITUTIONS AND CULTURE

In general terms, we know that overall economic conditions matter for entrepreneurship. Levels of entrepreneurship tend to track the economy's ups and downs. [36] During recessions, entrepreneurship fades because people have a lower risk threshold and less capital is available. Conversely, entrepreneurship and innovation tend to rise when businesses find themselves needing to respond to steady increases in labor costs in a given economy. [37]

But it is the very nature of entrepreneurship which indicates what some of its key stimulants might be. Many entrepreneurs are intrigued by the actual process of creating something new. But they also generally want to make a profit. It follows that if entrepreneurs are not allowed to keep most of the profits of their venture, their entrepreneurial instinct may not be "turned on" in the first place. Worse, it is possible that people's entrepreneurial drives will find outlets in economically unproductive areas. Individuals can be entrepreneurial in many spheres in life: that includes bureaucratic empire-building or securing privileges from governments. Many crony capitalists are superb entrepreneurs insofar as they see opportunities for regulatory capture that others don't. [38] Incentives thus matter for entrepreneurship, but it also matters *where* the incentives are located. Much of that is determined by the legal and political environment in which entrepreneurs are operating.

Context is thus vital for economically creative entrepreneurship. It is one thing for a new idea, product, or service to be a technically realizable proposition. That, however, does not mean that it is commercially feasible. This has to be determined in the marketplace so as to gauge whether the innovation is profitable. [39] But while commercial feasibility relies on whether consumers like or want the product, it also depends upon the existence of institutions which help secure the rewards of innovation: i.e., the type of guarantees associated with strong private property rights, secure contracts, and the rule of law. Absent such circumstances, some entrepreneurs who want to be economically creative will simply leave to find institutional environments more conducive to such innovation. [40]

While the importance of legal and political settings for entrepreneurship has been known for some time, we have learned in more recent years that the cultural settings in which these institutions are located are equally important. For a long time, modern economics struggled to grasp the significance of culture for economic activity insofar as cultural dynamics are untidy, constantly changing, and often hard to quantify. The absence of firm markers for such things didn't, however, prevent Tocqueville from recognizing that the value ascribed by Americans to entrepreneurship and their positive attitudes towards freedoms of exchange, movement, and association had helped make America economically different to his native France: a country where fewer people were attached to such liberties and more inclined to let state actors take the initiative in the economy. [41]

On one level, culture embodies the informal attitudes and unspoken expectations which have been in place in a society for some time. These shape how people interact in the economic settings of Greece, for instance, compared to those of Denmark. Such attitudes may be difficult for Greeks or Danes to articulate precisely because they are so deeply internalized in people's habits of thought and action. But those living in a society in which economic security is generally prioritized over liberty, and where the state is considered the primary institution responsible for securing such security, are more likely to trade off various economic liberties in return for economic security via the government—the long-term price being gradual stagnation. In short, it matters where the balance of sentiment about such questions is tilted.

Attention to culture's significance for the economy also widens our horizons when we think about incentives. Not all incentives are financial or economic. In his *Theory of Moral Sentiments*, Adam Smith observed how people value others' esteem and will go a long way to attain it. Some people don't care what others think of them—but most do. If a society is inclined to associate achievement primarily with attaining high rank in the civil service, there will be fewer "esteem-incentives" to be economically entrepreneurial.

Cultural dispositions consequently have implications for how Americans think about entrepreneurship. Changing laws and policies is important if one is to incline an economy in particular directions. Yet, as the Nobel economist Douglass North discovered, "Informal constraints (norms, conventions, and codes of conduct) favorable to growth can sometimes produce economic growth even with unstable or adverse political rules."[42] This particular idea is central to observations made by Edmund Phelps in his explanation of why entrepreneurship remains strong in America.

The United States continues to rate highly in world rankings of levels and intensity of entrepreneurship. It has been consistently ranked as number one in the world for overall entrepreneurship in the well-respected Global Entrepreneurship Index.[43] This is remarkable, considering that America's overall economic freedom level is not outstanding by international standards. The 2022 *Index of Economic Freedom* ranked America as only the world's twenty-fifth freest economy, down from a ranking of twenty in 2021.[44] So why does entrepreneurship continue to be so strong in America?

Phelps's answer is that much of it comes back to cultural inclinations. Comparing Western European economies with that of America, Phelps noted that many factors discouraged productivity in the former. These included heavy labor-market regulation and weaknesses in those factors that bolster growth like vibrant capital markets. At the same time, Phelps added, modern European nations "were not a bunch of banana republics." They did not lag behind America in crucial predictors of growth like the rule of law and property-rights protections.[45] Judging from the 2022 *Index of*

Economic Freedom, many Western European countries are in better shape than the United States in these areas.

Through comparing data that surveyed American and Western European attitudes towards variables like views of change, embrace of new ideas, and the desirability of economic liberty, Phelps's research found that most Americans generally have a more positive understanding of such things than many Europeans. "I came away," Phelps wrote, "with the impression that differences across countries with respect to certain well-defined institutions were not as important as the prevailing differences in economic culture."[46] As he stated in his 2006 Nobel Prize lecture, "various attributes of a country's economic culture serve to animate entrepreneurs and, more broadly, to encourage them by offering them a willing workforce and a receptive marketplace for their innovations."[47]

Phelps's research over the past twenty years indicates that the American economy remains predisposed "for cutting-edge innovation . . . *fertile* in coming up with innovative ideas with prospects of profitability; *shrewd* and *adept* in selecting among these ideas for development; finally, *prepared* and *venturesome* in evaluating and trying the new products and methods that are brought out."[48] By contrast, he found that many European economic cultures stressed stability, social cohesion, protection for existing businesses, professions and organized labor, and an emphasis upon gaining assent from existing stakeholders. These priorities reflect the corporatist expectations described in Chapter Four.

Given entrepreneurship's ongoing strength in America despite all the obstacles, we should consider how much more dynamism could be added to the U.S. economy if the political and legal environment for entrepreneurship was more favorable than it is at present. Attitudes may sometimes be more important than policies, but policies still matter. The list of changes which could be made is lengthy. They range from better enforcement of property rights to diminishing the incentives to become a political entrepreneur. Here, however, are three particular measures that would bolster an entrepreneurial culture focused on economic growth rather than the endless rent-seeking which characterizes state capitalism.

DEREGULATE, DEREGULATE, DEREGULATE

Americans love to complain about regulation. Economist Russ Roberts observes that the overall rate of regulation in America has grown inexorably over the past seventy years. Between 1950 and 2018, the number of pages in the Federal Register[49]—the rules administered by the federal government's regulatory agencies—grew from just less than 10,000 pages to more than 186,000 pages.[50]

This number disguises the fact that some industries have experienced significant deregulation, while others have been subjected to more. Under the Trump administration, it should be noted, the flow of new regulations was much smaller than under the previous two administrations. There was also progress in working with Congress to promote more deregulation through the legislature.[51] But the overall number of completed deregulatory actions under Trump was small. In their study of this question, Keith B. Belton and John D. Graham report that the combined total for FY 2017 and FY 2018 "was 243 out of the 68,846 total regulations adopted in the last 24 years." [52]

In short, the long-term overall trend in America has been towards more regulation. There are no fewer than 260 federal agencies that impose regulations, and many of their rules overlap. [53] To this we must add the numerous regulations implemeneted by state and local government agencies. [54] Looking at trends in data compiled by the Organization for Economic Co-operation and Development (OECD) over recent decades, economists Germán Gutiérrez and Thomas Philippon found that while "European countries have substantially improved their regulatory process ... the US has not." [55]

Excessive regulation has deeply negative consequences for entrepreneurship. First, the burden of regulatory compliance can become a major distraction for start-ups trying to focus their attention on innovation. [56] Second, it makes entry barriers into the marketplace for new entrepreneurs higher than they should be. These individuals find themselves having to expend capital on buying equipment that allows them to adhere to regulations while also hiring experts and compliance officers to help them work their way through the rules. Some regulations may even force entrepreneurs to pay wages and benefits that, at least at an early phase, they cannot really afford. [57] Large existing businesses can more easily absorb such costs than start-ups. Such regulation thus helps solidify the control of existing businesses over a given economic sector. Third, regulation can influence the directions in which people's entrepreneurial instincts are directed. In heavily regulated economies, many innovative people will gravitate towards seeking new ways to engage in regulatory capture, thereby engaging their talents in effecting wealth appropriation rather than wealth creation.

This is not to claim that all regulation is bad. Many regulations, such as food-safety standards, serve good purposes. [58] Much regulation is, however, unrelated to such commendable goals. A prominent example is occupational licensing. While often justified in the name of consumer safety, the evidence indicates the contrary. As one Treasury Department study produced under the Obama administration concluded, "most research does not find that licensing improves quality or public health and safety." [59] This suggests that such licensing is maintained in place to protect the status quo from being challenged by new entrepreneurs. It follows that if we want America to retain its edge in entrepreneurship, one focus should be upon reducing the size and scope of regulation at the local, state, and federal level so as to tilt creative individuals away from trying to capture a greater share of existing wealth, and towards creating new and refined products.

CAPITAL, CAPITAL, CAPITAL

Enhancing entrepreneurship in America involves more than removing barriers. We must consider what fuels and sustains entrepreneurship over time, especially at the beginning. Entrepreneurship in market economies does not result only from sharp-minded creators of new products. Providers of capital need to be persuaded to understand the same entrepreneurial insight and embrace the risks associated with trying to realize it. Without capital, most entrepreneurial initiatives will not get off the ground. More than one injection of capital is often needed to sustain a new enterprise.[60] Venture capital—a form of private equity that investors provide to start-ups and small enterprises viewed as having long-term growth potential—is particularly associated with higher levels of innovation, and it has a positive impact on the number of new firms established, their aggregate income, and the employment they generate.[61]

Fortunately, if there is one thing that Americans understand, it is capital. America was blessed that several critical Founders—most notably, Alexander Hamilton[62]—understood that the ability to attract and mobilize domestic and foreign capital would be fundamental to America's economic development. The long-term result was Wall Street's emergence as the world's financial center. This makes it all the more curious that new entrepreneurial ventures in America face considerable difficulties in accessing the capital that they need at the beginning of the enterprise and at critical growth points. If you ask American entrepreneurs about their greatest challenges, you can be sure that gaining access to capital features on their list of concerns.

On average, approximately two-thirds of new economic endeavors rely heavily on personal and family assets for start-up capital. At the time of startup, 83 percent of these enterprises have not accessed venture capital or bank loans.[63] In 2008, the drop in American housing prices contributed to a fall in the rate of start-ups because so many start-up entrepreneurs use the equity value in their house as collateral for business loans; the greater the fall in housing values in any one area, the more the start-up rate declined.[64]

It's tempting to think that one way to make capital more available would be for the federal and state governments to become direct lenders through entities like the Small Business Administration. Unfortunately, their track record in providing capital to successful ventures is mediocre.[65] They also help crowd out private capital. An example of this were the attempts by the Department of Energy in the late 2000s to provide loan guarantees to clean energy projects deemed too risky to attract private investment. Starting in 2009, it invested over $34 billion in such projects in less than four years. This was almost $2 billion more than the total private venture capital investment in the field. The effect was to crowd out private capital as it waited on the sidelines to see what directions the public funds would go. As a consequence, clean tech energy fell from 14.9 percent of private venture capital investment in 2009 to 1.5 percent in 2019.[66]

This is not a peculiarly American phenomenon. From the mid 2010s onwards, the Chinese government tried to increase the amount of venture capital available for new businesses via government departments and state-sponsored venture capital funds. By 2017, Beijing was claiming that it had directed something like $1.8 trillion into these vehicles. Again, the results were unimpressive. It also created a venture capital bubble which subsequently collapsed. This was followed by an ongoing slowdown in Chinese venture capital investment. From a high of 45 percent of venture capital invested worldwide in the early 2010s, Chinese companies had fallen to 15 percent of that total by the middle of 2019.[67]

Why does it matter if private venture capital is crowded out or its share of overall venture capital is diminished? The answer is that there are real problems associated with trying to deliver capital through government vehicles. Political leaders and government officials are not especially adept at identifying worthy entrepreneurial ventures to support, as evidenced by their track-record in supporting failed enterprises. [68] As economist Josh Lehner states, "If dozens of Ph.D.s poring for years over econometrics models with mountains of historical data have been unable to show how to target industries, how can the typical government leader identify good prospects in a compressed time period and with limited information?" [69] Even more problematic is the tendency for public officials to support whatever happens to be the latest trend in capital investment—especially if the latest trend coincides with whatever is politically fashionable. This is closely related to a third difficulty: any form of public funding is prone to being captured by those with good political connections. In seeking to secure government capital for a new enterprise, political connections generally matter more than whether the proposed venture is deemed commercially feasible. [70] That creates particular disadvantages for entrepreneurs [71]—such as those immigrants who constitute a disproportionately high number of America's entrepreneurs—who lack precisely such connections.

Given these problems, one way forward is to increase the availability of private capital and diminish the regulatory obstacles which make it harder to access. Some policymakers have tinkered with the regulatory framework to make it easier for private investment funds to start. Others have sought to provide tax breaks for capital investors in new ventures so as to increase the incentives to lend. But perhaps the most optimal way to increase the flow of private capital to entrepreneurs is to encourage private creativity in how capital is provided.

Crowdfunding is a good example of innovation in the provision of private capital to budding entrepreneurs. The first instance of successful crowdfunding occurred in 1997 when a British rock band funded a reunion tour by appealing to fans to support them. The practice acquired major traction in America from 2009 onwards and its emergence occurred very much from the bottom up. By 2020, there were more than six hundred different crowdfunding platforms in the world, most of which were located in America. Prominent examples of enterprises initially capitalized through crowdfunding include the data collector Bitvore, the gaming headset Oculus VR, and the high-tech 3D printer Glowforge.[72]

Crowdfunding platforms establish venues for connecting entrepreneurs who need capital with many small-to-medium scale investors and lenders, thereby facilitating the direct flow of private capital to entrepreneurs. The absence of a mediator helps reduce costs and gives investors the opportunity to decide personally whether they want their capital to take the form of debt, equity, or even a donation. Through debt crowdfunding, investors provide loans to businesses directly. In the case of equity crowdfunding, entrepreneurs raise capital from investors who effectively buy into profit-sharing arrangements. Backers receive shares of a company in exchange for the pledged capital, thereby establishing securities-based relationships between entrepreneurs and investors.[73] Crowdfunding has even allowed the emergence of reward-based crowdfunding. Entrepreneurs effectively "presell" a good to start the business without incurring debt or sacrificing equity/shares. Future customers become the business's backers by providing working capital in return for which they receive a "reward" like pre-purchasing the good or service being developed. [74]

The beauty of crowdfunding is its entrepreneurial nature. Crowdfunders are mostly individuals who like to seek, select, and support entrepreneurial initiatives to which they are attracted. Sometimes it opens up possibilities for becoming involved in developing and marketing the product, often by spreading information about it through their various communities. This creates forums for feedback on the product and allows entrepreneurs to begin establishing a profile. Crowdfunding is thus more than just a way for entrepreneurs to acquire capital; it also allows investors to exercise patronage, become directly involved in new commercial ventures, and, hopefully, make money—all while reducing transaction costs by diminishing the need for middlemen.

Like any investment method, crowdfunding has its own risks. For example, due diligence of those looking for investors is often harder. The point, however, is that crowdfunding illustrates that we can be creative in developing different ways of generating and directing capital. The entire history of the financial sector, going back to the medieval period, [75] is one in which innovation has been a constant—but only if it is allowed to be. This history suggests that part of the business of enhancing the supply of capital to entrepreneurs is to permit as much entrepreneurship as possible in the field of capital itself. Will there still be entrepreneurial losses in this area? Yes. Will frauds be committed? Undoubtedly. Will some new forms of providing capital fail? Of course. But the more innovation we allow in this area, the more likely it is that more entrepreneurs will acquire the capital that they need.

MIGRANTS, MIGRANTS, MIGRANTS

While enhancing the flow of financial capital to entrepreneurs is important, another form of capital is equally important. Over the past fifty years, there has been growing appreciation among economists of the importance of "human capital." Many dislike the phrase, but it simply means the stock of intelligence, talents and skills, accumulated experience, and education embedded in and acquired by human beings as individuals and communities. It also reflects the insight that, as economist Julian Simon once wrote, "the ultimate resource is people, especially skilled, spirited, hopeful young people who will exert their will and imagination for their own benefit and in doing so . . . benefit the rest of us."[76] Gauging the quantity of human capital in a society is hard. But America undoubtedly possesses enormous amounts of it, thanks to its population size, skill base, and educational resources.

Predicting what human capital will be most optimal in the future is difficult. The economic value of different types of human capital changes over time. Each stage of America's transformation from a highly agricultural economy to one in which the industrial sector dominated, and then to an economy characterized by services, has involved some forms of human capital becoming more valuable than others. There is, however, one form of human capital that never grows obsolete and isn't dependent upon particular training: entrepreneurship. There is no shortage of American entrepreneurs. But there are many millions of entrepreneurs outside America who would flourish far more easily in many parts of America than in Buenos Aires, Damascus, or Tehran. It follows that if human capital is so valuable, America would do well to acquire as much of it as possible. That suggests that addressing America's challenges vis-à-vis entrepreneurship involves asking ourselves how we can incorporate more such people into the United States.

Since 1970, the number of foreign-born residents in America has grown steadily from about 5 percent of the total U.S. population in 1970 to approximately 14 percent in 2018.[77] It's not unusual for migration to be regarded as adding more people to those already competing for a slice of the existing economic pie. But another way to reflect upon immigration is to consider how much human capital has been added to the U.S economy by migration, and how so many migrants have become successful entrepreneurs who have helped to multiply the pie over time and provided incomes and jobs to millions of native-born Americans.

Throughout America's history, entrepreneurs have come from an astonishing range of migrant backgrounds. Many of them have left countries in which the political, legal, and cultural conditions are simply not amenable to the type of entrepreneurship that creates wealth. Think of the waves of Jewish migrants from Eastern Europe and Czarist Russia who came to America in the late nineteenth century to escape anti-Semitism; or those Latin Americans who have fled repressive Communist and socialist regimes in

Cuba and Venezuela; or the Christian Arabs who have fled corrupt secular-nationalist and Islamist regimes in the Middle East. Millions of such people have come to America asking not for a hand-out but simply the chance to exercise their creativity.

It is therefore hardly surprising that immigrants to America are disproportionately represented among entrepreneurs in America and are much more likely to start new businesses than native-born Americans.[78] Between 2010 and 2017, immigrants founded approximately 25 percent of all start-ups in America, and they proved especially successful in the high-tech sector.[79] Of the new science-, technology-, and engineering-related companies established between 1995 and 2005, one-quarter had at least one immigrant founder.[80] Back in 2010, the OECD noted that "In the United States, skilled migrants outperform college-educated natives in terms of starting companies, per-capita patenting, commercializing, or licensing patents. In particular, for patenting, there is evidence that immigrants' success has positive spill-over effects on natives."[81]

There is something predictable about this. In many cases, the choice to migrate to America represents a decision by individuals to strike out into the unknown, pursue new opportunities, and change their status quo. Many of these individuals have taken significant risks to come to America, and a willingness to take risks is central to entrepreneurship. Indeed, we know that highly motivated individuals are far more likely than others to emigrate and to plan on becoming entrepreneurs at some point in their lives.[82]

Lastly, there are demographic dimensions to boosting entrepreneurship in America. In 2021, economists Michael Peters and Conor Walsh found that declines in population growth contributed to a reduction in creative destruction, increased the average firm size and concentration, and diminished aggregate economic growth in the long-term.[83] Applying these findings to America, they demonstrated that the slowdown in America's population growth since the 1980s had weakened the country's economic dynamism. The projected continuation of this trend, they added, would reduce the entry of new firms into the economy.[84]

Put bluntly, fewer people can mean fewer entrepreneurs. There is even research suggesting that America's declining birthrate has negatively impacted the rate at which start-ups occur.[85] Nor is an aging population good for entrepreneurship. The incentives to start new businesses tend to decline as a work-force ages.[86] It is also the case that younger people are about 50 percent more likely to switch their consumption products. Older populations are by contrast generally less interested in new products or variations on existing goods and services.[87] This makes it harder for entrepreneurs and start-ups to build a customer base.

Absent a decision by more Americans to have more children, one way to address these negative demographic effects upon entrepreneurship is for America to accept more immigrants. Between 1783 and 2019, approximately 86 million immigrants entered the United States legally.[88] Though not all of them became entrepreneurs, many did. Large numbers of these migrants were also young, and all of them became consumers. Such are the ways in which immigration can help address America's entrepreneurship challenge today on multiple levels.

SOVEREIGNTY AND IMMIGRATION

Immigration is central to the American story. But that story goes beyond the economy. Important questions of social cohesion associated with migration cannot be ignored. The failure of many European governments to address this dimension of immigration sufficiently (often because of reluctance to acknowledge that not all cultures are equally amenable to freedom, the rule of law, constitutionalism, etc.) has created enormous political tensions throughout the Old Continent which are not disappearing soon.

Under international law, migration policy remains the prerogative of sovereign nation-states. National governments have the responsibility of determining how many immigrants enter a given country, and of deciding the composition of those migrants. Indeed, the concept of national sovereignty provides critical parts of the framework required by any country, including America, if it is to embrace the opportunities associated with migration and minimize the challenges.

On one level, the origins of national sovereignty are to be found in groups who regard themselves as members of one national community rather than another. Shared cultural factors such as language, beliefs, memories, association with a particular territory with recognized boundaries, or a patrimony of ideals (something especially applicable to America), cause people to identify with a single nation. Members of this group adhere to the laws of that nation, and they are prepared to make sacrifices for their fellow citizens, such as defending their country from aggression or paying taxes to provide common services for those living within its

sovereign borders. Put another way, American citizens are committed to America's common good in ways that they are not committed to Mexico's common good. This is despite the fact that
many Americans living along Mexico's northern border are geo-
graphically closer to Mexican citizens who live in Monterrey than
Americans who live in New York. It isn't that Americans have no
duties in justice to Mexicans. Rather, it is that they have particular
responsibilities to their fellow American citizens that they don't
have to Mexican citizens—and vice versa.

There is, however, another dimension to national sovereignty
that complements the existence of these common bonds and
sympathies. This is illustrated by way of analogy—one made by
philosophers as different as John Rawls and John Finnis—with
some of the arguments for private property developed by figures
like Thomas Aquinas. [89] For these thinkers, sovereignty is the public equivalent of private property. One of Aquinas's arguments for
private property's legitimacy is that experience shows how the
resources with which all of humanity has been endowed are nor-
mally made more fruitful when divided and possessed by individuals rather than owned in common. [90] The indisputable economic
degradation associated with socialist regimes underscores the
truth of this observation. Likewise, the international order is better
organized when the world is divided into sovereign states made up
of peoples who share common bonds that facilitate order within a
territory recognized as their own.

There's no indication that the conditions exist now or in the
foreseeable future which would allow some type of world authority to assume responsibility for maintaining order for humanity as

a whole. Few Israelis, Australians, Poles, Americans, or Chinese would voluntarily risk their lives for the UN. Yet does anyone doubt that plenty of Israelis, Australians, Poles, Americans, and Chinese would be willing to defend Israel, Australia, Poland, America, and China respectively?

The parallels between sovereignty and private property do not end there. Private property's ability to achieve its end of ordering the use of the world's resources by all people is dependent on each owner's liberty to exclude others from using his property as well as his freedom to decide how he wants to use his property, subject to restraints of just laws. Without these powers, private property is effectively nullified, and we are plunged into the tragedy of the commons. So too with national sovereignty: the government of a nation of twenty million people may rightly decline to admit ten million migrants who suddenly appear at its borders on the reasonable grounds that immediately admitting all these migrants would severely disturb the nation's internal harmony. Likewise, if a country doesn't possess the freedom to exclude those potential migrants whose beliefs or actions threaten the nation's well-being—those with no intention of abiding by its laws, or who reject or want to destroy that nation's patrimony—then the order and stability that sovereignty protects is undermined. This is why a sovereign state may apply conditions of residence to non-citizens that are not applicable to citizens, refuse to admit non-citizens, or choose to expel non-citizens—again, subject to due process of law.

It may well be that a sovereign state determines that its well-being will be enhanced by an increase in population occasioned by immigration, or the entry of migrants with particular skills, or the admission of large numbers of migrants who simply want to work and pursue economic opportunities less available to them in their homelands. Such policies have contributed to the economic prosperity and common good of America, not least because it has brought many aspiring entrepreneurs to the United States. Recognizing a sovereign state's authority to implement these policies is, however, entirely different from claiming that a sovereign state *must* admit, as a matter of right, any non-citizen who presents herself at its borders and demands entry, no questions asked. No such right can be derived from the criteria listed above.

Another way in which the private property-sovereignty analogy helps us order immigration policy is with regard to emergency situations. In cases of extreme necessity—which, Aquinas specifies, means "a person is in some imminent danger, and there is no other possible remedy" (rather strict criteria)—Aquinas stated that private property becomes common to the extent that this will meet the immediate need. [91] Applying this logic to the case of migration, we can say that those facing imminent danger because of war, persecution, or famine in their country and who don't possess any other reasonable remedy for their plight can rightly seek refuge in another nation. A sovereign nation's power to exclude non-citizens thus isn't absolute. But it doesn't mean that a given sovereign nation is duty-bound to admit any migrant who simply asserts that he confronts imminent danger if he remains in his native land. Nor does it imply that genuine refugees can demand asylum in whatever country they happen to choose. No one who migrates to escape imminent danger can claim that her need for a permanent refuge can *only* be fulfilled by, say, America or *only* by France or *only* by Singapore, and not by any other nation whatsoever.

If immigration is going to be part of the solution to America's entrepreneurial challenges, immigration policy needs to be grounded in a coherent legal framework. Bad or disorganized institutional settings have a way of generating perverse results.

While the U.S. Constitution does not list immigration policy as one of the powers inherent to the United States as a sovereign nation-state,[92] it has fallen to Congress to determine immigration policy since the 1790s. Its implementation has largely been an Executive Branch responsibility. American immigration law has undergone numerous changes since the Founding. It has also been subject to multiple interpretations and modifications by the judicial and executive branches. These changes and interpretations have been influenced by economic factors like a desire to meet demands for labor, but also darker forces—like the insistence by prominent progressives between the 1890s and 1930s that certain ethnic groups be refused entry to America on explicitly eugenicist grounds.[93]

But whether you favor more or less immigration, it is hard to dispute that, as Andrew M. Baxter and Alex Nowrasteh point out, America presently possesses "an archaic and barely coherent immigration system."[94] America's immigration policy presently makes it hard to migrate legally to the United States, and it incentivizes people to enter and stay in the country illegally. The waxing and waning of enforcement of immigration laws by the federal government, combined with the sheer plethora of contradictory pieces of legislation and interpretations applied to immigration policy, has created serious rule of law problems in this area. There is something especially pernicious about this, given how many people want to migrate to America to escape societies in which the rule of law is at best winked at.

Much more could be said about American immigration policy. But the United States should be capable of addressing many of the problems associated with its presently confused and upside-down immigration laws in a manner consistent with the principles outlined above. This would allow more would-be entrepreneurs to migrate legally to America, with the clear understanding that they will (1) obey all the laws of the United States and (2) affirm the American experiment in ordered liberty to which migrants to America—including Founders such as James Wilson, Alexander Hamilton, John Witherspoon, Robert Morris, and Thomas Fitzsimons—have contributed from the Republic's beginning. Migrants have always been and should continue to be part of the story of entrepreneurship in America: a story that has also involved a commitment to the rule of law.

Entrepreneurship in America has played out in varying ways for different people. Many entrepreneurs are content to enjoy the fruits of their success. Others have a restless disposition and move on to other ventures. Some, however, find themselves working harder simply to maintain their position. They know that there are thousands of other actual and potential entrepreneurs out there in the economy, many of whom are likely to come up with new ideas that make existing products obsolete, or alternatively, available in greater quantities but of a better quality and at a lower price. These real and potential competitors are what keep many entrepreneurs awake at night, but also alert to new opportunities.

We've seen that institutions, culture, the regulatory environment, capital, and immigration matter if we want entrepreneurship to flourish in America. For Wilhelm Röpke, however, one contextual factor was especially important. To his mind, business could be defended "more confidently and effectively if more entrepreneurs embrace free competition, which makes them servants of the market and causes their private success to depend upon their services to the community." Röpke then ominously added, "Otherwise they stab us in the back."[95] Röpke's point was that competition is indispensable if entrepreneurship is to work its magic, and if business is to remain focused on serving consumers rather than contributing to the growth of state capitalism. Bolstering competitive pressures in the economy must consequently be part of America's future.

CHAPTER 6

COMPETITIVE NATION

In general, if any branch of trade, or any division of labor, be advantageous to the public, the freer and more general the competition, it will always be the more so.

—ADAM SMITH

The competitive instinct is innate to humans. Whether we admit it or not, we constantly assess how we are doing in light of others' achievements. Everyone wonders how they are performing relative to their peers. Many societies are unenthusiastic about acknowledging these realities. America, however, is different.

Just as Americans have a reputation for entrepreneurship, they are also viewed as enthusiasts for competition. In the 1830s, Tocqueville commented on how "the competition of all"[1] pervaded America, and the ways in which a competitive spirit expressed itself in every aspect of American life, ranging from religion to politics. That spirit, Tocqueville noted, distinguished the American republic from many European nations in which competition was often considered inimical to social cohesion, as something that challenged traditional hierarchies, and often as rather vulgar.

But how much is this American reputation for a full-throated embrace of competitiveness merited today? In Chapter Four, we identified corporatism and its guarded view of competition as part of the background influence upon the stakeholder capitalism that some want America to embrace. Edmund Phelps points out, however, that the American economy has already experienced several waves of corporatism, all of which have negatively impacted competition throughout America. One wave occurred in the 1930s, when unions acquired significantly more institutional power following the New Deal and then used it to diminish competitiveness in labor markets. Another upsurge ensued in the 1950s and 1960s, when many large modern American corporations grew close to the federal government as a consequence of Cold War military spending and used their position to inhibit competition in industries such as aircraft manufacturing. A third corporatist wave, Phelps states, began in the 1980s, as expansive stakeholder theory gained traction in universities and worked its way into corporate America.

But Phelps maintains that another form of corporatism began spreading throughout the U.S. economy in the late 1980s and early 1990s. According to Phelps,

> The new corporatism . . . goes beyond the groups of
> classical corporatism—the groups that may bargain

collectively and the groups yoked together in "con-
certed action"—by embracing the idea of a social
compact: every person in a society is a signatory to
an implicit contract with the others—its terms understood by all—and according to this contract, no person
may be harmed by others without receiving compensation. . . . This new element of corporatism goes beyond
the classic demand for state control that improves the
conditions of society—national growth through state
direction and industrial peace through "concertation"
and co-determination—to the demand that the course
of development at no time set back some while propel-
ling the rest. The new thinking sees the state as undertaking to protect everyone from everyone else—or as
close to it as is practicable. [2]

Phelps then listed how this new corporatism manifested itself,
whether through "an ocean of persons and companies ready to lit-
igate," the encouragement of lobbyists who "submit requests for
legislation, regulations, and interpretative rulings," and, above all,
redoubled efforts to freeze in place the position of existing companies "producing the same old products."[3] Put differently, this variant of corporatism reflected even more wariness of competition's
effects upon social stability than its preceding variants. For competition brings with it social upheaval and tension, not all of which is
easily borne by individuals, communities, and nations. The trouble
is that, absent competition, economies and the nations in which
they are grounded are doomed to stagnation.

IS AMERICA COMPETITIVE?

Given how many waves of corporatism which have swept across the U.S. economy over the past one hundred years, we are bound to wonder about the state of competition in America. By one set of measures, the American economy remains quite competitive. In his 2021 analysis of the U.S. Census Bureau's 2017 Economic Census data for more than 850 industries, Robert D. Atkinson found that

> Just 35 of 851 industries are highly concentrated, with the top four firms' sales accounting for more than 80 percent of industry sales (this is called the C4 ratio). In 2002, 62 percent of industry output was from industries with low levels of concentration (a C4 ratio below 50 percent), but by 2017, 80 percent of industries had low concentration. Moreover, of the 115 industries with a C4 ratio of 60 percent or more in 2002, the majority got less concentrated. Overall, the average C4 ratio for American industry increased only slightly, from 34.3 percent to 35.3 percent.[4]

These numbers suggest that competition in America is relatively healthy. Nonetheless, other indicators suggest that not everything is as it should be. In their 2018 analysis of competition in America, economists Jay Shambaugh, Ryan Nunn, Audrey Breitwieser, and Patrick Liu pointed to several problems in this area. In 1979, they noted, between 11 percent and 18 percent of firms were new in any given industry. By 2014, however, only 4 percent to 9 percent of businesses fit that description. That included the high-tech sector. In the mid-2010s, Shambaugh et al. added, American businesses aged ten and younger were employing a much smaller share of the labor force (19 percent) than they did in the mid 1980s (33 percent). [5] This was attributed to the declining share of new firms in the economy overall and their declining size relative to older businesses. These falloffs went together with America's biggest firms increasing their market share. Looking across nearly every sector of the U.S. economy, Shambaugh and his colleagues found that

> the largest firms have more market share than they did in the late 1990s. At the same time, the most profitable firms earn far higher returns than they used to, and those returns are persistently high, undiminished by competition. These larger, more dominant firms may make it harder for start-ups to gain traction; conversely, fewer start-ups mean that there is less competition to take market share and profit opportunities from incumbents. [6]

Similar arguments were made by the French economist Thomas Philippon in his widely read book *The Great Reversal: How America Gave Up on Free Markets* (2019). Declining performance throughout much of the American economy, Philippon stated, owes something to degrading competitiveness. This was especially expressed, in his view, in growing levels of concentration across many sectors of the American economy. This "lack of competition," he added, "has hurt U.S. consumers and workers: it has led to higher prices, lower investment and lower productivity growth." [7] To demonstrate his point, Philippon compared competition in America with European nations, and illustrated that competition was healthier in several European countries—something that tracks America's steady fall on several indices of economic freedom over the past decade and its lower rankings than European states like Ireland, Denmark, Britain, the Netherlands, and Finland. [8]

At the political level, worries about deteriorating competitiveness in the U.S. economy began being given more vocal expression in the mid-2010s. In 2016, President Obama's Council of Economic Advisors (CEA) issued a report outlining where it believed uncompetitive practices had become prevalent, especially in labor markets. "Reduced competition," the Obama CEA stated, gave "employers power to dictate wages—so-called 'monopsony' power in the labor market." [9] In the CEA's view, "The presence of a limited number of firms in the market for a particular type of labor may give each of these firms some power in setting wages." [10] When one economic sector is dominated by a small number of firms, it suggested, they can collude to keep wages lower than they would be otherwise. The CEA also pointed to growing market concentration in the U.S. economy as evidenced, it argued, by the fact that "between 1997 and 2012, the majority of industries have seen increases in the revenue share enjoyed by the 50 largest firms." [11]

Five years later, the Biden administration engaged the subject of competition but with a broader focus. In an Executive Order issued on July 9, 2021, it stated that wider anti-competitive trends were apparent throughout the U.S. economy. The Executive Order argued that industry consolidation had

- "[I]ncreased the power of corporate employers, making it harder for workers to bargain for higher wages and better work conditions."
- Resulted in farmers being squeezed "between concentrated market power in the agricultural input industries—seed, fertilizer, feed, and equipment—and concentrated market power in the channels for selling agricultural products."
- Enabled "a small number of dominant Internet platforms [to] use their power to exclude market entrants, to extract monopoly profits, and to gather intimate personal information that they can exploit for their own advantage."
- Forced Americans to pay "too much for prescription drugs and healthcare services."
- Required Americans to "pay too much for broadband, cable television, and other communications services, in part because of a lack of adequate competition."
- Caused "consumers [to pay] steep and often hidden fees" in the financial-services sector. [12]

It isn't difficult to find similar concerns expressed by prominent progressive and conservative politicians. In her 2021 book *Antitrust: Taking on Monopoly Power from the Gilded Age to the Digital Age*, Democrat senator Amy Klobuchar maintained that large swaths of the American economy were dominated by a small number of businesses. Referencing President Teddy Roosevelt, she subsequently argued for more aggressive antitrust action. [13] In his own 2021 book *The Tyranny of Big Tech*, Republican senator Josh Hawley claimed that Big Tech's sheer scale enabled it to shut down

competition, thereby allowing companies to manipulate and cen-
sor information to promote progressive causes, marginalize conservative views, and compromise privacy. [14] Like Klobuchar, Hawley's
proposed solutions included using antitrust powers to break up
Big Tech *à la* Teddy Roosevelt and barring "dominant" firms from
acquiring or merging with other such firms. Hawley also argued
that regulators should be allowed to look beyond the consumer
welfare standard (usually defined to mean maximizing overall economic growth) that has governed antitrust policy since the Reagan administration. The protection of democratic self-governance
should, Hawley maintained, be added to the grounds for initiating
antitrust actions.

One question prompted by Klobuchar and Hawley's claims concerns the association of market concentration with the suppression
of competition. But is this necessarily the case? Arriving at a correct answer to this question matters because erroneous conclusions could generate policy responses that actually help entrench
businesses intent on blurring politics and profit. Determining the
truth about this, however, requires understanding what competition is, and why it is so important.

COMPETITION AS
CONSUMER SOVEREIGNTY

In many economics textbooks, what is called "perfect competition" is the market that achieves an efficient allocation of available resources. In the real economy, however, competition has two

dimensions. First, it is a device for regulating and ordering the economic system. Second, it is a way to stimulate individuals and groups to be more entrepreneurial, effective, and efficient in what they do.

Competition realizes both of these dimensions simultaneously in the condition of market economies. As economist Don Lavoie wrote, "It is the competitive quest for profit that directs productive activity in a market, and it is the complex configuration of consumers' wants as registered in their expenditures which dictates where profits are made." [15] Market competition thus provides ongoing incentives for businesses to maximize their performance, while also bringing a type of order to economic life by allowing for the formation of prices that reflect the availability of goods and services (supply) in light of people's wants and needs (demand).

It's also the case that in a highly competitive economy, every business—small, medium, or large—knows that its viability as an enterprise is perpetually open to challenge from existing and potential rivals. Competition forces businesses to assess over and over again what they are doing and why they are doing it. It subjects them to unrelenting pressures to innovate, shrink costs, streamline their organization, find less-expensive inputs, take their goods and services into new markets, reorganize their distribution systems, offer better sales services, and lower their prices. In these circumstances, no business can presume unqualified fidelity from their customers.

This state of affairs produces an ongoing tug-of-war between thousands of businesses, and an insecurity that incentivizes people to work harder and innovate. While there is no respite from this remorseless discipline, it creates new or refined products, which businesses hope—but do not know—will generate revenue that covers costs and produces a profit. Competition is inherently unsettling, but it makes others in the same industry or economic sector respond and adapt, including large established businesses. [16] By contrast, ignoring your competitors leads to losses because it means allowing others to serve consumers better than you can. Ongoing failure to oblige consumers will likely result in eventual expulsion from the marketplace. Indeed, every "victory" over your rivals in competitive markets is only temporary because the competitive fray is unending.

Understood this way, robust market competition is synonymous with the sovereignty of consumers. [17] Every dollar expended by a consumer is a "vote" for one business and against others. Those who benefit from the never-ending contest not only include companies that embrace competition and make a profit; it is also the millions of consumers who get greater access to new and refined products for which, in many cases, they pay ever lower prices over time.

Then there are competition's beneficial side effects upon economic life. In the first place, competition functions as a type of "discovery procedure," to use Hayek's famous phrase. It stimulates us to think differently, to take the risk of incurring the costs associated with pursuing useful knowledge, and to test the validity of that information in the marketplace. Thousands of people are thus stimulated to search for knowledge on a second-by-second basis without any state official telling them how and where to find it. When my competitors produce something faster, better, or cheaper

COMPETITIVE NATION   203

than I do, they are informing me that I am doing something less efficiently or effectively than they are. I thus learn from my marketplace rivals. Likewise, when competition results in consumers starting to abandon me and gravitating towards other businesses, I learn that I must solve my deficiencies. As I do so, my competitors will have to react. Hence, while competition doesn't produce perfect knowledge, it does help to reduce everyone's ignorance levels over time.[18]

A second side effect of competition is that it engenders flexibility and adaptability throughout an economy. Businesses in competitive economies quickly accentuate what consumers like and discontinue what they do not. They are also more proficient at reacting to the impact of new ideas, technological developments, ups-and-downs in the supply of capital, and alterations in income levels. The same flexibility helps companies to absorb the business cycle's highs and lows as well as external shocks coming from the global economy.

When inflexibility prevails within an economy, rigidities build up over time. Addressing these invariably produces economic, social, and political tensions. Confronting a union's monopoly of the labor supply in a particular market, for instance, is never easy. That makes many politicians reluctant to embark on change in the first place. Conversely, in economies where businesses are accustomed to adjusting to competitive pressures, it is much harder for rigidities to develop in the first place. This obviates the need to engage in the difficult work of having to dismantle them.

A third benefit of competition is its undermining of the ability of companies to maintain everlasting dominance of an economic sector. No matter how big their capitalization or market share, every company is under some degree of challenge in a competitive economy. A big firm can certainly respond by buying out competitors, or through paying big money for someone else's innovations and then integrating them into its own products and operations. But these are manifestations of the large company's need to react to competitive pressures if it wants to keep its customers and market share. The same business knows that there is every likelihood that there is an entrepreneur or business "out there" who, as the economist of innovation Joseph A. Schumpeter famously wrote, "commands a decisive cost or quality advantage and which strikes not at the margins of the profits and the outputs of existing firms but at their foundations and their very lives." [19] There is thus *always* the possibility that someone will come up with a new idea or product that decisively shifts consumer sentiment away from an Amazon or Facebook or BlackRock and adds seemingly omnipotent companies to the long list of once-great but now-small—or dead—businesses.

FALSE SOLUTIONS

Competition's benefits for Americans, whether producers or consumers, are real. But so too are the effects of diminishing competition. For once competition starts to weaken, the pressures to which it subjects businesses also begin receding. Companies consequently become lax about innovation and cost control, their structures start weakening, and their distribution networks become inefficient. The end result is less economic growth, growing inflexibilities throughout the economy, and, above all, businesses becoming less incentivized to care about what consumers think and want. If one wants to understand, for example, some of the reasons for manufacturing's decline in the "Rust Belt"—the heavy manufacturing region bordering the Great Lakes—there is much evidence suggesting that the lack of competitive pressures in its labor and output markets played a major role in depressing the incentives of firms "to innovate and thereby raise productivity." [20]

How can America avoid becoming uncompetitive? Thomas Philippon has argued that one way to augment competition in America is through more extensive antitrust action. This was central to the Obama administration's approach. In one Executive Order, it called for greater use of antitrust action to make labor markets more competitive by investigating collusion between employers concerning wages. It also suggested: (1) reforming occupational licensing to make it easier for people in one state to work in other states; (2) limiting the applicability of non-compete agreements; and (3) loosening land-use regulations so that housing markets could respond more quickly to growing demand, thereby making it easier for workers to move to different parts of America. [21]

There was, however, a schizophrenic dimension to the Obama administration's competition policies. Its Executive Order reflected no recognition that antitrust action can be easily abused by governments to protect favored businesses by accusing their competitors of monopolistic behavior. The same Executive Order also called for increasing the minimum wage, more paid sick leave, and strengthening the presence of unions in the workplace.[22] Whatever their merits, it is hard to see how such measures would bolster labor market flexibility and competition. But the biggest sign of confusion in the Obama administration's approach to competition was that while its Executive Order stressed the need to "eliminat[e] regulations that create barriers to or limit competition," the administration had, at the time of issuing this Executive Order, added six of the seven highest-ever annual page counts to Federal Registrar of Regulations.[23] As we will see, one of the greatest drivers of declining competition is regulation.

This incoherence pales, however, next to that of the Biden administration's position on competition policy. Though President Biden's Council of Economic Advisers (CEA) stated that his Executive Order on competition was promoting "more than 70 specific actions that will remove barriers to entry and encourage more competition,"[24] most of the Order sought to improve competition by adding more regulation.[25] It called for a "whole of government" approach in which agencies ranging from the Department of Treasury to the Department of Transportation would intervene to reinvigorate competition across the economy. This included closer monitoring of mergers and acquisitions, strengthening regulations to address practices deemed unfair, and specific regulatory interventions into particular sectors: broadband service providers, airplane baggage fees, hearing aids, health insurance, generic drugs, consumer finance products, independent brewers, winemakers, distilleries, and aerospace-based transportation technologies, to name just a few. While agreeing on the need to reform occupational licensing, the Biden Executive Order insisted that "many occupational licenses are critical to increasing wages for workers."[26]

As observed by economists Daren Bakst, Gabriella Beaumont-Smith, and Peter St. Onge, the Biden Executive Order effectively:

- Empowered government officials to micromanage how companies operate and serve their customers by seeking to dictate airline and shipping practices, meddling with private railroad contracts, and making it harder for businesses to grow through mergers and acquisitions.
- Encouraged cronyism by encouraging failing or failed market players to seek assistance from the government.
- Discouraged technology start-ups from getting off the ground by hindering the most popular "exit strategy" for start-up firms; "namely, getting acquired. Some of the most dynamic new businesses in America came out of this process, and slamming that door shut might slam the door altogether on the next generation of innovators."[27]

To this list one could add that the Biden Executive Order reflected a failure to grasp how market consolidation sometimes promotes greater efficiencies in particular economic sectors. It claimed, for instance, that "consolidation in the agricultural industry is making it too hard for small family farms to survive." But one reason why the number of small farms continues to decline is that bigger farms are generally more efficient.[28]

FALSE PROBLEMS

Unfortunately, the Obama and Biden administrations' approaches to competition were not outliers. Not long before he died, Nobel economist George J. Stigler stressed that public regulation had long been "the preferred choice in America" for promoting competition, "beginning with the creation of the Interstate Commerce Commission in 1887 and extending down to municipal regulation of taxicabs and ice companies." The problem, Stigler noted, is that most public regulation had "the effect of reducing or eliminating competition rather than eliminating monopoly. The limited competition—and resulting higher profits for owners of taxis—is the reason New York City taxi medallions sold for more than $150,000 in 1991 (at one point in the 1970s, a taxi medallion was worth more than a seat on the New York Stock Exchange)." [29]

Beneath Stigler's observation is an awareness that using regulation to address anti-competitive tendencies often reflects misunderstanding of economic phenomena like monopolies. The strict definition of a monopoly is a particular entity being the only supplier of a particular good or service. The existence of this state of affairs in an economic sector, however, need not mean that there is insufficient competition. It may simply be that no one else has yet proved capable of producing the same product as effectively or efficiently.

Similar observations may be made of what is called a "monopsony" (one entity's control of a market to purchase a good or service), or "duopolies" and "oligopolies" (two or several entities controlling the market for a given product). Again: the fact that these may

prevail in a given sector doesn't necessarily indicate a lack of competition. Why? Because market concentration is not the same thing
as an absence of competition. Former Federal Trade Commissioner
Maureen K. Ohlhausen observes that "One should be careful before
insisting that there is a causal relationship—from consolidation to
market power to supracompetitive rents." [30] The Chicago economist
Harold Demsetz, she reminds us, "showed that scale economies can
produce a concentrated industry structure, in which efficient firms
enjoy cost advantages and hence higher profits. [31] President Obama's
CEA acknowledged this point, stating that "rising concentration
can reflect increased efficiency from economies of scale." [32] Between
2002 and 2017, prices actually rose less in industries with higher
concentration levels of than they did in the overall economy. [33]

Economist David Henderson uses the case of Amazon to elaborate on this point. Many believe, he states, that when an economic
sector is concentrated (a conventional measure of monopoly and
market power being the share of revenue earned by the 50 largest
firms in various industries), it is easier for firms to collude and keep
new entrants out. By this standard, many believe that competition
has declined in the retail trade in America because of Amazon's entry
into that sector. But, Henderson notes, this reflects misunderstanding of how Amazon changed the nature of competition in retail:

> Before Amazon became important, what typically mat-
> tered for you as a retail customer was the amount of
> competition in your local market. So, if you lived in San
> Francisco and wanted a lawn chair, you might go to Sears...,
> Home Depot, or your local hardware store. But after

Amazon came into being, you had another major choice: saving a lot of time traveling from store to store and, instead, sitting at your desk or kitchen table, or even lounging on your old lawn chair, and ordering from home. Not only did you save time but also the odds are that you got a lower price. In short, Amazon made the relevant market for you much more competitive. And it did that even while, at times, wiping out local competitors. [34]

How then did Amazon rise to dominance? According to Henderson,

It got there with innovation that slashed retailing costs and then by sharing much of the cost reduction with consumers. The point is that Amazon became such a major player by innovating. And its market share is a reward for innovation. Other companies in other industries got large market shares for innovating also and did better than Amazon on the earnings front. Their large profits are their reward for innovating. [35]

A similar picture emerges with regard to Big Tech. Between 2002 and 2017, only eight of the 135 advanced-technology industries met the technical definition of concentration. [36] Of those eight that were concentrated, Thomas Philippon states, "most . . . actually got to where they are today by being better than their competitors." [37] Economist Ryan Bourne's explanation for how and why Big Tech companies achieved their market share is similar:

What we know for certain is that these tech companies
engage in extensive research and development spending
and are continually diversifying into new product markets. All regularly outline their fears of being disrupted
by insurgent firms and technologies. They compete with
one another in serving non-consumers or the low ends
of markets. None of this behavior would be expected
from entrenched monopolies planning to harm consumer welfare. [38]

Unlike Bourne, Philippon is willing to contemplate antitrust
action against Big Tech in the interests of creating "some space for
new entrants." Yet Philippon hesitates before recommending this as
the way forward with Big Tech [39] because he accepts that these companies' dominance has not emerged out of anti-competitive practices.

From this standpoint, the number of companies in an industry
and their respective share of that market is not sufficient to determine whether competition has been shut down. When competition is understood as a process of continuous striving to attract
consumers, monopoly no longer means one or two firms' dominance of a market. Those one or two firms can only maintain
their position by continually outcompeting others' efforts to offer
something to consumers. Yes, that may involve buying up new
products, technologies, or other businesses in the same economic
sector, but such actions are all responses to competitive pressures.
In other words, as Don Lavoie stated, "To say that there is less
than an infinite number of competitors is not to say that there is
no competition." [40]

CRONY TIME

Dominance of an economic sector by a relatively small number of companies is therefore not necessarily indicative of an uncompetitive state of affairs. If competition is ultimately a situation in which current and potential producers are serving consumers, an uncompetitive economy is one in which this situation is reversed: when the constant striving by producers is replaced by a situation of: (1) permanently protected positions for particular businesses by virtue of privileges and regulations that favor them; and (2) the creation of political obstacles that inhibit others from entering a given market. In such situations, consumer sovereignty is extinguished.[41] Elaborating on this point, Röpke comments:

> There are in fact not many monopolies in the world which would not exist without privileges having been consciously or unconsciously granted by the state or without some sort of legislative or administrative measure, legal decision, or financial policy having been responsible for it, and the fact that hardly anyone today properly appreciates this connection makes it all the more dangerous because it makes the actual power which the state can exercise over monopolies appear much less than it actually is.[42]

On the basis of similar reasoning, Stigler defined monopoly as existing in an economic sector where the government uses coercion to restrain competition.[43] Writing in the 1970s, Stigler maintained that "Even today, most important enduring monopolies or near monopolies in the United States rest on government policies. The government's support is responsible for fixing agricultural prices above competitive levels, for the exclusive ownership of cable television operating systems in most markets, for the exclusive franchises of public utilities and radio and TV channels, for the single postal service—the list goes on and on."[44] If there were situations in which monopolies existed independent of government support, Stigler added, they were likely "due to smallness of markets (the only druggist in town) or to rest on temporary leadership in innovation."[45]

The literature illustrating how diminished competition results from rent-seeking[46] by businesses that establish barriers to entry is overwhelming.[47] Much of the evidence was laid out by Thomas Philippon and Germán Gutiérrez in 2017, when they showed how industry concentration increased with regulation[48] as dominant firms continued "to erect barriers to entry and increase market power."[49] Other economists point to strong correlations between cumulative regulation and the declining number of new firm entries into a given economic sector.[50] In their study of regulation's effects on competition, James Baily and Diana Thomas found that more-regulated industries experienced fewer new firm births and slower employment growth. The same regulations inhibited employment growth in small firms more than in large firms. Large firms, they stated, have the resources to navigate regulatory environments; smaller firms lack those resources.[51] The more numerous the regulations and the more costly the compliance, the harder it is for new firms to break into the market.

Even when a regulation appears neutral, competition can still be undermined, Henderson demonstrates, through economies of scale in compliance:

> A given regulation might cause a firm with $10 billion in sales to spend $10 million to help it comply. That expenditure is 1/1000 of sales. But to comply with that same regulation, a firm with only $100 million in sales might need to spend $1 million. That's 1/100 of sales, which is 10 times as much as the large firm's expense. This can force out small firms, making an industry less competitive than otherwise. [52]

Many established American businesses understand how regulation often makes it more difficult for new companies to enter or remain in a market. They consequently lobby for enhanced regulation of their industry. In his explanation of declining competition throughout the U.S. economy, Philippon specifies the main cause as political insofar as barriers to entry were being put in place, sustained, and increased via businesses lobbying politicians. Asked about this in an interview, Philippon reiterated that "with the data we have, the effects of lobbying are still very clear at the state level, at the federal level, across industries—when you see a big increase in lobbying, firms succeed in getting the regulations they want, or avoiding antitrust actions. The more we refine the data, the more it becomes consistent with this idea." [53]

Other research supports Philippon's claim. Seeking to determine what drove increased profits in publicly listed firms in America, James E. Bessen found that while R&D investment played a
major role, political factors such as lobbying (often backed up with
campaign contributions) accounted for much of the increase. After
2000, Bessen maintains, lobbying became an even more important driver of profit, with major increases of regulation appearing
to augment the profits of publicly listed firms who lobbied hard to
skew the regulatory environment in their favor. [54] The relationship,
Bessen argues, "appears causal: increases in regulatory complexity
appear to cause subsequent increases in profits" [55] for such firms,
presumably because such complexity makes entry by competitors
harder. Summarizing his findings, Bessen noted two particularly
problematic developments:

> First, the link between regulation and profits is highly
> concentrated in a small number of politically influential
> industries. Among non-financial corporations, most of
> the effect is accounted for by just five industries: phar-
> maceuticals/chemicals, petroleum refining, transporta-
> tion equipment/defense, utilities, and communications.
> These industries comprise, in effect, a "rent-seeking
> sector." Concentration of political influence among a
> narrow group of firms means that those firms may skew
> policy for the entire economy. . . . Second, while political
> rent-seeking is nothing new, the outsize effect of politi-
> cal rent-seeking on profits and firm values is a recent
> development, largely occurring since 2000. Over the

last 15 years, political campaign spending by firm PACs
has increased by more than thirty-fold and the Regdata
index of regulation has increased by nearly 50 percent for
public firms. However much political rent-seeking has
affected economic dynamism and inequality so far, the
effect is likely to be greater in the near future.[56]

This depressing picture underscores the imperative of diminishing regulation to make it easier for entrepreneurs and new businesses to break into economic sectors with new ideas, products,
and technologies and thereby challenge companies who enjoy
market dominance. Here it is telling that the heads of some Big
Tech firms—most notably, Facebook's Mark Zuckerberg—have
asked on several occasions for more regulation of their industry by
the government.[57] They understand that the resources which they
can devote to lobbying, combined with their present high-level
of access to legislators, gives them the ability to craft regulations
to stave off encroachments on their market share. While such big
firms will incur the costs associated with increased regulation,
they know that their size enables them to better diffuse the costs
than smaller companies.

Obviously it isn't only businesses that dislike competition who
bear responsibility for crony regulation. Many politicians have
strong incentives to protect market incumbents. By making themselves the centerpiece of decision-making through legislation,
executive orders, or regulatory ordinances, those holding public
office can signal their importance to everyone in a given industry. They thereby increase their ability to exercise patronage and

consequently reap financial support for electoral campaigns. Such individuals can also set themselves up for well-paying positions either as lobbyists or on the boards of firms who once lobbied them for favors in what amounts to an ill-disguised *quid pro quo*. There are few, if any, incentives for legislators to maintain a "no-favors" position in any industry or in the economy as a whole.

REAL SOLUTIONS

Many countries have used devices like trade practices legislation and competition agencies to try to address anti-competitive trends. But the effects can be mixed. The drafting of such legislation or the operations of these agencies can themselves be captured by market players and legislators. That includes antitrust agencies. Though Philippon believes that there is a case for using anti-trust action to improve competition, this is one reason why he is diffident about giving this remedy his full-throated endorsement.[58] Similar worries lay at the heart of Stigler's doubts about antitrust activity:

> The declining support for antitrust policy has been due to the often objectionable uses to which that policy has been put. The Robinson-Patman Act, ostensibly designed to prevent price discrimination (i.e., companies charging different prices to different buyers for the same good), has often been used to limit rivalry instead of increase it. Antitrust laws have prevented many useful mergers, especially vertical ones. (A vertical merger

is one in which company A buys another company that supplies A's inputs or sells A's output.) A favorite tool of legal buccaneers is the private antitrust suit in which successful plaintiffs are awarded triple damages. [59]

The other problem with antitrust policies is that even if a very large company is broken up in an effort to restore competition, the component pieces can reintegrate themselves over time into a wider whole. In 2021, Mark Weinstein, the founder and CEO of MeWe, an ad-free social network, described Facebook as a monopoly and argued that "A new approach in antitrust regulation is required to meet this challenge." He conceded, however, that "A Facebook breakup may even follow the same destiny as AT&T Corp., which was broken up by federal regulators into 'baby bells' in 1984, only to have many of its parts merged back together over the years." [60]

If the key problem with American competitiveness is regulation, and if much of that regulation has nothing to do with the common good and everything to do with businesses wanting to avoid competition and legislators happy to oblige them, the answer is clear. Consumer sovereignty must be reestablished through reducing regulation and limiting its spread. How might that come about? Here are five general suggestions.

First, Phillipon is surely right to contend that "any new regulation contemplated in the U.S. should be judged in part according to the basic question, 'Is it going to create barriers to entry?'" [61] Even if the answer to that question is "Yes," then at least it will be a matter of public record. People will be able to judge whether the cost to competition is worth it and identify the firms who benefit from the regulation. The point is to establish transparency about a regulation's effects and identify who is benefiting at everyone else's expense.

Second, the judicial branch provides opportunities for countering business-legislator collusion. As demonstrated by Ohlhausen, one of the most successful ways in which the Federal Trade Commission "has opposed private restrictions on competition cloaked as government action [is] through successive wins at the Supreme Court." [62] These cases have made it harder for competition to be inhibited at the state level by forcing state legislators and regulators to be up-front about what they are doing. "[I]f states wish to limit competition," she writes, "they must do so without ambiguity, pursuant to a 'clearly articulated and affirmatively expressed' policy to displace competition." [63]

Third, we should explore ways to shift competition law away from a regulatory focus. Competition law "should not," Ohlhausen says, "intervene to order more competition or to reengineer market structure. Rather, it should protect the competitive process by which firms vie for sales opportunities by offering superior prices, terms, technology, and so on." [64] That means, she adds, "nurturing the incentives bestowed by the capitalist system, which rewards success and punishes failure." [65] It also implies ensuring that the rules of competition are kept as simple as possible. This limits the ability of CEOs and politicians to use regulatory complexity to close markets to new entrants.

Fourth, we should consider decentralizing the regulatory process to prevent a small number of intermediaries and incumbent political leaders from dominating it. If more individuals and groups are involved in the decision-making process, economist Luis Zingales observes, it becomes harder for lobbyists, incumbent businesses, and legislators to skew the process. This makes it more likely that the rules will reflect a type of minimum consensus focused on general principles rather than a plethora of complex details.[66] Some economists have even suggested employing methods of direct democracy to diminish opportunities for insiders to dominate the regulatory process. To the extent that direct democracy diminishes the role of intermediaries—especially legislators happy to connive with businesses looking to suppress competition—it offers some potential for achieving this goal.[67]

Fifth, we need wider recognition that competition cannot flourish and regulation will not be diminished without broader and general acceptance of certain norms of conduct. That includes, I'd argue, a willingness on the part of businesses to decline to invoke state power to curtail competition.[68] American businesses should make it a point of pride not to ask legislators and regulators to limit competition. Nor should Americans be kind to businesses which attempt to regulate competition out of the economy—even if it means naming and shaming American companies which play these games. Granted, that won't deter some American business executives from seeking to rig the market through regulation. Few of them, however, will enjoy being publicly labelled for what they are: rent-seeking cronies. Such rhetoric would also remind American consumers that competition is about making business work for them—not for the mercantilists of our time and their political enablers.

Translating these recommendations into concrete proposals, legislative or otherwise, is easier said than done. But we can take solace in economic history, which indicates that even when competition is far from robust it is difficult for businesses to maintain market dominance for long periods. Certainly such companies can try to establish such a preponderance through means like mergers and acquisitions, or through buying new technologies or companies, selling their products at a loss until their rivals give up and exit the market, or even integrating suppliers into their organization. But as Ryan Bourne's analysis of the fate of very large American firms over extended periods demonstrates, such methods have failed to guarantee lasting market dominance.

"Over the past century," Bourne writes, "large businesses operating in industries similar to today's tech firms were regularly labeled as unassailable monopolies. Retailers, social networks, mobile phone producers, camera manufacturers, and internet browser and search engine companies have all been thought likely to dominate their sectors perpetually, based on similar economic reasoning to that heard about tech companies today." [69] And yet, Bourne states, "predictions of unassailable market dominance that we hear in relation to today's tech giants, often explained by appeals to economic phenomena such as network effects, economies of scale, tying of products, or other cost barriers to entry, have been heard many times before in similar industries. The forecasts have proven ill-founded." [70]

Businesses are unable to maintain long-term market dominance partly because innovation and competitors often come from completely unexpected places. Once upon a time, entire markets for private transport in cities were dominated by companies that had secured transferable permits (taxi-medallions) from

city-governments. Then Uber and Lyft appeared. No one predicted their emergence, and no government official planned for
this to happen. Nonetheless, these businesses shattered what were
many taxi companies' market-dominance in numerous towns and
cities throughout America. The ultimate beneficiaries were American consumers.

The importance of reestablishing consumer sovereignty via
competition over and against today's mercantilists goes beyond
making markets serve consumers. There is another, more political
reason why America needs to enhance its economy's competitiveness. Economic strength is insufficient for a country to be a great
power, but it is indispensable for such greatness. Paradoxically, one
way of maintaining and even increasing that economic strength is
through understanding that a commitment to open trade and the
competition that it generates serves America's interests as a nation
rather than degrades them.

CHAPTER 7

TRADING

NATION

It is the maxim of every prudent master of a family, never to attempt to make at home what it will cost him more to make than to buy. . . . What is prudence in the conduct of every private family, can scarce be folly in that of a great kingdom.

—ADAM SMITH

In few areas is the reality of economic policy's inseparability from politics more manifest than in global trade. In the period immediately following ratification of the U.S. Constitution, for example, trade debates within the Washington administration became quickly entangled with arguments about what should be America's stance vis-à-vis the spreading global conflict between France and Britain in the French Revolution's wake. Similarly, when Congress and the Executive Branch today develop or modify trade policy, whether in a liberalizing or protectionist direction, it inevitably has political ramifications for both America's allies and its opponents in the world.

One element of statesmanship involves accurately identifying and understanding the most relevant facts confronting a country as it pursues its national interests. Though economics forms an important part of that calculus, the legislator must take other criteria into account. What implications, for instance, does the government's responsibility to uphold national security have for the type of products freely exchanged between American businesses and their foreign counterparts?

In Chapter Two, we saw how America has adopted protectionist practices at different periods to attempt to shape the nature of Americans' economic interactions with businesses and nations through the world. Also detailed was the subsequent harm inflicted upon the American economy. But if the prime alternative—free trade—is to be advanced successfully in twenty-first-century America, it needs to occur in a manner fitted up for present geopolitical circumstances rather than those of the 1980s or 2010s. That does not mean downplaying the economic case for free trade. Nonetheless it does necessitate reexamining our assumptions about the environment in which that case is advanced.

TRADE IN AN IMPERFECT WORLD

Following World War II, America committed itself to an agenda of trade liberalization between developed nations. This was not simply a question of American policymakers believing that free trade would deliver better economic results for America. It reflected the conviction that protectionism had exacerbated radical-nationalist trends in Europe in the 1920s and 1930s and thereby helped fuel the march to war. Rightly or wrongly, greater trade between nations came to be associated with greater peace. With this agenda being embraced by successive presidential administrations after 1945, the scale and depth of tariffs and quotas applied to imports by America fell. As noted in Chapter Two, the picture is more mixed than this broad trend suggests, but the overall trajectory away from protectionism was clear.

By the mid-2010s, however, free trade was on the defense throughout much of America. While this owed something to perceptions about trade liberalization's domestic effects, it also reflected broader disagreements about the nation-state's place in a more economically integrated world and related questions concerning sovereignty. For some Americans, support for free trade had become associated with dreams of a borderless planet in which nation-states would be subordinated to supranational organizations like the EU as an ever-extending integration of national economies brings universal peace in its wake.

The irony is that there is no necessary association between free trade and ambitions of a peaceful, nation-free world.[1] This was well understood by some of the leading figures of the movement most associated with the rise of free markets which exercised tremendous influence upon many of those at the heart of the American Founding. Scottish Enlightenment thinkers like Adam Smith and David Hume neither desired nor envisaged the disappearance of nations; they were also skeptical about strong correlations between free trade and a more peaceful world. Grasping their reasons for thinking so is, I'd suggest, important for how America thinks about trade openness in our time.

Both Hume and Smith were careful observers of international relations. Several of their commentaries focused on Britain's relationship with its American colonies. But their starting point on these matters was always sovereign-states—not aspirations towards a pan-European federation of the type sketched out in 1713 by the Abbé de Saint-Pierre in his *Projet pour rendre la paix perpétuelle en Europe* and developed by Immanuel Kant in his 1795 *Perpetual Peace: A Philosophical Essay*. Hume and Smith were certainly part of the Enlightenment's transnational world of letters. By eighteenth-century standards, they lived cosmopolitan lives. Yet they did not develop cosmopolitan affections, let alone sympathy for universal peace projects. Their approach to foreign relations was marked by deep realism about human nature.

Hume primarily explored foreign affairs through the prism of a balance of power between nations. This was the best basis, he believed, for a relatively peaceful world. I say "relatively" because Hume thought that human imperfectability meant there would always be tensions between countries that would occasionally spill over into outright conflict. Establishing a balance of power,[2] he thought, was the most realistic way of limiting such tensions and would help restrain military conflict from escalating to the global proportions that he and other Scots witnessed during the Seven Years' War.

Hume also doubted that the extension of free trade between nations, of which he was a strong advocate, would necessarily produce a more peaceful world. More countries, he reasoned, would become wealthier through free trade. Their governments could therefore maintain and increase their armies and navies and absorb the costs of war for longer periods.[3] One finds traces of this insight in George Washington's observation that "in modern wars the longest purse must chiefly determine the event."[4]

Adam Smith's views on these matters were not far removed from those of Hume. In his *Theory of Moral Sentiments*, Smith didn't argue that our sympathy for others stopped at borders. Smith did, however, believe that sympathy necessarily became feebler once it moved beyond the national level. Empathy for the human race and love of country weren't, to Smith's mind, incompatible, but they were not the same thing. "The love of our country," Smith wrote, "seems not to be derived from the love of mankind. The former sentiment is altogether independent of the latter, and seems sometimes even to dispose us to act inconsistently with it."[5] Nations, according to Smith, are more part of our everyday cultural and historical reality than a generic humanity as a whole. Placing your country's well-being before that of other nations was thus to be expected, even natural,[6] and Smith regarded fighting and dying for one's country as deeply honorable.[7] Certainly Smith was no enthusiast for war. Part V of his *Wealth of Nations* details the substantial economic burdens which it imposes on nations. Nonetheless Smith agreed with Hume that such conflicts were part of the human condition.

Part of Smith's critique of eighteenth-century mercantilism was that it exacerbated the potential for international conflict. Thanks to its beggar-thy-neighbor conception of wealth, mercantilism encouraged governments to think that national prosperity could only come at others' expense. This mindset stimulated national rivalries, whether it concerned territory in Europe or colonies and trading rights in the Americas, Africa, and Asia. To the extent that free trade undermined many of these sources of conflict, Smith thought that it could encourage greater peace among nations.

Nevertheless Smith didn't imagine that free trade would render either war or nations obsolete. In the first place, Smith was skeptical that economic integration would gradually neutralize humanity's propensity for conflict. Trade might ameliorate some of the international tensions associated with cultural and religious differences, but it wasn't going to produce perpetual peace. This realism manifests itself in the exceptions which Smith—much like Alexander Hamilton two decades later—made to his otherwise comprehensive advocacy of free trade. These included the use of retaliatory economic restrictions during trade wars, and protecting industries and technologies essential for a nation's war-fighting capacities. These aren't the conclusions of a crypto-pacifist who thinks that growing trade freedom will eventually dissolve the likelihood of clashes between countries.

Likewise, Smith's advocacy in *The Wealth of Nations* of professional armies wasn't just a question of him applying the division of labor principle to national security issues. He also thought that professional armies were more effective than militias at conducting war and deterring aggression. The implication was that Smith didn't believe that war or nations were likely to dissipate amidst a universal commercial pacifism. Indeed, Smith elaborated on Hume's thesis that the increased wealth generated by free trade would allow countries to enhance their military capacities. Free trade, Smith believed, would make countries rich, but such wealth could be used to manufacture and buy weapons as well as build armies and navies.[8] Echoing Hume, Smith specified that the growth in a nation's "consumable goods" from an increasingly efficient economy would permit that country to support "fleets and armies in distant countries" and "carry on foreign wars,"[9] whether through an enhanced capacity for military expenditures or a greater ability to sustain debt for longer time periods.[10]

An example of what Smith envisaged might be the stupendous economic growth experienced by nineteenth-century Britain. This accelerated after the 1846 repeal of tariffs (colloquially known as the Corn Laws which had hitherto restricted food imports into Britain and kept food prices high) and successive British governments' commitment to further trade liberalization. What's often forgotten is that, absent the enormous wealth facilitated partly by free trade, it's doubtful that Britain could have maintained the powerful navy which enabled it to enforce the *Pax Britannica* throughout much of the nineteenth-century world. Free trade had certainly helped enrich Britain, and some of that wealth gave Britain a capacity to project military force around the globe on a scale unmatched by any other nineteenth-century power.

MISTAKES AND EXPECTATIONS

This excursion into eighteenth- and nineteenth-century history illustrates how some of the most important advocates of free trade refrained from overstating its positive effects. That circumspection went together with a conviction that countries were here to stay and that imperfect human beings would always be prone to some degree of conflict.

Why is this relevant for our time? The answer is that many American policymakers and free marketers oversold the case for free trade from the 1980s onwards. By that, I do not mean that their economic arguments for free trade were wrong. But there was a tendency to overestimate free trade's capacity to help shift many countries towards greater liberty, the rule of law, constitutionalism, and other Western ideals.

The biggest fish that many hoped would be caught in the free trade–free society net was China. Many American policymakers calculated that a steady integration of China into the global economy would not only be of mutual economic benefit for China and Western nations. They also held that trade might further a growth of commercial freedoms inside China. This in turn would soften the regime's authoritarian character, gently create space for other domestic liberties, and help pacify China's external impulses.

Certainly, this consideration was not necessarily at the forefront of American policymakers' minds at the time. Trade negotiations are hard-headed affairs in which one-world sentimental humanitarianism is put firmly to the side as national representatives seek to secure the best bargain for their country. As Scott Lincicome points out, analysis of Clinton administration speeches and policy documents illustrate that "creating a liberal democracy in China was not a primary reason for the U.S. government's approval of China's WTO accession."[11] Multiple domestic and foreign policy objectives, ranging from better market access for U.S. companies to promoting stability in the Taiwan Strait, were being pursued.

That said, one need only read various presidential statements at the time to see that a more freedom-friendly China *was* part of the hopes, if not a mild expectation. This can be observed in President Bill Clinton's speech of March 9, 2000, at John Hopkins University explaining why, in his words, "Supporting China's entry into the WTO. . . . is about more than our economic interests." China certainly represented an enormous opportunity for American businesses and lowered the costs of many products for American consumers. Yet Clinton also maintained that it would help in shifting China towards becoming a freer country. "Membership in the WTO, of course, will not create a free society in China overnight or guarantee that China will play by global rules," Clinton commented. "But over time, I believe it will move China faster and further in the right direction, and certainly will do that more than rejection would." [12]

That same year, the Republican contender in the 2000 presidential election made similar comments. Alongside claiming that China's ascension to the WTO would serve America's national and economic interests, George W. Bush argued that China's further integration into global markets could help move the country toward greater domestic liberty:

> First, trade with China will promote freedom. Freedom is not easily contained. Once a measure of economic freedom is permitted, a measure of political freedom will follow. China today is not a free society. At home, toward its own people, it can be ruthless. Abroad, toward its neighbors, it can be reckless. . . . I view free trade as

> an important ally in what Ronald Reagan called "a for-
> ward strategy for freedom." The case for trade is not just
> monetary, but moral, not just a matter of commerce, but
> a matter of conviction. Economic freedom creates hab-
> its of liberty. And habits of liberty create expectations of
> democracy. There are no guarantees, but there are good
> examples, from Chile to Taiwan. Trade freely with China,
> and time is on our side.... Simply put: China is most free
> where it is most in contact with the world economy. [13]

Clinton and Bush were careful to insert caveats throughout their respective comments. They were *not* saying that enhanced participation in global markets was guaranteed to push China towards broader embrace of the habits and institutions of freedom. Nonetheless, this was a period in which many policymakers were influenced by the thesis outlined by Francis Fukuyama in *The End of History and the Last Man* (1992): that the collapse of Communist systems in 1989 foreshadowed a coming "end-point" in "mankind's ideological evolution," this being the eventual "universalization of Western liberal democracy as the final form of human govern-ment." [14] There might be temporary lapses on this Hegelian high road to liberal order and the journey might be long, but the destina-tion was settled. More-or-less liberal democracies and more-or-less market economies were the future.

Things did not quite turn out that way in China. As Ste-phen Ezell explains in detail, China did not abide by some of the very basic commitments expected by any WTO mem-ber "on issues such as industrial subsidization, protection of

foreign intellectual property, forcing joint ventures and technology transfers, and providing market access to services industries"—so much so, there is good reason to doubt that China
ever intended to keep its promises. [15] Instead of adopting the
broad market liberalization agenda expected of WTO entrants,
Chinese economic policies were more akin to those of an
eighteenth-century mercantilist state. More generally, political
liberalization never materialized.

American recognition of these facts was signaled by the
National Security Strategy issued by the Trump administration
in 2017. Many national security and foreign policies of previous
administrations, it stated, had been "based on the assumption
that engagement with rivals and their inclusion in international
institutions and global commerce would turn them into benign
actors and trustworthy partners." But, the document then added,
"For the most part, this premise turned out to be false." [16] This
conclusion was not one limited to conservative Americans. One
year later, two former senior Obama administration officials
stated in a *Foreign Affairs* article that Democratic and Republican
administrations "had been guilty of fundamental policy missteps
on China." [17] That included mistaken assumptions about trade's
long-term effects on China.

Parts of this assessment may be quibbled with. Jeffrey Bader
and Ryan Hass note that America's relationship with China had
competitive dimensions long before Xi Jinping's ascension to
power in 2012. There have also been areas in which China has
quietly cooperated with the United States since President Richard Nixon went to China in 1972. [18] Nonetheless, while trade with

China has delivered considerable economic benefits to Americans, political and economic trends in China did not shift in the anticipated direction. By the late-2010s, the Chinese regime had become even more authoritarian, increasingly less market-orientated in its domestic economic policies, even less transparent about the true state of Chinese businesses and the economy, and more aggressive in its approach to other nations.

The question thus becomes: where does America go from here vis-à-vis free trade in general and China in particular? A fair amount of rhetoric presently inhibits clear reflection upon the optimal way forward for America vis-à-vis China. On parts of the right, we hear calls for an "immediate" decoupling of the Chinese and U.S. economies. [19] Fewer are outlining precisely how that might occur or acknowledging the subsequent costs that would be incurred by American consumers and businesses. [20] From sections of the left we hear a parroting of Xi's lines about China's deep commitment to international law. [21]

To my mind, there are two preconditions to any successful path forward. First, there must be recognition that America's approach to trade cannot return to a 2000-2016 outlook or set of expectations. Second, Americans need to reexamine the relationship between trade liberalization and national security in a manner cognizant of: (1) basic economic truths about how trade benefits American consumers, businesses, and workers; and (2) the fact that trade policy cannot be separated out from foreign policy considerations. That, I concede, is an extraordinarily difficult balancing act, but it should not be beyond us.

HOW AMERICA
WINS THROUGH TRADE

Any resetting of trade policy requires recognition of the very real benefits that free trade can and does confer upon the United States. America's long-term economic prosperity and international competitiveness is, I submit, significantly dependent upon openness to international trade. One key to grasping why this is the case is the concept of comparative advantage. This was briefly discussed in Chapter Two's critique of protectionism but now requires elaboration.

Given embryonic expression in Smith's *Wealth of Nations* before being further developed by the British classical economist David Ricardo in his *Principles of Political Economy and Taxation* (1817), comparative advantage is the capacity of a country to produce a particular good or service at a lower opportunity cost to itself than another nation. This means that a nation gains by: (1) exporting what it has a comparative advantage in producing; and (2) importing those things which other countries have a comparative advantage in producing. Trade conducted on this basis makes each country better off because, Pierre Lemieux notes, "each country produces what it can produce at lower cost and imports what others produce at lower cost."[22] This holds even if a country possesses an absolute advantage in every single sector of its economy over another nation. Israel might be able to produce more manufacturing goods and technology than Australia. It's still, however, the case that Israel can obtain more manufactured goods from Australia by specializing in technology and trading some of that output for imported manufactured goods.

America therefore benefits by specializing in the production of goods and services in which it has a comparative advantage. America's comparative advantage in high-tech, for instance, enables it to produce and sell high-tech faster and at more competitive prices than anyone else to Americans and millions of others around the world. That is good for American companies and workers in such sectors. People and industries in other countries do the same in other areas like clothing. They benefit from our technology; we benefit from their clothing.

Capitalizing on comparative advantage can also involve companies in different nations producing particular parts of a given product, other businesses in other countries assembling the parts, and the marketing and distribution of that product being undertaken by yet other companies in a third set of nations. Many parts for planes made by American companies, for instance, are built and assembled in a series of countries and then integrated together in the United States.[23] The overall effect is to reduce costs and increase efficiencies across the board for American businesses, thereby reducing prices for American consumers.

This does not mean that America's comparative advantages vis-à-vis other nations are somehow fixed. Economists have always recognized that comparative advantage isn't static.[24] It can be affected by institutional factors like corrosion of the rule of law in a given country, or economic developments fueled by entrepreneurial discoveries or improvements in a nation's competitiveness. It doesn't, however, follow that government officials can somehow predetermine America's comparative advantage in international markets. The very fact that a country's comparative advantages are developing and changing vis-à-vis that of other nations makes this extremely difficult.

Trade openness helps American businesses to maximize the benefits of pursuing comparative advantage insofar as it provides them with greater access to foreign markets in which to trade and sell their products: the bigger the potential market, the greater the capacity for sales and profits. This is a major reason why so many American businesses were anxious for China—a market of 1.4 billion people—to enter the WTO in 2001. At the same time, trade openness brings more and more competitive pressures to bear upon the American economy, and thereby amplifies the benefits which go along with enhanced competition for American consumers and businesses. As for American workers, trade openness has a positive effect on labor productivity. That matters because in a developed nation like America, a higher degree of average labor productivity generally translates into higher average wages.[25]

Critics maintain that, in conditions of free trade, American workers cannot compete with Chinese workers without enduring substantive wage reductions. But this argument misses two points. First, under free trade, more and more workers will gravitate over time to different and more productive and often less physically intensive economic sectors along with the higher wages associated with that. Second, the value of the *real* wages of American workers will increase insofar as they are able to buy more things which have become less and less expensive, thanks to free trade.[26]

Lastly, there is a crucial and broad benefit of free trade to the United States: it increases GDP growth; that is, the growth of total income over time. It has been estimated, for instance, that between 1950 and 1998 "countries which liberalized their trade regimes experienced annual average growth rates that were about 1.5 percentage points higher than before liberalization."[27] Or, as an IMF/WTO/World Bank study of the relationship between trade and growth stated, "In advanced economies . . . the rising living standards that came with greater trade openness lent widespread support to the view of trade as a key engine of economic growth."[28] The extent to which this occurs is, we should note, influenced by factors like the quality of institutions in a given country. Nonetheless tariff reductions do appear to contribute to higher growth, which translates into expanding wealth, jobs, and consumption.

This is good news for Americans and magnified by the fact that trade across borders significantly contributes to increases in per capita income: i.e., average income earned per person in a given area in a specified year. The IMF/WTO/World Bank report cited above observed how "Cross-country evidence suggests that the effect of trade on income has remained consistently positive over time, although it has somewhat diminished since the global financial crisis." It then estimated that "a one percentage-point increase in trade openness raises real per capita income by 2 to 6 percent."[29] The same trade openness also results in lower consumer prices, whether through a lowering of tariffs imposed on imported goods and related pro-competition effects, or, more indirectly, through the associated productivity gains by domestic and foreign firms.[30] Significantly, the pay-off is greater for *less-wealthy* American consumers. Not only do they benefit from lower prices; those on lower incomes tend to spend proportionately more on internationally traded goods like manufactured and agricultural goods, while wealthier Americans spend more on goods like health and education that are less traded across borders.[31]

WHAT ABOUT ADJUSTMENTS?

The tangible economic benefits for America which flow from trade openness have positive spillover effects in other areas. If America did not enjoy steady economic growth over time, for example, its capacity to fund (as Hume and Smith understood) a strong military would degrade alongside its ability to project power abroad. It's also the case that the more the American economy grows, the greater its ability to attract foreign capital and reduce the size of its public debt as a proportion of GDP. Certainly, trade openness isn't responsible for all or even most of America's growth, but it does make a substantive contribution. We are sometimes inclined to take economic growth for granted, but it is not the norm in human history. Even a one percent difference in economic growth (up or down) can have substantive implications (positive or negative) for the American economy, which itself is an indispensable (though insufficient) basis for America's status as a world power.

But as observed in Chapter Two, many Americans question whether such benefits have, in the greater scheme of things, been worth it. One effect of trade liberalization is that, like entrepreneurship and competition, it introduces dynamism into society.

Not everyone copes as well as others. Once-protected industries can find themselves in deep trouble as tariffs are lowered. Many American businesses thrive as they embrace the opportunities created by the opening-up of export markets across the world, and all Americans benefit from lower prices. But some companies close because they can't compete or adjust. In such cases, some people lose their jobs. Not all of them find new employment easily, often because of their age or lower demand for their skillset.

This, however, needs to be put into perspective. Despite the disruption caused by increased competition and imports from China in the 2000s and the negative impact this had on some areas with significant numbers of less-educated workers, Scott Lincicome illustrates that the majority of U.S. regions ultimately found themselves better off as far as jobs and economic output was concerned. [32] A similarly positive picture can be found in Alan Berube and Cecile Murray's 2018 analysis of how older industrial towns in regions like America's Northeast and Midwest have fared since the 1970s. Of the 185 U.S. counties they identified as having a disproportionate share of manufacturing jobs in 1970, Berube and Murray illustrated that approximately 115 had managed to switch successfully away from manufacturing by 2016. Of the other seventy, forty had exhibited "strong" or "emerging" economic performance between 2000 and 2016. [33]

The fact that there are far fewer permanent rust-belt towns than supposed is a helpful corrective to popular narratives, but it is not to trivialize the adjustment costs. There was considerable upheaval in those four decades between the 1970s and 2010s. Moreover, while the number of such people and places negatively affected in a lasting and deep way is fewer than often supposed, neither can it be treated as collateral damage. Yet it would also be irresponsible to sacrifice most of the benefits of open trade in order to protect particular jobs in one industry at the expense of more than 330 million American consumers by deploying measures like industrial policy, which have poor track records in realizing their stated goals and perpetuate deep economic and political dysfunctionalities.

One way in which America and other countries have sought to smooth the process of change is through baking trade adjustment programs into trade treaties. These endeavors, however, have had mixed and sometimes counterproductive results. As one team of economists reported:

> Trade Adjustment Programs . . . aim to provide additional and temporary support to workers displaced by trade, including for retraining. These programs can play an important political role, enabling trade agreements to be ratified when they would not otherwise, but the experience with them has been largely disappointing. It is not always evident who is displaced by trade or by domestic competition or automation. The US program, for example, has been found to have only limited uptake . . . [34]

These programs may thus help secure trade deals, but they are hard to target. How do you determine which individuals have been let go because of trade liberalization, and distinguish them from those who lost jobs because of the introduction of new technology? Indeed, there is much evidence to suggest the dislocation generated by trade represents only a small part of job churning. [35] Adjustment programs can also have unintended negative consequences. In some cases, they slow down the flow of the benefits of trade openness. There are also many instances of temporary adjustment measures morphing into yet more permanent government programs. [36]

A better way of addressing these problems is to increase ease of mobility for labor and capital among firms in the same economic sector, across such sectors, and between regions and localities. Americans are more inclined to move for work than, say, Western Europeans. At different points of American history, this has taken on mass proportions, such as when millions of African-Americans moved from the segregationist South to Northern states, or when Americans migrated across the continent from Eastern states to the West throughout the nineteenth century. In both instances, the movement primarily consisted of people at the lower end of the income scale who stood to gain by moving to areas where there was more widespread economic opportunity. [37]

Moving, however, is not made easy when it incurs high transaction costs. Harvard economists Edward Glaeser and David Cutler point out that between 2007 and 2020, geographic mobility in American decreased by one-third, with fewer than 4 percent of Americans changing counties annually. The primary reason for this, they maintain, is that insiders in some of the country's most prosperous regions and cities actively use regulations and laws to make it difficult for outsiders from other parts of America to enter these communities. The more, for instance, the housing market is regulated via zoning rules or significant restrictions on further development, the higher the price of housing and the lower the likelihood of people with less means being able to find somewhere to live. [38]

Increasing mobility thus means decreasing transaction costs. This requires making it simpler and less expensive for people to access capital, accept new jobs, or acquire new skills through education. There are also very specific measures which can be taken, whether it is eliminating unnecessary licensing requirements that make it harder for people from one state to pursue jobs in other regions, or, as Glaeser and Cutler suggest, states legislating to allow local government only to impose regulations and rules that have been subject to rigorous cost-benefit analysis. [39]

None of this is to pretend that mobility is a cost-free exercise, psychologically or economically. Even necessary or good change can be hard. That is part of the human condition. But if we want the U.S. economy to grow and flourish, mobility is essential, and we increase mobility by removing barriers to movement. Here we should recall that the entire history of economic development is one of mobility and transition: from rural areas to cities, from agriculture to factories, and from factories to service-provision. If the American economy is to continue growing and competing with the rest of the world, people and material resources must continuously shift to higher value-added sectors, and, within specific sectors, to the more efficient firms. There are trade-offs associated with this, but they are generally worth it—not least because of the many drawbacks associated with the protectionist alternative. It is frankly imprudent to encourage Americans to stay in industries losing comparative advantage or to remain in occupations that

competitive pressures from abroad and, even more so, technological change are making redundant.

DEFENSE TRUMPS OPULENCE

Questions surrounding the adjustment costs associated with free
trade featured prominently in American public debate in the 1990s
and 2000s. Beginning in the 2010s, however, much of the debate
around free trade in America gravitated towards national security
questions.

This is not the first time that the trade dimension of national
security issues has figured in American policy disputes. For
decades, there were lively arguments inside successive presidential
administrations about American trade with the Soviet Union.[40]
In the 1950s, outspoken free trade supporters like Wilhelm Röpke
cautioned against Western companies trading with the U.S.S.R.,
its satellites, or its allies. Communist states, Röpke argued, were
devoted to the destruction of capitalist economies. They regarded
trade with Western nations as a way to extract—and steal—
resources and technology from the West. The more Western businesses traded with their Soviet counterparts, he argued, the more
trade relations would be corrupted by regimes that saw no inherent
value in playing by the rules of the game if those rules impeded the
spread of Communist revolution.[41]

In the case of America and the Soviets, the volume of trade was
never extensive or large. The United States imported very little
from the Soviet Union, while American exports to the U.S.S.R.

were focused on particular albeit vital agricultural products like grain.[42] Soviet trade policy was itself characterized by a mixture of autarchic aspirations and efforts to limit trade as far as possible to Warsaw Pact nations.[43]

U.S.–China trade is of an entirely different scale. China ranked as America's largest goods trading partner in 2020, and America's third largest goods export market that same year. In 2020, China was also the United States' largest supplier of imported goods. America's foreign direct investment (FDI) in China was $123.9 billion in 2020. That amounted to a 9.4 percent increase from 2019. Such investment was led by manufacturing, wholesale trade, and finance and insurance.[44]

In one sense, these are big numbers. It's also worth noting the Department of Commerce estimated that U.S. exports to China supported an estimated 758,000 jobs in 2019.[45] To put this in perspective, however, U.S. exports to China accounted for 8.7 percent of overall U.S. exports in 2020.[46] This means that 92.3 percent of U.S. exports went to other countries.

The question of the volume of U.S.–China trade is thus not the most pressing issue for America's national security. Other questions weigh more heavily. The possibility, for instance, that technology transfers from American companies to Chinese businesses will undermine the U.S. military's ability to outpace the technological sophistication of the People's Liberation Army cannot be lightly dismissed.

Free marketers have always acknowledged that national defense is a legitimate reason for state intervention—including in trade. Adam Smith held that "defense . . . is of much more importance than opulence."[47] One of "two cases in which it will generally be advantageous to lay some burden upon foreign for the encouragement of domestic industry," Smith stated, is "when some particular sort of industry is necessary for the defense of the country."[48] These are the grounds on which Smith supported what were called the Navigation Acts.[49]

The Navigation Acts reflected the geopolitical reality that, for long stretches of time in the seventeenth and eighteenth centuries, Britain was at war with one or more of three of Europe's leading powers of the period—The Netherlands, France, and Spain—all of whom had large and powerful navies and the will to use them. This meant that trade routes between Britain, its colonies, and the rest of the world were often subject to interdiction by the Dutch, French or Spanish navies and thus needed to be defended. Such defense necessitated Britain possessing British-owned ships and experienced seamen to sail them in times of war. London sought to achieve this objective via the Navigation Acts.

The Acts effectively gave British shipping companies a type of monopoly over trade between Britain and other countries. They also specified that 75 percent of the crews of British ships should be British or colonial. There was a significant economic cost to this insofar as the Acts diverted wealth to British shipping companies at the expense of consumers in Britain and its wider empire. The Acts also limited the export of certain types of goods deemed strategic or essential—naval stores, copper, pig-iron, etc.—produced in the colonies to the market of the mother country.[50]

It's important to recognize that Smith's endorsement of the Navigation Acts was *not* a result of him holding that the state should intervene in these industries and sectors of British commerce in order to develop them economically. Smith supported the Acts because he believed that it was a question of *military* necessity for an island trading-kingdom that risked being blockaded into submission by rival powers during wartime.[51] But Smith also maintained that it would "very seldom" be "reasonable" to pursue protectionist policies—"to tax the industry of the great body of the people"[52] so as not "to depend upon our neighbors for the supply"[53]—for all the reasons stated in Chapter Two. He also believed that trade restrictions associated with the Navigation Acts would eventually become economically "oppressive and insupportable"[54] for the American colonies as their economic development accelerated. In the long term, Smith thought, these colonies would decide that the restraints imposed on their trade and manufacturers by the Navigation Acts outweighed the benefits of being part of the British Empire. That, possibility, however, lay in the future. Given the geopolitical tensions of the time, Smith believed the Acts were in the interests of Britain's national security.

ABUSING NATIONAL SECURITY

Fast-forwarding to more recent decades, we discover that Milton and Rose D. Friedman broadly followed Smith's line on national security and trade: "it cannot be denied," they wrote, "that on occasion it might justify the maintenance of otherwise uneconomical productive facilities."[55] They warned, however, that there is some distance between "this statement of possibility" and establishing "in a specific case that a tariff or other trade restriction is justified in order to promote national security." In their view, serious analysis was always needed to "compare the cost of achieving the specific security objective in alternative ways and establish at least a prima facie case that a tariff is the least costly way." They also opined that "Such cost comparisons are seldom made in practice."[56]

Numerous American industries and political leaders have appealed to the necessity of nations' preserving vital capacities that they may need in time of national emergency or war as a basis for tariffs. Under Section 232 of the 1962 Trade Expansion Act, the President may restrict imports for national security reasons. Part of the process involves the Commerce Department undertaking an investigation about whether a good is "being imported into the United States in such quantities and under such circumstances as to threaten to impair national security."[57] This power was exercised rarely until Donald Trump was elected president in 2016.

One of President Trump's first Section 232 actions was to impose 25 percent tariffs on steel and 10 percent tariffs on aluminum. This decision came despite advice from the Defense Department that the U.S. military only needed 3 percent of total domestic steel and aluminum production, and that broad-based import restrictions were unnecessary. It was also the case that most steel and aluminum imports into America came from American allies.[58]

The rationale for these steel and aluminum tariffs was outlined in a Department of Commerce report. There was considerable resistance in the Executive Branch to making the report public. This only occurred in July 2021, after much pressure applied by Congress. The first paragraph of the report's executive summary explains the reluctance: "The Secretary in this investigation again determined that 'national security' includes the 'general security and welfare of certain industries, *beyond those necessary to satisfy national defense requirements*'." [59] This interpretation amounts to a license for any administration to invoke national security as the basis for curtailing free trade in areas of the U.S. economy tangentially related to national security: in this case, the car industry.

The Commerce Department report advanced assertion after assertion about how automobile technology contributes to defense, yet provided little evidence to support these claims. Rather, it emphasized how much American car companies had outsourced many of their operations to countries like Mexico and Canada and were importing many parts from abroad. The fact that such outsourcing has occurred was certainly true. Less obvious is how this threatened national security. In the end, the report was reduced to claiming that "the 'displacement of domestic products by excessive imports'—in particular, the displacement of automobiles and certain automobile parts manufactured by American-owned firms" weakened America's domestic economy, which in turn might "impair national security." [60] That amounts to arguing that the American economy is weakened whenever American businesses follow the logic of comparative advantage and decide to focus on what they do comparatively better than their domestic and foreign competitors. But we have already seen that pursuing comparative advantage is the path to economic growth and strength, not the opposite.

A variant of this type of national security argument is to claim that protectionist measures should be used to ensure that certain vital industrial capacities remain in America so that no one can threaten American and international supply chains during a crisis. Neither Smith nor Friedman ruled this out. But it is important to recognize that open and competitive economies are extraordinarily adept at adapting to sudden crises precisely because, like all forms of competitive pressure, free trade encourages such flexibility. When Covid-19 struck in 2020, small and large manufacturers in America were able to overcome shortages of goods that suddenly became seen as essential and meet high demand for products like disinfectants, hand-sanitizer, and masks by retooling their operations quickly.[61] A nation unaccustomed to a significant degree of exposure to the disciplines that flow from foreign competition, I suggest, might have struggled to adapt so quickly.

National security is indeed something that no advocate of free trade should ignore or trivialize. But we ought to acknowledge that appeals to national security can be effective in giving legislators cover for supporting measures which are at best marginally relevant to national security, and in which the real objective is to secure favors for businesses in their district or state at everyone else's expense. A good example of this is the Jones Act.

Passed in 1920, the Jones Act mandates that cargo which is shipped between different parts of the United States be carried on ships which are American-built, owned, and crewed. Much like Britain's Navigation Acts, its purpose was to maintain the American merchant marine as well as spare shipbuilding capacity for war. At the time, national security analyst Mike Watson points out, American-built ships "cost 20% more than foreign ones." In the wake of World War I, that extra expense may have seemed worth it. But as Watson goes on to note:

> A century later, American-made tanker ships are nearly 400% more expensive than foreign-made ones. And yet the Jones Act remains in place. As a result, American civilian shipyards cater almost exclusively to clients held captive by the Jones Act's requirements: Between 2007 and 2017, over 900 ships were built in the United States, but only 80 were exported. Since the act sustains 650,000 American jobs in various congressional districts, repealing it is a political non-starter. [62]

Rather than propping up such arrangements, Americans serious about national security should focus their attention upon the *export* of certain forms of technology. Many contracts between American and foreign companies involve the former selling or giving technology to the latter. Problems emerge when the business to whom a form of technology is transferred is controlled directly or indirectly by a regime hostile to the United States and with a track-record of trying to use such technology to enhance its military capacities.

Most such sales or transfers are usually of technology at least two or three generations behind whatever is state-of-the-art. It is rarely in American companies' self-interest to sell or give away any decisive technological advantage. This is why the Chinese government and companies regularly resort to theft to attempt to secure such information, or why they break China's commitment under

the terms of its entry into the WTO not to precondition investments on technology transfers.[63]

Bans already exist in the United States on the export of particular commercial technologies which might be easily used to develop
conventional arms or weapons of mass destruction, or to otherwise
facilitate terrorist activities.[64] Numerous federal agencies oversee
and enforce these prohibitions.[65] The challenge is that many technologies have multiple uses, including for military purposes. But
this has always been the case. The military potentialities of trains
and planes were quickly understood when these technologies were
in their infancy. This is not grounds to never ban particular types
of technology transfers. It is simply recognition that there are limits to what such embargos can achieve and that it is always more
important to be developing cutting-edge technologies as well as
preventing its theft by hostile governments.

FREE TRADE REALISM
AND CHINA

Questions like technology transfers exemplify how the inevitable
links between trade policy and national security create conundrums
for American political leaders. While foreign policy cannot be
reduced to trade questions, nor do we want opportunities for greater
trade between America and the rest of the world to be undermined
by incumbent American businesses and their political allies appealing to elastic conceptions of national security to protect themselves
from competition. Trade openness consequently helps ensure that

national security doesn't become confused with the prosperity of those companies which happen to be better rent-seekers than others.

It takes particular skills to bolster free trade in ways cognizant of these national security concerns. But one dimension of such economic statesmanship involves recognizing how much Beijing's accelerated embrace of its version of state capitalism is likely to undermine China's economic growth. Between 2002 and 2019, publicly listed Chinese state-owned enterprises persistently showed far less productivity than publicly listed firms in which Beijing has no ownership stake. [66] It follows that if China continues to shift its economy in the direction of state enterprises, the decline in productivity will accelerate. Likewise the increasing uncertainty in the legal environment generated by growing state authoritarianism will make China an increasingly risky place for Americans and others to invest and do business. [67]

China's state-driven growth model is also likely to exacerbate all the problems associated with state mercantilism. Some of the more prominent include market-access restrictions which discourage foreign investment; severe misallocations of capital by state-controlled banks lending to inefficient state enterprises as they try to outguess markets; industrial policies that breed cronyism and corruption; and an overall diminishment of the disciplines which emanate from domestic and international competition. These are likely to exacerbate the disastrous consequences of the one-child policy adopted by China between 1980 and 2015. China is, as Ryan Hass writes, "at risk of growing old before it grows rich." [68] Its working-age population is on track to shrink by 170 million people over the next thirty years. As the number of retirees grows, China will need to spend increasing amounts on social security and healthcare benefits. This will weaken consumption demand and crowd out expenditures on research and development, infrastructure, and defense.

A prominent instance of Beijing's state capitalism hurting China concerns its much-touted Belt and Road Initiative (BRI). Initiated in 2013, BRI involves the Chinese regime making foreign investment decisions driven primarily by its perceived geopolitical needs, such as control of strategic corridors in Central and Southeast Asia. The means for achieving this are infrastructure development in areas like new railroads, energy, ports, and shipping lanes funded by investments and loans made by enterprises partially or fully owned by the Chinese state.

The actual amounts invested by China in BRI are murky, with estimates ranging from $1 trillion to $8 trillion between 2013 and 2018. That raises questions about how much of BRI is real and how much is state propaganda.[69] There is nevertheless significant evidence that BRI has backfired economically and politically insofar as it has (1) produced little return on the significant investments made by state-directed Chinese companies involved in this project; (2) resulted in significant political backlashes against China's presence in countries like Burma, Pakistan, Malaysia, Bangladesh, Sri Lanka, and the Maldives; and (3) accelerated the corruption in Chinese political and business circles in a nation already awash in corruption.[70]

This array of problems with Chinese state capitalism is likely to facilitate some decoupling of much of the American and Chinese economies without the U.S. Government lifting a finger. By 2021, this process was underway. Some major American businesses pulled out of China altogether. Others hedged their bets by withdrawing from particular sectors of the Chinese economy while increasing involvement in those sectors where state capitalism seemed less advanced.[71] Yet other American businesses began transferring their operations from mainland China to Taiwan.[72]

How and to what extent such decoupling occurs, it could result in significant price increases for many consumer goods for Americans. Let's not forget that one reason for many supply chains being in China in the first place is that it was less expensive to make, source, or assemble certain goods in China than in America. At a minimum, obstacles should not be put in the way of American companies who disengage from China from shifting their operations and investments to other, friendlier countries where production or sourcing costs for particular goods are lower than in America. Here it's worth recalling that open and competitive global markets make it easier and more efficient for American companies to switch supply chains when it becomes apparent that a once-productive trading relationship has become politically toxic and economically inefficient. Protectionism makes such adaptation slower, more difficult, and more costly.

REFINING THE CASE
FOR FREE TRADE

Plainly, the challenges associated with America's trade relationship with China require some recasting of how the case for free trade is presented to Americans. Such a reframing, I believe, needs to be developed around four axioms.

First, advancing the argument for free trade requires those in favor of liberalization to be more measured when stating what free trade can and cannot do for America. Advocates for free trade should, for example, avoid claiming that trade will somehow inevitably and eventually make countries like China with a four-thousand-year political culture of authoritarianism "just like us." The determinism underlying such assertions should be repudiated. Acknowledging these realities while simultaneously underscoring the positive aspects of free trade and the negative aspects of protectionism would, I'd argue, make the case for free trade more plausible to many Americans skeptical of its benefits.

Second, those who support free trade in America should focus their fellow Americans' minds on how trade openness serves *America* economically and politically as a nation. This is not a question of indulging jingoists. It's a matter of seizing the mantle of patriotism—something that's quite different from xenophobia and which can't be condescendingly dismissed as mere tribalism—from protectionists. It would also help to create a context in which more Americans are willing to absorb thoroughgoing economic and political critiques of protectionism: especially the fact that protectionist policies are all about elevating influential sectional interests over the economic well-being of all Americans.

Third, we must distinguish those aspects of trade with other nations which constitute legitimate economic activities from those that don't. Trade competition is one thing. Theft is quite another. Chinese businesses and nationals, for example, have been engaged in aggressive theft of intellectual property in the service and knowledge sectors of the U.S. economy for some time.[73] In March 2020, the Chairman of Huawei Technologies Inc.—a company credibly deemed to be effectively owned by the Chinese regime—[74]warned America to "expect countermeasures from the Chinese government if it further restricts the technology giant's access to suppliers."[75] What he did not mention is that those restrictions were imposed as a result of Huawei being indicted for racketeering and intellectual property theft in January 2019 and February 2020.[76]

The Huawei case points to a wider issue: that, as one strategic analysis illustrated, Chinese technology companies "not wholly owned by the state" but with "deep ties to the Chinese state security apparatus" operate in ways that blur "commercial imperatives" with "the strategic imperatives of the party-state."[77] Huawei and other Chinese technology companies have been accused of aiding the regime's security forces in carrying out repression inside China.[78] If true, it's reasonable to assume that these companies' subservience to the regime continues beyond China's borders. This suggests that the more evidence that emerges of a Chinese company (or any foreign business) engaging in activities like intellectual property theft or outright espionage, the more such companies should be formally blacklisted. Such blacklisting—which (1) prohibited American companies from transferring and selling materials and technology to, or investing in, named Chinese companies (including Huawei and other major telecommunications businesses) and their affiliates; and (2) required U.S. companies to divest themselves of investments in these companies—was implemented by the Trump administration and extended by the Biden administration.[79]

Another instance of rethinking the U.S.–China trade relationships along these lines was the Holding Foreign Companies Accountable

Act. Passed by unanimous voice vote in the House and unanimously in the Senate and signed into law by President Trump in December 2020, this legislation requires "certain issuers of securities to establish that they are not owned or controlled by a foreign government" and allows the U.S. Public Accounting Oversight Board to review the financial audits of these companies which have been carried out in foreign jurisdictions. The Act also mandates disclosure of "any board members who are officials of the Chinese Communist Party, and whether the articles of incorporation of the issuer contain any charter of the Chinese Communist Party." Failure to comply with these provisions within three consecutive years will result in such a company being banned from trading and delisted from exchanges.[80] That sent a message to Chinese companies that if they want to do business in America, they have to identify who are their real owners and subject their financials to American scrutiny. Otherwise, they risk losing access to U.S. financial markets, which remain a key source of capital for companies around the world—including those in China.[81]

Fourth, free traders must reiterate that American companies trading with foreign entities, or which have operations based abroad, need to avoid directly bolstering the military and security forces of regimes deemed hostile to the United States. There is considerable evidence that some major American corporations have become entangled in relationships with Chinese government entities and military-linked business partners working in explicitly military and state security-relevant domains.[82]

One reason for American businesses to extradite themselves from these situations is that they risk violating U.S. laws.[83] More fundamentally, no American company should be knowingly and directly contributing to the capacity of regimes demonstrably hostile to the United States to carry out espionage, military, or terrorist actions against America.

Those words "knowingly" and "directly" are important. Not everything is foreseeable. It is not easy to predict, for instance, the use to which your trading partners might put particular technologies. As for capital, it is by nature fungible. This can make tracing the precise way in which an American investment in a Chinese enterprise is being put to work very difficult. Once, however, an American business becomes aware that its commercial relationship with a foreign entity is directly aiding an America-hostile regime to develop military and surveillance capabilities that could be used against the United States, it needs to withdraw from that relationship. This is not simply a question of avoiding possible legal prosecution back home. There is something intrinsically wrong with American businesses, whose emergence and prosperity owe so much to hard-won liberties such as the freedom to trade abroad, helping hostile regimes to acquire the ability to compromise or undermine those very same liberties.

POLITICAL ECONOMY
AS IF IT MATTERED

Much of the burden for rearticulating the arguments for free trade falls on intellectuals, economists, journalists, and business leaders who believe that trade liberalization is good for America. At some point, however, any recasting needs to be embraced by political leaders. Political economy is ultimately a science of the legislator, and that applies to free trade as much as any other dimension of economic policy. American political leaders can, however, learn from those examples of statesmanship in which a commitment to trade liberalization was pursued with an attention to the political realities in which all trade liberalizations occur. Here Adam Smith's friend and admirer, but also a legislator and major thinker in his own right, Edmund Burke, provides us with considerable insight.

The political and economic life of the eighteenth-century European world is notable for two phenomena that increasingly preoccupied many European thinkers and rulers. One was the emergence of Britain as a global power with an empire. The second was the spread of sustained criticisms of the mercantilist arrangements which dominated Western economic life and the growing conviction that free trade was preferable. By "free trade," it's important to recognize that this was not understood as "no tariffs." It was accepted that the state could tax trade to raise revenue. Rather, free trade meant that governments did not make merchants from one country pay more duties than others simply because they were Prussian rather than French. [84]

This growing challenge to mercantilism could not be limited to economic thought and policy. It had implications for how European leaders viewed the world politically. If, for example, wealth lay not in possessing more gold and silver than others, part of the argument for conquering wide swaths of the earth to acquire more quantities of such metals no longer made sense.

But as strong as such intellectual arguments were, the business of putting them into effect meant navigating numerous geopolitical realities. There were three factors in play that no late-eighteenth-century British statesman anxious to advance trade openness could ignore. The first was that Britain *did* possess an empire. That empire had been acquired at a considerable spillage of blood and treasure over 170 years. This made it unlikely that any parliament or government would even consider suddenly abandoning colonies and territories located in every continent, however compelling the economic case for doing so might be.

Second, despite growing inclinations to see Britain's empire as one interconnected whole, the economic and political arrangements prevailing within that empire differed significantly from place to place. The economic conditions and political systems of the free-spirited American colonies—which considered themselves linked to Britain by a common language, history, religious bonds, and allegiance to the person of the monarch (and not by the binding authority of the King-in-Parliament)—were vastly dissimilar to those prevailing in the Indian possessions controlled through that most mercantilist of outfits, the British East India Company.

Further muddying the waters was the fact that other European powers—most notably, Bourbon and then Revolutionary France—had foreign policy ambitions that, if realized, would result in diminishment of Britain's global influence and ability to maintain a balance of power in Europe.

These three considerations only grew in importance following Britain's comprehensive victory over France and Spain in the Seven Years' War and the ensuing addition of vast possessions across the globe to Britain's already extensive empire. They also created significant political and economic dilemmas. What, for instance, should London do if (as frequently occurred) the East India Company ran into financial difficulties? Should London, pressured by share-holding merchants, parliamentarians, and government officials, regulate trade in ways that sought to corral American colonists into buying tea from the Company, despite the disadvantages this would visit upon independent American tea-importers, as well as doubts as to whether Parliament even possessed the authority to legislate for American colonies in such a manner? Or should London undertake a sustained reform of the East India Company? This would involve confronting numerous interest groups, many of whom numbered among the government's own parliamentary supporters, and would require expenditure of vast amounts of political capital.

This was the context conditioning Edmund Burke's efforts to promote greater commercial freedom within Britain's Empire and between Britain and other nations. Like any politician, Burke's involvement in these matters was shaped by legislative maneuvering and deal-making that were, and are, part-and-parcel of political life. But the picture that emerges is one of an economic liberalizer who was nonetheless attuned to political realities. Burke's most well-known and specific treatment of economic questions, his *Thoughts and Details on Scarcity* memorandum of 1795, is notable for its strong advocacy of economic liberty and free exchange. The context of this document, however, is domestic and focused on a specific sector: farmers and laborers in Britain's domestic grain market. [85]

As the historian of ideas Gregory A. Collins observes, "because of his defense of the British Empire and the political constraints imposed on him as an elected legislator," Burke "was not what we today would call a champion of 'free trade' absolutism." [86] Yet Burke was far from neutral about such matters. "Burke leaned strongly," Collins states, "though not wholly, in favor of liberal commercial intercourse between nations—particularly those within the British Empire—throughout his adult life, even prior to his entry into Parliament in 1766." [87] Nonetheless, there were occasions when Burke subordinated trade considerations to the Empire's other needs, particularly its security and integrity. The Navigation Acts are one example of a security consideration. By "integrity" Burke had in mind what he regarded as the rightfulness of Parliament's authority over the Empire's disparate parts. [88]

Burke thus found himself having to advance an agenda of trade liberalization within the complex politics of the British Empire. Burke subsequently used policy debates to educate his fellow parliamentarians, government officials, and the reading public in the arguments favoring greater commercial liberty at a time when such arguments were still in their early development. He also actively pressed for legislative changes that would move the needle towards economic liberalization at home and abroad, but in a manner cognizant of the domestic and international realities then facing Britain.

Burke's brand of economic statecraft is exemplified by his involvement in the first Rockingham ministry's drafting and promoting of the Free Ports Act, passed by Parliament on June 6, 1766. Put briefly, this legislation created six free trade ports in the British Caribbean: four in Jamaica and two on the island of Dominica. These functioned as places in which there were much lower duties and far fewer trade restrictions for merchants importing and exporting many commodities to and from these ports to British North America and Western Indian markets—and not just British Caribbean colonies but French and Spanish colonies as well. It thus marked a break with prevailing mercantilist doctrines about trade and represented a shift away from regulatory policies which had sought to protect existing West Indian monopolies of British merchants by restricting foreign imports and foreign merchants' navigation rights. In effect, the Free Ports Act embodied the idea that, as one historian of the period writes, the British Empire's economic prosperity "was best promoted by *not* regulating all aspects of colonial exchange."[89] Note that this occurred ten years before Smith's comprehensive attack on the mercantile system.

One feature of the Act's drafting was that it involved extensive consultation with merchants. That included those North American merchants who wanted to trade more freely throughout the Caribbean,[90] but also West Indian traders who recognized that establishing free ports in the Caribbean would undermine their dominance of particular markets.[91] At the time, such discussions were not common practice; the government was even criticized for soliciting people's views on the matter.[92] Burke nonetheless made a point of asking merchants for their thoughts, and convened meetings to gauge their opinions on the Act's likely effects.[93]

The Free Ports Act embodied compromises that maintained some mercantilist regulations in place, partly because the legislation's early drafting was influenced by merchants likely to be negatively impacted by it.[94] In later life, Burke told a correspondent that he would have liked to have pushed for even greater enlargements of commercial liberty "if more had been permitted by events."[95]

By "events," Burke appears to have meant the government's focus upon repealing the Stamp Act that had created such problems in the American colonies. Nonetheless the Free Ports Act did amount to "conscious movement in the direction of freer commercial intercourse." [96] Burke even claimed that as a consequence of the Act, "The trade of America was set free from injudicious and ruinous Impositions—Its Revenue was improved, and settled on a rational Foundation—Its Commerce extended with foreign Countries; while all the Advantages were extended to Great Britain." [97]

For all Burke's retrospective frustration, his contributions to the passing of the Free Ports Act reveal much about how he weaved together his pursuit of political and economic objectives. Despite its limitations, the Act did advance freer commerce throughout the British Empire and between Britain and other nations, thereby serving the long-term interests of consumers in Britain and its colonies. Just as importantly, the process of drafting and debating the Act had generated wider and critical reflection in political and commercial circles upon the mercantilist practices of the period. One benefit of talking to merchants, in Burke's view, was that it helped garner wider support for the Act in the West Indian and North American colonies, even if not all merchants were persuaded to back the legislation. [98] This was part of the process of educating people from different parts of the Empire in what Burke believed to be the case for economic liberty over and against the zero-sum mercantilist outlook.

Therein lies the essence of Burke's approach to the economic issues that loomed large in his time and became even more important in the nineteenth century. It combined awareness of political facts, commitment to what might be called the regime of the Empire, belief that mercantilism was flawed, confidence in free trade's generally positive effects, and the willingness to invest time and energy in shifting political and commercial opinion in a direction that he thought would serve the interests of the Empire as a whole.

Burke's prudence should not be understood as pragmatism, let alone *realpolitik* or a penchant for deal-making. It was more a reflection of what Collins calls Burke's "political temperament." In the realm of economic policy, this was actuated "by a purposeful attempt to move towards realization of a principle and yet tolerate, however regrettably, the policy results that followed given the constraints of political circumstances."[99] Clearly Burke was neither a mere ideologue spouting simplistic formulations nor someone content to manage a mercantilist status quo and personally profit—as many parliamentarians did.

NATIONS AND MARKETS

The period in which Burke sought to widen access to markets throughout the British Empire was in some respects similar to the situation in America today. People in Britain were fiercely divided over questions of political economy. Intellectual defenders of the mercantilist status quo lined up against those convinced of the case for liberalization. Then, as now, there was no shortage of businesses doing their best to diminish competition by securing protection and favors from governments. There was also no organized constituency for economic liberalization beyond groups of scholars like Smith and legislators like Burke who understood how markets made businesses earn their profits by serving consumers. Nonetheless, the intellectual robustness of these ideas gave such individuals their own form of power.

As for geopolitical rivalries, these were just as intense in Burke and Smith's time as in ours. Britain was locked into costly cycles of war and peace with France. Following Britain's defeat at the hands of the American Revolutionaries and their French, Spanish, and Dutch allies, many believed that Britain's time of global political preeminence was over. It was by no means obvious that, within a few decades of the deaths of Smith and Burke, Britain would emerge as the world's leading economy, awash with new entrepreneurs and businesses, unafraid of competition, fully committed to trade liberalization, and only rivaled economically by the United States.

This transformation didn't emerge spontaneously. It required breaking opposition from powerful mercantilist lobbies and their political allies, persuading government ministers and parliamentarians that change was necessary, and making appeals to vast numbers of ordinary people that the growth of economic freedom was in their own interests *and* tied to Britain's identity and well-being as a country. This was not achieved simply through the articulation of economic arguments, as important as these were. It involved those who favored markets linking their case to broader concerns. These included Britain's security as a nation-state at a time of quintessential European great power rivalry which had already assumed global proportions, as well as its self-understanding as a country that took certain values seriously. The same challenge confronts those who want America to retain its position as the world's leading economy through a renewed commitment to markets, but also through its distinct place in the world as a particular type of nation. Fortunately, as this book's final chapter shows, the pursuit of these two commitments can be mutually complementary if enough Americans have the imagination and will to make it so.

CHAPTER 8

A COMMERCIAL REPUBLIC

*Young man, there is America—which at this day serves
for little more than to amuse you with stories of savage
men and uncouth manners; yet shall, before you taste of
death, show itself equal to the whole of that commerce
which now attracts the envy of the world.*

—EDMUND BURKE

America featured a great deal in the writings of Edmund Burke and
Adam Smith. The American Revolution was one of the defining
points of their public lives. Not only did they understand the extent
to which debates about political economy underlay the tensions
between Britain and its American colonies. Both men were aware
of the colonies' potential as a power that the world would have to
reckon with, especially if they became a single sovereign nation
defined in important ways by its attachment to commerce and trade.

In the 1790s, key American Founders sought to create a republic in which the habits and institutions of commercial freedom,

industry, enterprise, competition, and trade would be integral to its identity. These habits and institutions were also to mark America as a political entity different from most other European nations and from the Spanish territories to its west and south. Yet it was not inevitable that things would turn out this way. As noted in Chapter One, some Founders had dreams of America as an agrarian idyll that would gradually grow across the limitless West and thus develop "horizontally" through physical space rather than "vertically" via means such as the division of labor, intensive capital markets, and organizations such as the corporation.

Thomas Jefferson's initial preference for a confederation of mostly agrarian polities populated by rural yeomen owed much to ideas going back to the Roman Republic concerning the supposedly corrupting effects of urban commerce, especially when money lending was involved. Classical books like Cato the Elder's *De agri cultura* portrayed commerce and banking as risky, even somewhat dishonorable practices while waxing lyrical about the virtues associated with agriculture. Almost 1800 years later in another hemisphere, such ideas resonated among many Americans. "Those who labor the earth are the chosen people of God," wrote Jefferson, "[and] generally speaking, the proportion which the aggregate of the other classes of citizens bears in any state to that of its husbandmen, is the proportion of its unsound to healthy parts, and is a good enough barometer to measure its degree of corruption." [1]

Against such outlooks were Founders like Alexander Hamilton. Just as learned in Greco-Roman sources as your average Virginian gentleman-planter, Hamilton had no patience with rural romanticism. For him, America's future success depended upon economic modernization, a sophisticated financial sector, and the pursuit of internal and foreign trade. It was better, Hamilton thought, to work with people's economic self-interest rather than viewing self-interest as the road to corruption. The aspiration underlying this outlook was summed up by George Washington, who in a 1788 letter envisaged America as "a great, a respectable & a commercial nation."[2]

PATRIOT GAMES

It is fair to say that Hamilton's commercial vision initially won out in much of the country. Nevertheless, debates about the U.S. economy continued in subsequent decades. Many early-nineteenth-century Americans wanted government involvement far beyond anything envisioned by Hamilton, let alone Jefferson. To this end, influential politicians like Henry Clay laid out an agenda for re-orientating the U.S. economy via state intervention in order to realize what he called "a genuine AMERICAN SYSTEM."

In his famous March 1824 speech to Congress, Clay presented proposals that involved far more than simply public works to bind the country together through common infrastructure. Instead, Clay proposed (1) a very high tariff whose purpose was explicitly protectionist rather than revenue-raising; (2) the preservation and extension of the Bank of the United States so that it could police banks that took on excessive risk; (3) mandating high prices for land-sales to generate more federal revenue; and (4) subsidizing the development of canals, roads, public works and other internal

improvements that Clay deemed necessary for what he called "balancing" the development of America's agricultural, commercial,
financial, and industrial sectors. Though Clay never argued for
autarky, he demanded that America prioritize its home market over
foreign trade to create an economy that was highly self-sufficient.
Clay maintained that this would have to happen through the federal government escalating its role in the economy.[3]

What concerns us is less the specific policies advocated by Clay
and other proponents of the American System than the political
garb in which they clothed their economic ideas. One impetus for
their program was the conviction, expressed directly by Clay in
an 1832 speech entitled "Defending the American System," that
free trade meant a type of colonial subservience to Britain.[4] This
address was littered with hostile remarks about other countries,
and claimed that the ability of Americans to compete with the rest
of the world depended upon them receiving significant protection
from foreign imports.

Clay's rhetoric, however, was not in the main negative. Generally he sought to present his American System in positive terms.
In his 1824 address, Clay even associated his preferred political
economy with the country's very identity. Nowhere is this more
apparent than in his speech's final sentences:

> [T]he cause is the cause of the country, and it must and
> will prevail. It is founded in the interests and affections
> of the people. It is as native as the granite deeply imbo-
> somed in our mountains. And, in conclusion, I would
> pray God, in his infinite mercy, to avert from our country

the evils which are impending over it, and, by enlighten-
ing our councils, to conduct us into that path which leads
to riches, to greatness, to glory. [5]

Clay's invocation of patriotic rhetoric of greatness and glory did
not prevent other Americans from criticizing his economic nation-
alism. Congressman Daniel Webster of Massachusetts immediately
stood up after Clay's 1824 speech to argue that economic growth
had to be driven by free enterprise, unlimited by the restrictions on
trade desired by Clay. Protectionism, Webster bluntly reminded
his audience, involved trying to protect and promote one part of
the American economy at the expense of other sectors, especially
those focused on foreign markets. Webster feared that if Clay's
economic reasoning was followed through to its logical conclusion
that it would result in the prohibition of imports altogether. [6] South
Carolina's Robert Hayne described Clay's "scheme of promoting
certain employments at the expense of others as unequal, oppressive, and unjust, viewing prohibition as the means and the destruction of all foreign commerce the end of this policy." [7]

Clay's full scheme was never realized. A watered-down compromise was eventually signed into law, [8] and the implementation
process was anything but noble. The internal improvements to be
constructed were largely determined by Congressmen and Senators pursuing pet projects justified, as economic historian John
L. Larson illustrates, "on increasingly dubious claims of national
significance." [9] Likewise, the setting of tariffs by Congress accentuated regional tensions between North, Midwest, and South as
politicians struggled to devise a tariff schedule that could reconcile

basic conflicts of interest between industrial good manufacturers, raw material producers, and those in the agricultural sector. [10]

But Clay's heady mixture of patriotic sentiment and protectionist arguments left a mark on the American polity. Almost two hundred years later, in his 2021 Henry Clay Lecture in Political Economy, Senator Marco Rubio called for "A new American Century ... in many ways not unlike the vision laid out by Henry Clay almost two hundred years ago." [11] Rubio's rhetoric and proposals played off the same type of equivalence made by Clay between love of country and support for specific economic policies—policies that, this book has argued, are likely to inflict considerable damage upon the U.S. economy and corrode the integrity of its political institutions.

The ongoing resonance of claims made by figures like Clay and Rubio among many Americans today has placed those who believe in the merits of market economies in the position of having to defend themselves from accusations of not caring about America, or of prioritizing other nations' well-being over their own country. These charges have not only come from some on the American right. Prominent progressives have also embraced the language of patriotism to legitimize their own varieties of state capitalism. The economic program outlined by Senator Elizabeth Warren of Massachusetts in her 2020 presidential campaign is a prime example. The opening of Warren's speech introducing her employment policy went like this:

> I come from a patriotic family. All three of my brothers joined the military. And I'm deeply grateful for the

opportunities America has given me. But the giant "American" corporations who control our economy don't seem to feel the same way. They certainly don't act like it.

Sure, these companies wave the flag—but they have no loyalty or allegiance to America. Levi's is an iconic American brand, but the company operates only 2% of its factories here. Dixon Ticonderoga—maker of the famous No. 2 pencil—has "moved almost all of its pencil production to Mexico and China." And General Electric recently shut down an industrial engine factory in Wisconsin and shipped the jobs to Canada. The list goes on and on.

These "American" companies show only one real loyalty: to the short-term interests of their shareholders, a third of whom are foreign investors. If they can close up an American factory and ship jobs overseas to save a nickel, that's exactly what they will do—abandoning loyal American workers and hollowing out American cities along the way.

Politicians love to say they care about American jobs. But for decades, those same politicians have cited "free market principles" and refused to intervene in markets on behalf of American workers. And of course, they ignore those same supposed principles and intervene regularly to protect the interests of multinational corporations and international capital.

The result? Millions of good jobs lost overseas and a generation of stagnant wages, growing inequality, and sluggish economic growth. [12]

The differences here between Warren's analysis and policy prescriptions and some of those preferred by economic nationalists on the right are marginal. If anything, Warren's patriotic rhetoric (albeit with a sharper class-conscious edge) exceeded that of some market-skeptic conservatives. In terms of content, what Senator Warren called her "agenda of economic patriotism"[13] involved the possible use of tariffs,[14] creating more conditionality before America entered trade deals, promoting "Buy American and other programs designed to develop local industry" as well as "strong rule-of-origin standards to promote domestic manufacturing,"[15] especially green manufacturing.[16] Industrial policy was also built into Warren's program. This included massive expansions of the federal government's support for R&D, using federal dollars to create and sustain domestic industries, and establishing a Department of Economic Development[17] whose functions resembled those of Japan's long-defunct Ministry for International Trade and Industry. Warren also proposed numerous regulations including "provisions . . . legally requiring big American corporations to focus on the long-term interests of all of their stakeholders—including workers—rather than on the short-term financial interests of Wall Street investors."[18]

MORE THAN THE MARKET

Many of the assumptions underlying Warren's economic patriotism program, like her assertion that the decline in manufacturing jobs was not driven by technology but rather by outsourcing,[19] have been subject to critique[20] on many of the same grounds that I have suggested that protectionism, industry policy and stakeholder capitalism will not revitalize America's economy. Warren had, however, learned a vital political lesson from Donald Trump: that debates about the economy have become heavily overlain with issues of identity. Warren grasped that questions like "Where do I come from?," "Who is my community?," or "Where do my loyalties lie?" had become central to Western political debates. In such an environment, a focus on liberty as the normative basis for free markets could not help but lose much of its potency. At the best of times, the marshalling of economic facts, however accurate, is always going to struggle to compete with the emotional pull associated with national identity.

Yet it does not have to be this way. Broad arguments for economic freedom need not be at odds with attachment to one's country or strong affirmations of national sovereignty. Nineteenth-century Britain illustrates this especially well.

From the 1820s onwards, Britain moved its economy decisively in the direction of economic liberalization, a process epitomized by repeal of the Corn Laws. Britain swiftly emerged as "the workshop of the world." The intense competition generated by free trade helped to ensure that its goods were produced with such efficiency and at such low cost that British products outsold locally manufactured comparable goods in most of the world's marketplaces. These were the fruits of Britain's embrace of entrepreneurship, competition in ideas and technology, and its pursuit of dynamic trade openness.

But there was also considerable popular support for Britain's journey down the path of economic liberalism. While large swaths of Britain's elites had become convinced of the case for free markets by the 1820s, proponents of liberalization were equally successful in popularizing the notion that it benefited millions of ordinary Britons. They also became proficient at politically mobilizing large numbers of the populace.[21] Britain itself consequently became identified in many people's minds with a strong commitment to domestic and international commercial freedom. A symbiosis emerged between the type of political economy in which economic freedom was accorded high priority, and other values concerning what it meant to be British. These included a distrust of arbitrary power, the embrace of scientific discovery and technological development, a revival of intense religiosity (especially among the growing middle-class), and openness to political and social reform.

To be sure, this was also a period in which socialist ideas emerged and started spreading, and when capitalism began to be associated with the dark images portrayed in Charles Dickens's novels. But the integration of a particular vision of political economy with Britain's self-understanding proved strong. It also helped Britain project political confidence abroad. The *Pax Britannica* meant more than just the Royal Navy's ascendency over the world's oceans. It also expressed and symbolized the dominance of *British* bankers, *British* industry, and *British* companies across the globe as *British* goods were traded extensively through the world and *British* capital was invested in every corner of the earth.

Therein lies lessons for Americans who want their country to embrace free trade over protectionism, and competition and entrepreneurship over industrial policy and stakeholderism. The case for free markets will lose if it remains narrowly economic in its content and emphasis. Instead, that case needs to be wrapped into a broader story about America. For if American defenders of markets can only offer an argument for "more stuff produced more efficiently for more people," if they allow free markets to become associated with borderless utopias, or if they trivialize the very real bonds that many Americans have to their country and communities, millions of Americans will not listen to them—no matter how compelling the economics.

A NEW SOCIETY

Throughout the twentieth century, some of the most compelling arguments for markets were made by classical liberals like F.A. Hayek. Much of this was presented in economic terms, though often complemented with philosophical defenses of the free society. In the midst of this, questions about nations, national identity, and national sovereignty received little attention. Hayek himself was ambiguous about this topic. In 1939, Hayek argued that "the abrogation of national sovereignties and the creation of an effective international order of law is a necessary complement and the logical consummation of the liberal program." [22] That sounds suspiciously like the language of Kantian perpetual peace. Yet five years later, Hayek expressed worries about the potential tyranny of supranational states over "the national communities." [23] It's likely that he had the U.S.S.R. in mind. Two decades later, Hayek dedicated his most important work of political philosophy, *The Constitution of Liberty*, "To the unknown civilization that is growing in America."[24] He apparently had some confidence that America might embody some of the ideals that he considered important for civilizational development.

The number of post-war intellectuals who sought to integrate arguments for the free economy into the American story was relatively small. It was not, for example, an exercise in which Milton Friedman invested much time. Perhaps it is the case that economists are generally not well-suited to undertake this task. One individual who had, however, some success in this area was the theologian and philosopher Michael Novak. Author of the influential 1982 book *The Spirit of Democratic Capitalism*, Novak is primarily remembered as the first to produce a strong theological defense of free markets. His book shaped the outlook of two generations of Jewish, Catholic, and Protestant believers looking to integrate their economic ideas into their religious commitments. Less commented upon is that Novak's book also offered a defense of the market economy rooted in a distinct idea of America, and that it articulated a vision of political economy very different to Clay's American System.

Novak's starting point was with the French theologian, Jacques Maritain. Novak noted that Maritain had written about America's economy and its underlying spirit in his 1958 book *Reflections on America*.[25] Ordinary Americans, Maritain saw, were nowhere near as materialistic as Europeans typically imagined them to be. Despite 1950s America being a country in which the New Deal's effects still weighed heavily, Maritain recognized that Americans continued to associate enterprise, commerce, and the pursuit of wealth with ideals reflective of the American mind.[26]

Reflecting on what Maritain meant by this, Novak argued that the moral and political structure underlying American capitalism had been articulated by Founders like Washington and Hamilton, as well as by eighteenth-century philosophers like Montesquieu and Adam Smith. It is not that these individuals worked out a "theory," as we understand that word today, for American capitalism. But they did develop a vision of a commercial civilization that they hoped would arise in America. While this ideal did not pretend that commercial society lacked blemishes, it identified serious deficiencies in "the civic orders of ancient Greece and Rome, in those of the Holy Roman Empire, and in the various *ancien regimes* of their experience."[27] Such orders, Novak wrote, appeared to these Americans as endowing

> each man of high birth and inherited status with false notions of "self-sufficiency and absurd conceit of his own superiority" [quoting Adam Smith]. They sold too short the capacities of commoners to direct their own activities, to form their own practical judgments, and to make their own choices. Moreover, they overlooked the tremendous economic potential of practicality, inventiveness, and enterprise on the part of free individuals.[28]

The Founders whom Novak had in mind did not deploy terminology like "democratic capitalism" to describe their alternative polity. The civilization to which they referred was summed up by the social philosopher Ralph Lerner in a 1979 essay as "a commercial republic."[29]

As Lerner describes it, the commercial republic envisaged by key Founders was one that placed the habits crucial for a free and commercially oriented economy at the center of its social and political life. These Founders did not, Lerner cautions, regard commerce as the whole of life. They also recognized that the viability of commercial societies was highly dependent upon particular practices (courtesy, promise-keeping, courage, etc.) and institutions (functional families, the rule of law, etc.) whose roots were traceable to older customs, philosophical perspectives, and religious sources such as the Jewish and Christian faiths. Nor were they unaware of the temptations associated with wealth, ranging from avarice to hedonism. Nevertheless, such Founders did seek to give economic freedom, and the pursuit of the prosperity that ensues from it, a more central place in public rhetoric, practice, and institutions than most pre-modern societies in which birth and inherited hierarchies counted for everything.

The centrality of this ethic of commerce, Novak and Lerner maintained, encourages the spread of habits and outlooks which have spillover effects in politics, society, and even international relations. Commercial societies stress practicality, thereby putting political tendencies to utopianism firmly in their place. The commercial ethic also recognizes the importance of incentives and self-interest, and it understands that these cannot be limited to the economic realm and affects how we approach politics and international relations.

That same ethic also breaks down the notion that public service is the monopoly of people born into a particular caste. People in commercial societies increasingly recognize that, through entrepreneurship, competition, and sheer hard work, they can constantly aspire to things that were beyond their parents' generation, albeit with no guarantee that this will be simply a matter of course. Then there are the particular virtues associated with commercial orders: prudence, industriousness, thrift, creativity, self-restraint, and the willingness to trust people we have never met before. Certainly, the fullness of the virtues go beyond these particular habits of action, but their presence in society and the economy is central to the type of polity that Lerner and Novak believed key American Founders were in the business of establishing.

COMMERCIAL, REPUBLICAN, AMERICAN

Of crucial importance for Lerner and Novak was that this particular constellation of ideas was expressed in a distinctly American setting between the 1760s and 1790s and, in many cases, with a direct view to shaping an emerging American body politic. Nowhere was this more expressed than in that most influential set of writings, *The Federalist Papers*. Famous for its defense of the U.S. Constitution and its explanation of how the federal government's three branches would function, few other sources have so well explained the Constitution's original articles and how they relate to each other. Much time has been expended bringing to light the deeper sources informing it, ranging from the Jewish and Christian inheritance, natural law and natural rights thought, and the influence of the moderate Enlightenment.

That, however, is only part of the story. *The Federalist* contains much that falls squarely into the realm of political economy. Much of this amounts to a brief for a commercial republic that the authors thought would serve America well in economic and extra-economic ways. Though *The Federalist*'s vision of America is often described as "nationalist," this did not mean what it does today. Those who wrote *The Federalist* were concerned with explaining why a loose confederation of states should integrate themselves into a more unified and modern sovereign state grounded on certain ideas and embodying a particular type of political and economic culture.

In envisioning the nation as a commercial republic, *The Federalist* had several things in mind. First, the American regime was to be *republican*. This term itself embodied several ideas, one of which was that the polity needed to be guided by public reason [30] rather than fickle majority opinion. It also meant that the governed were to be regularly consulted and public affairs would be conducted via accepted procedures which impeded the exercise of arbitrary power, whether from above or below. To this extent, "republican" also meant self-government.

That same republic, however, was to be primarily *commercial*, rather than one possessing a heavily military character like that of the late Roman republic. Neither the times nor America's particular circumstances, Hamilton specified, suited the United States for that type of regime. [31] Republican government would thus be combined with a modern private enterprise economy undergirded by property rights and in which merchants were subject to the disciplines of competitive markets.

Yet the deeper meaning of this type of regime went beyond according preeminence to commerce and trade. The unleashing of enterprise, an ever-increasing division of labor, and the subsequent deepening of domestic and international trade was envisaged as contributing to the ongoing refinement of commerce as a central element of modern civilized countries. "A landed interest, a manufacturing interest, a moneyed interest, with many lesser interests, would," *Federalist* 10 states, "grow up of necessity in civilized nations." [32] As Anthony A. Peacock writes, *Federalist* 8 hints at a strong parallel between the republican virtues promoted by the Constitution and those of commerce: "a self-governing discipline of enterprise consisting of character traits such as industry, innovation, economy, self-restraint, honesty, prudence, and so on." [33] The habits which made for commercial success would thus reinforce republican virtues against those habits which threaten republican practice—indolence, hubris, venality, and absence of restraint.

In the late-eighteenth century, the practice of commerce remained associated in many people's minds with mercantilism. That outlook is not to be found in *The Federalist*. On a domestic level, *Federalist* 11 articulates an unabashed defense of free trade throughout the republic, so that "An unrestrained intercourse between the States themselves will advance the trade of each by an interchange of their respective productions, not only for the supply of reciprocal wants at home, but for exportation to foreign markets. The veins of commerce in every part will be replenished, and will

acquire additional motion and vigor from a free circulation of the
commodities of every part." [34]

Skepticism of tariffs vis-à-vis other nations also pervades *The
Federalist*. Though allowing them as a revenue source for the new
federal government, *Federalist* 35 underscores the negative effects
of tariffs insofar as they effectively force some members of the community to subsidize others and help particular businesses establish
"a premature monopoly of the markets." Tariffs "force industry out
of its more natural channels into others in which it flows with less
advantage." [35] They are, *Federalist* 35 adds, "prejudicial to the fair
trader" [36]—by which was meant those who *didn't* seek favors and
privileges. This sounds distinctly like Adam Smith's exposition of
the ways in which tariffs help prop up monopolies and prioritize
the interests of politically connected producers over consumers.
Indeed, many Americans of the time were instinctively hostile to
anything that smacked of mercantilism, as it was strongly identified with the country against which they had waged a war to gain
their independence. [37] After the Revolution, disapproving allusions
were regularly made to Britain's "love of monopoly" which, in some
cases, was cast as "unconstitutional." [38]

Nor does *The Federalist* articulate a positive view of what we
would call a regulatory state. In *Federalist* 62, for instance, we find
a concise summary of excessive regulation's deleterious effects:

> Another effect of public instability is the unreasonable
> advantage it gives to the sagacious, the enterprising, and
> the moneyed few over the industrious and uniformed
> mass of the people. Every new regulation concerning

> commerce or revenue, or in any way affecting the value of
> the different species of property, presents a new harvest
> to those who watch the change, and can trace its conse-
> quences; a harvest, reared not by themselves, but by the
> toils and cares of the great body of their fellow-citizens.
> This is a state of things in which it may be said with some
> truth that laws are made for the FEW, not for the MANY. [39]

The American commercial republic envisaged by *The Federalist*
thus runs counter to those merchants and legislators who would use
law and regulation to privilege themselves. Instead, *Federalist* 11
states, it would embody the "spirit of enterprise" that "characterizes
the commercial spirit of America" [40] combined with a bottom-up
economic dynamism and the relentless search for opportunities in
domestic and foreign markets. *The Federalist* had no hesitation in
describing this as essential to the life of civilized countries:

> The prosperity of commerce is now perceived and acknowl-
> edged by all enlightened statesmen to be the most useful as
> well as the most productive source of national wealth, and
> has accordingly become a primary object of their political
> cares. By multiplying the means of gratification, by promot-
> ing the introduction and circulation of the precious metals,
> those darling objects of human avarice and enterprise, it
> serves to vivify and invigorate the channels of industry, and
> to make them flow with greater activity and copiousness.
> The assiduous merchant, the laborious husbandman, the
> active mechanic, and the industrious manufacturer,—all

orders of men, look forward with eager expectation and
growing alacrity to this pleasing reward of their toils. [41]

The Federalist's treatment of these questions evinces no particular concern that the growth of commerce and a capital-intensive
economy might foster the social pathologies often associated with
the pursuit of wealth. Instead, entrepreneurship, trade, and economic modernization are presented as crucial prerequisites for
realizing distinctly non-economic goods, like the greater unity, justice, domestic tranquility, common defense, and general welfare
envisaged in the Constitution's preamble.

Undergirding all this is a distinct realism about the human condition. Federalist 6 cautions against "the deceitful dream of a golden
age" [42] and any illusions about human perfectibility. People may be
good, but they are also "ambitious, vindictive, and rapacious." [43]
The Federalist thus embodies a healthy respect for the workings of
self-interest, suggesting "that momentary passions, and immediate
interests, have a more active and imperious control over human
conduct than general or remote considerations of policy, utility,
or justice." [44] Novak made a similar point two centuries later. "At
one end of the market," he observed, "a certain heroic boldness is
required; at the other end, moderation is taught and realism is the
necessary rule. A commercial republic captures plenty of roman-
tics, but is not easy on romanticism." [45]

The realism pervading The Federalist embraces its treatment of
America's approach to the rest of the world. It presents commercial
republics as innovative, restless, risk-taking, acquisitive by nature,
and not inclined to insularity. America's commercial dynamism

couldn't help but flow over the republic's borders into international markets. By 1786, America had already emerged from the 1784–85 depression, and American merchants were trading extensively with other parts of the world—not just the New World and Europe, but as far abroad as Alaska, Africa, Russia, and East Asia. The 1780s were not, in fact, a period of economic bleakness. Despite a temporary decline in immigration, the population was increasing and expanding into the newly acquired Western territories.[46]

Federalist 4 affirms that the American spirit of enterprise was leading Americans to trade with China and India and challenge monopolies exercised there by European powers like Britain, France, and Portugal. These developments had consequently "excited uneasy sensations on several of the maritime powers of Europe,"[47] for few such countries welcomed American competition. Given such hostility, *The Federalist* proposed that America develop naval and military power commensurate with the geographical extent of that trade, not least, *Federalist* 7 stated, because American commercial endeavors would not "pay much respect to those regulations of trade by which particular states might endeavor to secure exclusive benefits to their own citizens."[48]

This un-Pollyannaish view of the world points to another aspect of *The Federalist*'s commercial republicanism: one which clashes with those like Montesquieu and Kant who believed that *doux commerce* would necessarily produce more peaceful relations between nations. *Federalist* 6 stresses that "the rivalships and competitions of commerce between commercial nations"[49] (whether ancient commercial republics like Carthage or modern ones like the Dutch Republic) had produced much warlike behavior. "Is not the love of wealth as domineering and enterprising a passion as that of power or glory? Has there not been as many wars founded upon commercial motives," *Federalist* 6 states, "as were before occasioned by the cupidity of territory or dominion?"[50] Here the *Federalist* mirrors Smith and Hume's moderate skepticism of the proposition that dynamic trade between nations necessarily facilitates peace among countries. *The Federalist* also tracks closely with Hume's claim that, while trade might lead to countries becoming less bellicose, the citizens of commercial societies would display greater military spirit than others if war became necessary, since their own prosperity and freedom would be at stake.[51]

"A FREE, ENLIGHTENED, AND AT NO DISTANT PERIOD, A GREAT NATION"

Holding the "commercial" and the "republic" parts of this American political equation together was never going to be easy. *The Federalist* acknowledged that the republic outlined in the Constitution presupposed the existence of people of integrity, talent, and character to lead it.[52] There was no guarantee that such individuals would rise to the top of politics. Much also depended upon the creation of a basic institutional infrastructure fit for a modern economy, such as sound public finances, a judicial system free of corruption, or the rules required for efficient money markets. Some of these prerequisites were secured during the Washington administration's first critical years, though only after overcoming tremendous opposition.

Then, as now, foreign affairs played into economic policy issues. The radical ideological turn taken by France from 1789 onwards had immediate implications for America's trading relations with the rest of the world. During Washington's Presidency, Jefferson and others called for "commercial discrimination" to enhance Franco-American trade, primarily because of their positive view of the French Revolution and their determination to hurt Britain. Hamilton, by contrast, maintained that trade policy should be driven by national interest—not specific factions' ideologically driven foreign policy preferences—and pointed out economic realities such as the fact that Britain was America's biggest trading partner and would likely remain so for some time into the future. Hamilton also stressed that international trade of the type envisaged and promoted by Smith did not yet exist and might, as Smith himself acknowledged, never emerge. Nations, especially a new country like America, could not ignore such facts of life.[53]

Given that he was the author of Federalist 35 cited above, Hamilton clearly had no illusions about protectionism's drawbacks. "He was," Douglas A. Irwin reminds us, "skeptical of high protective tariffs because they sheltered both inefficient and efficient producers, lead to higher prices for consumers, and gave rise to smuggling, which cut into government revenue."[54] This conclusion is echoed by Hamilton historian Michael P. Federici, who maintains that Hamilton "generally opposed tariffs and any policies that interfered with the free exchange of goods between nations, and he adamantly opposed using trade sanctions as an instrument of foreign policy."[55] Contra the mercantilist outlook of his time, Hamilton *didn't* want to discourage imports—especially imports of capital—because this was the basis on which he wanted to fund America's public debt. Hamilton also wanted to avoid a trade war with Britain.[56] His subsequent choice not to go down the high tariff path played a major role in driving the votes of economic protectionists away from the Federalists and towards the Jeffersonian Republicans in the late 1790s.[57]

The often-fierce domestic debates occasioned by the nexus of trade and foreign policy which divided Americans and split his own cabinet weighed heavily upon America's first president. That is why it is all the more important to recognize that much of the ideal of America as a commercial republic expressed in *The Federalist* comes together in a succinct but powerful way in George Washington's 1796 Farewell Address. Much of it was based on drafting prepared by Hamilton (author of seven of the eleven *Federalist* papers cited in this chapter and possible author of two of the others) but also reflected Washington's own thoughts.[58]

Like all such documents, the Farewell Address sought to achieve several immediate goals, such as maintaining America's neutrality in the escalating war between France and Britain. But Washington also sought to lay down some long-term markers by trying to identify principles and ideas upon which he thought all Americans concerned with their country's general welfare should always reflect. That included articulating a particular conception of America as a commercial republic in which the word "republic" conveys much more than commitment to a sovereign regime of a particular type, while the word "commerce" provides an interpretative key as to how that republic understood its own character. At the same time, Washington portrays his ambition for America in the world: that of a sovereign nation freely trading with, and able to hold its own among, other countries.

The view of commerce articulated by Washington in the address's lengthy list of recommendations to America is overwhelmingly positive. He sought to teach Americans that the yet-to-come greatness of their country was inseparable from freedom of enterprise. Washington presents "unrestrained" trade between America's East, South, North and West as binding the country together, as each region capitalizes on its comparative advantages to meet the others' economic needs. This endows Americans with "greater strength, greater resource, proportionately greater security from external danger, [and] a less frequent interruption of their Peace by foreign Nations." [59]

Like *The Federalist Papers*, Washington's Farewell Address is infused with realism. Nations will always follow their own interests, and these interests don't always coincide. Certainly America should "Observe good faith and justice toward all nations." But America's conduct of foreign relations could not be grounded on what Washington called "disinterested friendship." Indeed, he thought America should avoid particular attachments. Commerce has a way of underscoring that point. "The great rule of conduct for us in regard to foreign nations," he stated, "is in extending our commercial relations to have with them as little political connection as possible." Thus while the Farewell Address rejects isolationism, autarky, imprudent international entanglements, and cynical *realpolitik*, America's national interest is firmly associated with American commerce's extension across the globe. Central to that outlook is a general commitment to free trade. As Washington elaborated:

> our commercial policy should hold an equal and impar-
> tial hand, neither seeking nor granting exclusive favors
> or preferences; consulting the natural course of things;
> diffusing and diversifying by gentle means the streams of
> commerce, but forcing nothing; establishing with pow-
> ers so disposed, in order to give trade a stable course,
> to define the rights of our merchants, and to enable the
> Government to support them, conventional rules of
> intercourse, the best that present circumstances and
> mutual opinion will permit, but temporary and liable to
> be from time to time abandoned or varied as experience
> and circumstances shall dictate . . . . [60]

Plainly, this is not a pure laissez-faire position. [61] Trade, Washington recognized, is subject to all the vicissitudes that characterize foreign affairs: a realm which, like any other, mirrors humanity's political and fallible nature. The fluctuations generated by wars, economic crises, natural disasters, and mass disease may occasionally require government intervention. Nor did Washington dispute the consensus of the period concerning the legitimacy of using tariffs to raise revenue. Nevertheless, the Farewell Address's outlook is far removed from the policy-prescriptions of an eighteenth-century mercantilist, let alone that of a twenty-first-century protectionist. The proposed norm is that of a sovereign nation whose citizens exuberantly, competitively and, as far as possible, freely trade with each another and across the world. Like *The Wealth of Nations*, it allows for exceptions. Still, Washington regarded trade openness as necessary if America was to become, to use his expression, "a free, enlightened, and at no distant period, a great nation."[62] The overall picture is one in which America allows its citizens to truck and barter where they see fit. Meanwhile government officials should work to ensure that all the conventional rules of international commerce are upheld, without forgetting that it is folly to imagine that other countries won't pursue their own interests.

Washington's confidence in the benefits of wide-ranging and free-flowing domestic and international commerce wasn't without qualifications. He preferred an intensification of interstate commerce to foreign trade because the former helped build up domestic unity at a time in which many Americans regarded their state as their country. Washington also wanted to ensure that America wasn't excessively reliant on allies for military supplies. Still, he recognized and accepted many Americans' anxiousness to trade with other countries. In 1786, Washington told his friend, the Marquis de Lafayette, that "liberal and free commerce" often helped to alleviate tensions between nations, and that it was in America's interests with its then agriculturally based economy to trade with those countries whose present advantage lay in manufacturing.[63]

In private, Washington occasionally worried about commerce's effects on public morals. In a 1784 letter to Jefferson, he referred to "those vices which luxury, the consequence of wealth and power, naturally introduce[s]."[64] The weight of such concerns, however, should not be exaggerated. Later that same year, while corresponding with Benjamin Harrison, Washington stated that, "A people . . . who are possessed of the spirit of Commerce—who see, & who will pursue their advantages, may achieve almost anything." [65]

The conception of the normative foundations of America as a commercial republic articulated in the Farewell Address and *The Federalist Papers* contrasts with Montesquieu's understanding of the same type of polity. His *Spirit of Laws* praised Britain for knowing "better than any other people upon earth how to value, at the same time, these three great advantages—religion, commerce, and liberty." [66] Montesquieu nevertheless maintained that the basis of "the laws of morality" in commercially focused societies was self-interest. What prevents such societies from disintegrating, Montesquieu argued, was that people's tendency to pursue their self-interest is tempered by that same self-interest.

While the commercial republic envisaged in *The Federalist Papers* and the Farewell Address takes the workings of self-interest for granted, these texts are far more explicit than Montesquieu concerning how much such polities need other reference points to survive and prosper. Their authors are likely to have read Sir James Steuart's warning in his 1767 book *Inquiry into the Principles of Political Economy* (closely studied by Hamilton [67]) that the moment when great trading states like Tyre, Carthage, and Venice attained their heights, "they immediately found themselves laboring under their own greatness." [68] While attaching a high premium to commercial success and displaying tremendous confidence in economic freedom's benefits, these Founding documents stressed the necessity of cultural and moral resources that motivate people to think directly about the well-being of their fellow citizens and the republic as a whole.[69]

The remedy for the challenges arising from vibrant commercial orders was not, from Washington's standpoint, anything like today's administrative state. The Farewell Address affirmed his belief in "a Government of as much vigor as is consistent with the perfect security of Liberty," but primarily emphasized "Religion and morality" as the "indispensable supports," as he called them, of "political prosperity." Washington also underlined the importance of "Institutions for the general diffusion of knowledge" and "refined education" for realizing that objective. These recommendations reflect an Anglo-American Enlightenment temperament and a belief that a republic in which commerce played a prominent role needed formation and foundations shaped and inspired by the Hebrew and Christian Scriptures as well as the concern for natural rights and natural law which were part and parcel of late-eighteenth-century American thought. They were, Washington held, essential for "private and public felicity."[70] The same, I'd suggest, is true today.

A NEW AGE

Twenty-first-century American economic life, profoundly influenced as it is by the legacies of the New Deal and the Great Society, as well as by ongoing faith in experts that persists on much of the left and some of the right, is far removed from the particular spirit and mind that animated the idea of America as a commercial republic.

So too are the proposals of those who are inspired by economic traditions like corporatism, or who put their trust in industrial policy, or who believe in the imperative of extensive government intervention into America's economy.

This being the case, some might ask: why should Americans look to particular Founders or important Founding documents for inspiration, if not direction as we reflect on our country's economic future? Given that we are more than two hundred years distant from the world of Washington, Jefferson, and Hamilton, it could be argued that too much has changed for their insights to carry much weight in today's America. Twenty-first-century America is less white, less Protestant, and less dominated by men. It is also more shaped by ideologies antithetical to the ideas concretized before, during, and after the American Revolution. In economic terms, today's American economy is neck-deep in state regulation and interventions bequeathed by American progressives, modern liberals, social democrats, and ostensive conservatives. The United States of today more closely resembles a European social democracy than many Americans are willing to admit.

The differences between the world of *The Federalist Papers* and the Farewell Address and that of contemporary America are real and profound. Some of them are for the better, insofar as they underscore that the blessings of the American experiment have not been limited to white men like me. It has proved capable of encompassing a wide plurality of individuals and groups who occupied very different social, political, and economic statuses in the eighteenth century by virtue of their ethnicity, religion, or sex.

This matters because America's ability to re-forge its economic direction along the lines suggested in this book relies upon much more than returning to sound economics. It is at least as much about affirming many of the ideals underpinning the American experiment and their enduring importance for us today. The Sino–US competition certainly concerns economics and national security, but it is also about whether the values of the United States will prove stronger than the very different outlook that drives Chinese state capitalism. Getting America's own house in order is the *sine qua non* not only for dealing with a belligerent China, but also for reattaching the market economy to a distinctly American political regime. This will not occur without a renewal of faith *by* Americans *in* the American experiment at every level of society. In the end, it is domestic self-confidence that allows nations to behave with self-assurance at home and abroad. Until Americans regain that self-confidence, the United States' capacity to shape its own economic destiny while taming dragons abroad will be limited.

This underscores two important reasons why we must ground the case for an economy of entrepreneurship, competition, and dynamic trade in these distinctly American ideals. First, it disassociates all the values and institutions that characterize this economic outlook from an opaque globalism, while simultaneously illustrating that those promoting a state-centric future for the American economy are out of step in important ways with the ideal of a self-confident America animated by the spirit of enterprise. Some of these individuals may cheerfully concede that this is the case. That, however, only helps clarify who stands where in the debates about the most optimal political economy for the United States, and why they do so.

Second, by reminding ourselves of the centrality of entrepreneurship, enhanced competition, and trade openness to the American enterprising spirit, we may advance advocacy for these things beyond economic considerations. This book has dwelt at length on the empirical dimension of contemporary economic debates because the truth of such matters is vital to deciding America's economic future. But economic truth is not sufficient to settle these questions. Americans are not simply economic beings, and America is more than an economy. The ideas expressed in the texts reviewed in this concluding chapter were written by people who took the then-embryonic social science of economics very seriously. Yet they connected these ideas to a distinct vision of America as a new type of self-governing political community. By itself, economics cannot do that, for economics cannot explain what it means to be an American, whether today or two hundred years ago, or why America matters for the rest of the world.

Is there a real possibility that an American commercial republic, equipped for twenty-first-century particularities, will emerge to shape America's future? To be honest, I do not know. The forces who want to push America towards even greater state intervention are real. More generally, while the idea of an American commercial republic repudiates state capitalism, whether from the left or right, it also rebukes those (again, on the left and right) who appear to have no particular affection for America and its experiment in freedom. Alas, significant numbers of Americans actively involved in public life today fall into one or both of these camps.

Despite these obstacles, I see no reason why America cannot embrace the habits, incentives, and disciplines associated with markets while also grounding them in the language, norms, and virtues of the American experiment. They are, for the most part, mutually reinforcing. Above all, the potential for a fresh economic page in America's history—a new Age of the American Commercial Republic—presents the United States with the possibility of embracing a political economy characterized by hope and grounded in confidence about the perpetual potentialities of the American way of liberty and virtue. And when there is hope, especially when grounded in something extraordinary like the story of America, nothing is definitively lost.

ACKNOWLEDGMENTS

Many of the ideas in this book have been developed in publications for whom I have written for many years. Here I must single out *Law and Liberty*, where I serve as a Contributing Editor. *Law and Liberty*'s superb editorial team are especially thanked for their thoughts and critiques. Other publications in which I have explored some of these ideas include *Public Discourse, The Spectator, Cosmos+Taxis, Revue Conflits, National Review, Fox Business, The National Interest,* and *The American Spectator.* I also thank the Real Clear network— *Real Clear Politics, Real Clear Markets, Real Clear World, Real Clear Books,* and *Real Clear Religion*—for disseminating many of these articles to even wider audiences.

Several institutions have helped me formulate my thoughts about the subjects discussed in these pages. First and foremost, the Acton Institute has provided a congenial environment for thinking through many of the questions to which this book responds. I want to single out Michael Matheson Miller, Alejandro A. Chafuen, Stephen A. Barrows, Dylan Pahman, Daniel Hugger, and Kris Alan Mauren for conversations about these and related topics. I also thank Sarah Negri for reading through the text, asking good

questions that caused me to revise particular sections, and for helping to compile the index.

Other organizations have provided forums to discuss and debate
the topics addressed in these pages. The Heritage Foundation has
provided many opportunities to do so. Other places include: The
Public Interest Fellowship, The Fund for American Studies, The
James Madison Program at Princeton University, The Philadelphia
Society, The Mont Pelerin Society, The Napa Institute, Catholic
University of America, American Enterprise Institute, American
Legislative Exchange Council, Intercollegiate Studies Institute,
Hillsdale College Free Market Forum, The Jack Miller Center, Ave
Maria University, Faulkner University, The Wisconsin Forum, The
Lynde and Harry Bradley Foundation, The Federalist Society, The
Tikvah Fund (America and Israel), The Argaman Institute (Israel),
Institut Français Centre Saint-Louis (Italy), Pontifical Urbaniana
University (Italy), Pontifical Gregorian University (Italy), Fran-
cisco Marroquín University (Guatemala), Instituto Fe y Libertad
(Guatemala), Instituto Acton (Argentina), Vienna University of
Economics and Business (Austria), Institut d'études et politique
(Liechtenstein), Libertad y Desarrollo (Chile), and Universidad de
los Andes (Chile).

Particular individuals have helped me, through conversation
and pen, reflect upon the many political and economic paradoxes
with which this book grapples, most notably: Richard M. Reinsch
II, Brian A. Smith, John G. Gore, Lee Trepanier, Bridgett Wag-
ner, Veronique de Rugy, William McGurn, Lenore Ealy, Carroll
Ríos de Rodríguez, Kim R. Holmes, William Ruger, Margarita
Mooney Suarez, Harry Z. Cohen, David L. Bahnsen, Iain Murray,

Anne Rathbone Bradley, Timothy Andrews, Alexander William Salter, Jay W. Richards, Conor Sweeney, Tonya Christina Greig, Roger Ream, Catherine Ruth Pakaluk, Rabbi Mitchell Rocklin, Thomas D. Howes, Jack Butler, and Scott Lincicome. So too has the music of Wolfgang Amadeus Mozart, especially at the most difficult of times.

This book is seeing the light of day thanks to the publisher of Encounter Books, Roger Kimball. The American public square has been enriched by his work for decades. I hope this book serves as an extension of that. Mary Spencer, Amanda DeMatto, Sam Schneider, Andrew Shea, and the team at Encounter are also thanked for helping to bring this book into the light.

Above all, there is the sustenance which has been provided by my family, near and far. Lastly, I have in mind the one who I will always adore. She will forever have my love.

NOTES

Chapter 1: It All Falls Down

[1] Adam Smith, *An Inquiry into the Nature and the Causes of the Wealth of Nations*, eds. R.H. Campbell and A.S. Skinner (Indianapolis: Liberty Fund, [1776] 1981), Vol. II, Par. IV.vii.c.66, 617.

[2] See Jiwei Ci, *Democracy in China: The Coming Crisis* (Cambridge, Mass.: Harvard University Press), 2.

[3] See Ryan Hass, *Stronger: Adapting America's China Strategy in an Age of Competitive Interdependence* (New Haven: Yale University Press, 2021), 46-47.

[4] See ibid.

[5] Bill of Rights Institute, "Jimmy Carter, 'Malaise Speech,' July 15, 1979," accessed October 8, 2021, https://billofrightsinstitute.org/activities/jimmy-carter-malaise-speech-july-15-1979.

[6] President William Jefferson Clinton, "State of the Union Address," U.S. Capital, January 23, 1996, accessed May 4, 1996, https://clintonwhitehouse4.archives.gov/WH/New/other/sotu.html.

[7] Patrick Buchanan, *The Great Betrayal: How American Sovereignty and Social Justice Are Being Sacrificed to the Gods of the Global Economy* (Boston, Mass: Little, Brown, 1998), 286.

[8] Robert L. Bartley, "Open NAFTA Borders? Why Not?" *Wall Street Journal*, July 2, 2001, accessed September 22, 2021, https://www.wsj.com/articles/SB994028904620983237.

[9] See Patrick Buchanan, "Globalists or Nationalists: Who Owns the Future?" March 13, 2018, accessed September 22, 2021, https://www.app.com/story/opinion/columnists/2018/03/13/globalists-nationalists-free-trade/418149002/.

[10] See Mohamed Younis, "Sharply Fewer in U.S. View Foreign Trade as Opportunity," Gallup, March 31, 2021, accessed September 24, 2021, https://news.gallup.com/poll/342419/sharply-fewer-view-foreign-trade-opportunity.aspx.

[11] Ezra Vogel, *Deng Xiaoping and the Transformation of China* (Cambridge, Mass: Belknap Press, 2011), 682.

[12] See Nicholas R. Lardy, "Issues in China's WTO Accession," Testimony. May 9, 2001, accessed May 5, 2021, https://www.brookings.edu/testimonies/issues-in-chinas-wto-accession/.

[13] Lingling Wei, "China's Xi Ramps up Control of Private Sector. 'We Have No Choice but to Follow the Party'," *Wall Street Journal*, December 10, 2020, accessed May 6, 2021, https://www.wsj.com/articles/china-xi-clampdown-private-sector-communist-party-11607612531?mod=searchresults_pos3&page=3.

[14] Heritage Foundation, "Overall Score, United States," *Index of Economic Freedom* (2022), accessed February 14, 2022, https://www.heritage.org/index/visualize?cnts=unitedstates|&src=country.

[15] Committee for Economic Development, *Crony Capitalism: Unhealthy Relations between Business and Government* (Arlington, VA: CED, 2015), accessed September 11, 2021, https://www.ced.org/pdf/Embargoed_Report_-_Crony_Capitalism.pdf.

[16] See Hunter Lewis, *Crony Capitalism in America: 2008-2012* (Edinburg, VA: AC2 Books, 2013).

[17] See Joseph Stiglitz, *The Price Of Inequality* (New York: W.W. Norton and Company, 2012), 39–51, 107.

[18] Luigi Zingales, "Crony Capitalism and the Crisis of the West," *Wall Street Journal*, June 6, 2012, accessed October 15, 2021, https://www.wsj.com/articles/SB10001424052702303665904577450071884712152.

[19] See Ann Schmidt, "The 20 wealthiest counties in the U.S., including these Washington, DC, suburbs: Report," *Fox Business*, December 18, 2019, accessed August 24, 2021, https://www.foxbusiness.com/money/washington-dc-suburbs-richest-counties.

[20] See Michael R. Strain, *The American Dream Is Not Dead: (But Populism Could Kill It)* (West Conshohocken, PA: Templeton Press, 2020).

[21] See Stephen Ezell, "False Promises II: The Continuing Gap between China's WTO Commitments and Its Practices," Information Technology and Innovation Foundation (July 2021), accessed October 16, 2021, https://itif.org/sites/default/files/2021-false-promises.pdf.

[22] See Samuel Gregg, "Young Americans Increasingly Prefer Socialism. Here's How to Change Their Minds," *National Review*, July 12, 2021, accessed August 30, 2021, https://www.nationalreview.com/2021/07/young-americans-increasingly-prefer-socialism-heres-how-to-change-their-minds/.

[23] Federalist 10, *Federalist Papers: Primary Documents in American History*, accessed May 10, 2021, https://guides.loc.gov/federalist-papers/text-1-10#s-lg-box-wrapper-25493273.

[24] See Samuel Gregg, "Stimulating Debate," *Claremont Review of Books* 18, 1 (2018): 61-63, accessed December 29, 2021, https://claremontreviewofbooks.com/stimulating-debate/.

[25] See R. La Porta et al., "The Economic Consequences of Legal Origins," *Journal of Economic Literature* 46 (2008): 285-332.

[26] Smith, *Wealth of Nations*, Vol. II, IV.vii.b.40, 581.

[27] See Gordon Wood, *Power and Liberty: Constitutionalism in the American Revolution* (Oxford: OUP, 2021), 6-62.

[28] See Sonia Mittal, Jack N. Rakove, and Barry R. Weingast, "The Constitutional Choices of 1787 and Their Consequences," in *Founding Choices: American Economic Policy in the 1790s*, eds. Douglas A. Irwin and Richard Sylla (Washington DC: National Bureau of Economic Research, 2011), 40.

[29] See, for example, Thomas Doerflinger, *A Vigorous Spirit of Enterprise: Merchants and Economic Development in Revolutionary Philadelphia* (Chapel Hill, NC: University of North Carolina, 1986).

[30] See Mittal et al., "The Constitutional Choices of 1787 and Their Consequences," 41.

[31] See Richard Sylla, "Comparing the UK and U.S. Financial Systems, 1790-1830," in *The Origins and Development of Financial Markets and Institutions, from the Seventeenth Century to the Present*, eds. J. Atack and L. Neal (Cambridge: CUP, 2009), 209-239.

[32] Douglas A. Irwin and Richard Sylla, "The Significance of the Founding Choices," in *Founding Choices*, 19.

[33] Smith, *Wealth of Nations*, Vol. I, IV.ii.43, 471.

[34] Milton Friedman, "The Future of Capitalism," February 9, 1977, accessed May 10, 2021, https://www.hoover.org/research/future-capitalism.

[35] Smith, *Wealth of Nations*, Vol. I, IV.ii.9, 456.

[36] Richard J. Shinder, "Capitalists against Markets," *American Greatness*, January 4, 2021, accessed May 11, 2021, https://amgreatness.com/2021/01/04/capitalists-against-markets/.

[37] Wood, *Power and Liberty*, 2-3.

[38] Ibid., 3-4.

[39] See Samuel Gregg, "Capitalism in the 1619 Project," Heritage Foundation Backgrounder no. 3576, January 26, 2021, accessed June 2, 2021, https://www.heritage.org/sites/default/files/2021-01/BG3576.pdf.

Chapter 2: Protectionism Doesn't Pay

[1] See Douglas A. Irwin, *Clashing over Commerce: A History of U.S. Trade Policy* (Chicago: University of Chicago Press, 2018), 80.

[2] Constitution of the Confederate States, March 11, 1861, accessed June 1, 2021, https://avalon.law.yale.edu/19th_century/csa_csa.asp.

[3] See Irwin, *Clashing over Commerce*, 217-218.

[4] See Kevin Phillips, *William McKinley* (New York: Times Books Henry Holt and Company , 2003), 42-44.

[5] See Joanne Reitano, *The Tariff Question in the Gilded Age: The Great Debate of 1888* (University Park, PA: Pennsylvania State University, 1994), 129.

[6] See Philippe Minard, *La fortune du colbertism: état et industrie dans la France des Lumières* (Paris: Fayard, 1998).

[7] Smith, *Wealth of Nations*, Vol. I, IV.ii.3, 453.

[8] *Papers of James Madison*, eds. William T. Hutchison and William M.E. Rachal (Chicago: University of Chicago Press, 1991), Vol. 12, 71.

[9] Smith, *Wealth of Nations*, Vol. II, IV.viii.49, 660.

[10] Ibid., Vol. II, IV.viii.54, 661-2.

[11] Adam Smith, "Letter to William Eden," in *The Correspondence of Adam Smith*, eds. E.C. Mossner and I.S. Ross (Oxford: Clarendon Press, 1977), 272.

[12] Smith, *Wealth of Nations*, Vol. I, IV.ii.2, 451.

[13] See Buchanan, "Globalists or Nationalists: Who Owns the Future?"

[14] See Douglas A. Irwin, "Tariffs and Growth in Late Nineteenth Century America," *The World Economy* 24, no.1 (2001): 15-30.

[15] See ibid.

[16] See J. Bradford DeLong, "Trade Policy and America's Standard of Living: An Historical Perspective," University of California at Berkeley, Economics Department, September 1995, Sixth Version, accessed June 9, 2021, https://pages.ucsd.edu/~jlbroz/Courses/POLI142B/syllabus/delong.pdf.

[17] See Douglas A. Irwin, "International Trade Agreements," *The Library of Economics and Liberty*, accessed June 2, 2021, https://www.econlib.org/library/Enc/InternationalTradeAgreements.html.

[18] Heritage Foundation, "United States," *Index of Economic Freedom* (Washington, D.C.: Heritage Foundation, 2022), accessed February 14, 2022, https://www.heritage.org/index/country/unitedstates#open-markets%20last.

[19] See United States International Trade Commission, *Harmonized Tariff Schedule of the United States Basic Revision 3* (Washington, D.C., April 2021).

[20] See Heritage Foundation, "United States," *Index of Economic Freedom* (2022).

[21] See "To Facilitate Positive Adjustment to Competition From Imports of Certain Steel Products: A Presidential Document by the Executive Office of the President on 03/07/2002," accessed June 2, 2021, https://www.federalregister.gov/documents/2002/03/07/02-5711/to-facilitate-positive-adjustment-to-competition-from-imports-of-certain-steel-products.

[22] See Douglas A. Irwin, *Free Trade under Fire*, 5th ed. (Princeton, NJ: Princeton University Press, 2020), 89-90.

[23] Wilbur Ross, "Mr. Trump Makes Some Good Points on Trade," *Wall Street Journal*, August 16, 2016, accessed June 6, 2021, https://www.wsj.com/articles/mr-trump-makes-some-good-points-on-trade-1471188728.

[24] Smith, *Wealth of Nations*, Vol. I, IV.iii.c.2, 488-489.

[25] See, for instance, Mary Amiti et al. "The Impact of the 2018 Tariffs on Prices and Welfare," *Journal of Economic Perspectives* 33, no. 4 (2019): 187–210; Eugenio Cerutti et al., "The Impact of US-China Trade Tensions," *IMFBlog Insights & Analysis on Economics and Finance*, May 23, 2019, accessed June 3, 2021, https://blogs.imf.org/2019/05/23/the-impact-of-us-china-trade-tensions/.

[26] See Aaron Flaaen and Justin Pierce, "Disentangling the Effects of the 2018-2019 Tariffs on a Globally Connected U.S. Manufacturing Sector," Finance and Economics Discussion Series 2019-086 (Washington, D.C.: Board of Governors of the Federal Reserve System, 2019).

[27] Douglas A. Irwin, "Trade Truths Will Outlast Trump," *Wall Street Journal*, November 19, 2021, accessed June 3, 2021, https://www.wsj.com/articles/trade-truths-will-outlast-trump-11605828052?mod=searchresults_pos3&page=1.

[28] See Shelly Jo Jacobs, "Trump's Metals Tariffs Added Some Jobs and Raised Consumer Prices," *New York Times*, May 30, 2019, accessed June 3, 2021, https://www.nytimes.com/2019/05/30/us/politics/norway-trump-aluminum-tariffs.html.

[29] Geoffrey Gertz, "Did Trump's tariffs benefit American workers and national security?" Brookings Institution, September 10, 2020, accessed June 3, 2021, https://www.brookings.edu/policy2020/votervital/did-trumps-tariffs-benefit-american-workers-and-national-security/.

[30] See Gary Clyde Hufbauer and Sean Lowry, "US Tire Tariffs: Saving Few Jobs at High Cost," Petersen Institute for International Economics, Policy Brief no. PB12-9, April 2012, accessed June 3, 2021, https://www.piie.com/publications/policy-briefs/us-tire-tariffs-saving-few-jobs-high-cost.

[31] Smith, *Wealth of Nations*, Vol. I, IV.ii.39, 468.

[32] Jennifer A. Dlouhy, "How China Beat the U.S. to Become World's Undisputed Solar Champion," *Bloomberg News*, June 4, 2021, accessed June 7, 2021, https://www.bloomberg.com/news/articles/2021-06-04/solar-jobs-2021-how-china-beat-u-s-to-become-world-s-solar-champion.

[33] Joan Robinson, *Essays in the Theory of Employment* (Oxford: Basil Blackwell, 1947), 158.

[34] See Robert Sobel, *The Age of Giant Corporations: A Microeconomic History of American Business, 1914–1970* (Westport: Greenwood Press, 1972), 87–88.

[35] See Douglas A. Irwin, *Peddling Protectionism: Smoot-Hawley and the Great Depression* (Princeton: Princeton University Press, 2011/2017), 144-183.

[36] See Scott Lincicome, "Manufactured Crisis: 'Deindustrialization,' Free Markets, and National Security," Cato Institute Policy Analysis no. 907, January 27, 2021: 5, accessed June 5, 2021, https://www.cato.org/publications/policy-analysis/manufactured-crisis-deindustrialization-free-markets-national-security?queryID=fecd5a4eacbc5f3571ed4f9c5b84b471#us-productive-capacity-remains-high.

[37] See Robert Z. Lawrence, "Recent US Manufacturing Employment: The Exception That Proves the Rule," Peterson Institute for International Economics Working Paper no. 17–12, November 2017, table 1.

[38] See Scott Lincicome, "Manufactured Crisis," 4.

[39] Ibid., 10.

[40] See ibid., 11.

[41] See Pierre Lemieux, *What's Wrong with Protectionism: Answering Common Objections to Free Trade* (Lanham, MD: Rowman and Littlefield, 2018), 46.

[42] See ibid., 49.

[43] See ibid., 47.

[44] Ibid., 48.

[45] Steven H. Woolf and Heidi Schoomaker, "Life Expectancy and Mortality Rates in the United States, 1959-2017," *Journal of the American Medical Association* 322, no. 20 (2019): 1996.

[46] Ibid.

[47] David H. Autor, David Dorn, and Gordon H. Hanson "The China Shock: Learning from Labor Market Adjustment to Large Changes in Trade," NBER Working Paper no. 21906, January 2016: 33-36, accessed June 9, 2021, https://www.nber.org/system/files/working_papers/w21906/w21906.pdf.

[48] Ibid., 38.

[49] See Charles Roxburgh et al., *Trading Myths: Addressing Misconceptions about Trade, Jobs, and Competitiveness* (New York: McKinsey Global Institute, 2012), 2, accessed June 9, 2021, https://www.mckinsey.com/~/media/McKinsey/Featured%20Insights/Employment%20and%20Growth/Six%20myths%20about%20trade/MGI%20Trading%20myths_ES_May%202012.pdf.

[50] See Michael Hicks and Srikant Devaraj, *The Myth and the Reality of Manufacturing in America* (Muncie, IN: Ball State University, Center for Business and Economic Research, June 2015 and April 2017): 2-7, accessed June 9, 2021, https://conexus.cberdata.org/files/MfgReality.pdf.

[51] See "Sharply Fewer in U.S. View Foreign Trade as Opportunity," March 31, 2021, accessed June 10, 2021, https://news.gallup.com/poll/342419/sharply-fewer-view-foreign-trade-opportunity.aspx.

[52] Smith, *Wealth of Nations*, Vol. I, I.xi.p.10, 267.

[53] Frank William Tausing, *The Tariff History of the United States: A Series of Essays* (New York & London: G.P. Putnam's Sons: The Knickerbocker Press, 1888), 229.

[54] Ibid.

[55] Ibid., 230-258.

[56] Irwin, *Peddling Protectionism*, 218.

[57] Ibid., 37.

[58] See Douglas A. Irwin and Anson Soderbery, "Optimal Tariffs and Trade Policy Formation: U.S. Evidence from the Smoot-Hawley Era," NBER Working Paper no. 29115, July 2021: 21, accessed August 10, 2021, https://www.nber.org/system/files/working_papers/w29115/w29115.pdf.

[59] Irwin, *Peddling Protectionism*, 99.

[60] Ibid.

[61] Ibid., 83.

[62] Irwin, *Free Trade Under Fire*, 203.

[63] Ibid., 202.

Chapter 3: The Trouble with Industrial Policy

[1] Clyde V. Prestowitz, *Trading Places: How We Are Giving Our Economic Future to Japan and How to Reclaim It* (New York: Basic Books, 1990), 493.

[2] See Aaron Wildavsky, "Industrial Policies in American Political Cultures," in *The Politics of Industrial Policy*, eds. Claude E. Barfield and William A. Schambra (Washington DC: AEI, 1986), 15.

[3] See Herbert Stein, "Commentaries," in *The Politics of Industrial Policy*, 87.

[4] Ellis W. Hawley, "'Industrial Policy' in the 1920s and 1930s," in *The Politics of Industrial Policy*, 63.

[5] Howard Pack and Kamal Saggi, "The Case for Industrial Policy: A Critical Survey," Policy Research Working Paper no. WPS 3839 (Washington, D.C.: World Bank Group, 2006), accessed June 18, 2021, http://documents. worldbank.org/curated/en/640951468138862957/The-case-for-industrial-policy-a-critical-survey.

[6] See Arthur Herman, "America Needs an Industrial Policy," *American Affairs* 3, no. 4 (Winter 2019), accessed June 18, 2021, https://americanaffairsjournal.org/2019/11/america-needs-an-industrial-policy/.

[7] See Robert B. Reich, *The Next American Frontier* (New York: Crown, 1983).

[8] Michelle Clark Neely, "The Pitfalls of Industrial Policy," Federal Reserve Bank of St. Louis, April 1, 1993, accessed June 18, 2021, https://www.stlouisfed.org/publications/regional-economist/april-1993/the-pitfalls-of-industrial-policy.

[9] World Bank Group, *The East Asia Miracle: Economic Growth and Public Policy* (New York: OUP, 1993), 6.

[10] See Edmund Phelps, *Mass Flourishing: How Grassroots Innovation Created Jobs, Challenge, and Change* (Princeton, NJ: Princeton University Press, 2013), 193-215.

[11] See Adam Thierer, *Permissionless Innovation* (Arlington, VA: Mercatus Center, 2014 and 2016).

[12] See Shane Greenstein, *How the Internet Became Commercial: Innovation, Privatization and the Birth of a New Network* (Princeton, NJ: Princeton University Press, 2015), 21.

[13] See ibid., 8.

[14] See "Mazzucato and the iPhone (II): The Myth of the Entrepreneurial State," accessed September 14, 2021, https://artir.wordpress.com/2015/08/21/mazzucato-and-the-iphone-ii-the-myth-of-the-entrepreneurial-state/.

[15] See Adam Thierer, "Industrial Policy as Casino Economics," *The Hill*, July 12, 2021, accessed September 23, 2021, https://thehill.com/opinion/finance/562525-industrial-policy-as-casino-economics.

[16] See Michael Beckley, Yusaku Horiuchi, and Jennifer M. Miller, "America's Role in the Making of Japan's Economic Miracle," *Journal of East Asian Studies* 18 (2018): 1-21.

[17] See Y. Kosai, "The postwar Japanese economy, 1945–1973," in *The Economic Emergence of Modern Japan*, ed. K. Yamamura (Cambridge: Cambridge University Press, 1997), 159-202.

[18] See K. Ohkawa and H. Rosovsky, "Capital formation in Japan," in *The Economic Emergence of Modern Japan*, 203-238.

[19] See Irwin, *Free Trade Under Fire*, 235.

[20] See Benjamin Powell, "Japan," *The Library of Economics and Liberty*, accessed June 16, 2021, https://www.econlib.org/library/Enc/Japan.html.

[21] See Arjan B. Keizer "Transformations in- and outside the internal labour market: Institutional Change and Continuity in Japanese employment practices," *The International Journal of Human Resource Management* 20, no.7 (2009): 1521-1535.

[22] See Robert Reich, *The Next American Frontier* (New York: Times Books, 1983), 50-55.

[23] Marcus Noland, "Industrial Policy, Innovation Policy, and Japanese Competitiveness," Peterson Institute for International Economics, Working Paper Series 07-4, May 2007: 6-10.

[24] Ibid., 10.

[25] See Irwin, *Free Trade Under Fire*, 234.

[26] Noland, "Industrial Policy, Innovation Policy, and Japanese Competitiveness," 11.

[27] See Richard Beason and David E. Weinstein, "Growth, economies of scale, and targeting in Japan (1955–90)," *Review of Economics and Statistics* 78, no.2 (1996): 286-95.

[28] David R. Henderson, "The Myth of MITI," *Fortune Magazine*, August 8, 1983, 113.

[29] Andrew Pollack, "'Fifth Generation' Became Japan's Lost Generation," *New York Times*, June 5, 1992, Section D, Page 1.

[30] Noland, "Industrial Policy, Innovation Policy, and Japanese Competitiveness," 11.

[31] Ibid.

[32] See Adam Thierer, "Japan Inc. and Other Tales of Industrial Policy Apocalypse," *Discourse*, June 28, 2021, accessed July 11, 2021, https://www.discoursemagazine.com/culture-and-society/2021/06/28/japan-inc-and-other-tales-of-industrial-policy-apocalypse/.

[33] See World Bank Group, "GDP Growth (annual %)-Japan," accessed May 5, 2021, https://data.worldbank.org/indicator/NY.GDP.MKTP.KD.ZG?end=2003&locations=JP&start=1991.

[34] Naoki Abe, "Japan's Shrinking Economy," Brookings Institution, February 12, 2010, accessed May 5, 2021, https://www.brookings.edu/opinions/japans-shrinking-economy/.

[35] See Issei Morita "Japanese Explode the Myth of MITI," *Financial Times*, June 27, 2002.

[36] Marco Rubio, "American Industrial Policy and the Rise of China," *American Mind*, October 12, 2019, accessed June 17, 2021, https://americanmind.org/memo/american-industrial-policy-and-the-rise-of-china/.

[37] Ibid.

[38] National Security Commission on Artificial Intelligence, "Final Report," March 19, 2021, accessed June 17, 2021, https://www.nscai.gov/wp-content/uploads/2021/03/Full-Report-Digital-1.pdf.

[39] Ibid.

[40] Ibid.

[41] Ibid.

[42] See Adam Thierer and Connor Haaland, "The Future of Innovation: Can European-Style Industrial Policies Create Tech Supremacy?" *Discourse*, February 11, 2021, accessed June 17, 2021, https://www.discoursemagazine.com/economics/2021/02/11/can-european-style-industrial-policies-create-technological-supremacy/.

[43] See Zuliu Hu and Mohsin S. Khan, "Why Is China Growing So Fast?" (Washington, D.C.: International Monetary Fund, 1997), accessed June 17, 2021, https://www.imf.org/external/pubs/ft/issues8/index.htm.

[44] See Yasheng Huang, *Capitalism with Chinese Characteristics* (Cambridge: Cambridge University Press, 2008).

[45] See Hu and Khan, "Why Is China Growing So Fast?"

[46] See Barry Naughton, *The Rise of China's Industrial Policy, 1978 to 2020* (Mexico City: National Autonomous University of Mexico, 2021).

[47] See ibid., 47.

[48] See Wei, "China's Xi Ramps Up Control of Private Sector."

[49] Lingling Wei, "Xi Jinping Aims to Rein In Chinese Capitalism, Hew to Mao's Socialist Vision," *Wall Street Journal*, September 20, 2021, accessed September 24, 2021, https://www.wsj.com/articles/xi-jinping-aims-to-rein-in-chinese-capitalism-hew-to-maos-socialist-vision-11632150725.

[50] See Hass, *Stronger*; and Michael Schuman "Don't Believe the China Hype," *The Atlantic*, June 16, 2020, accessed June 17, 2021, https://www.theatlantic.com/international/archive/2020/06/united-states-china-power-influence/612961/.

[51] International Monetary Fund, "People's Republic of China: 2021 Article IV Consultation-Press Release; Staff Report; and Statement by the Executive Director for the People's Republic of China," Country Report No. 2022/021, January 28, 2022: 11-12, accessed January 30, 2022, https://www.imf.org/en/Publications/CR/Issues/2022/01/26/Peoples-Republic-of-China-2021-Article-IV-Consultation-Press-Release-Staff-Report-and-512248.

[52] Ibid., 21-22.

[53] Naughton, *The Rise of China's Industrial Policy*, 108.

[54] See Michael Lelyveld, "China's Economic Growth Claims Raise Data Doubts," *Radio Free Asia*, October 23, 2020, accessed September 14, 2021, https://www.rfa.org/english/commentaries/energy_watch/recovery-10232020103243.html.

[55] See Liza Lin and Chu Han Wong, "China Increasingly Obscures True State of Its Economy to Outsiders," *Wall Street Journal*, December 6, 2021, accessed December 6, 2021, https://www.wsj.com/articles/china-data-security-law-ships-ports-court-cases-universities-11638803230?mod=hp_lead_pos5.

[56] See Scott Lincicome and Huan Zhu "Questioning Industrial Policy: Why Government Manufacturing Plans Are Ineffective and Unnecessary," White Paper, Cato Institute, Washington, D.C., September 28, 2021: 42-44, accessed September 29, 2021, https://www.cato.org/sites/cato.org/files/2021-09/white-paper-questioning-industrial-policy-updated.pdf.

[57] See Saheli Roy Choudhury, "China is still 'three or four generations' away from developing latest semiconductor tech, IDC says," *CNBC*, January 22, 2022, accessed January 30, 2022, https://www.cnbc.com/2022/01/20/idc-on-chinas-semiconductor-tech-ambitions.html.

[58] See Axel He, "After Decades of Catch-Up, China Needs to Rethink Its Innovation Strategy," Center for International Governance Innovation, October 26, 2020, accessed June 17, 2021, https://www.cigionline.org/articles/after-decades-catch-china-needs-rethink-its-innovation-strategy/.

[59] See Lincicome and Zhu, "Questioning Industrial Policy," 42-47.

[60] See also Michael Beckley, "The United States Should Fear a Faltering China," *Foreign Affairs*, October 28, 2019, accessed June 18, 2021, https://www.foreignaffairs.com/articles/china/2019-10-28/united-states-should-fear-faltering-china.

[61] See also Lily Fang, Josh Lerner, Chaopeng Wu and Qi Zhang, "Corruption, Government Subsidies, and Innovation: Evidence from China," NBER Working Paper no. 25098, September 2018, accessed June 17, 2021, https://www.nber.org/papers/w25098.

[62] Linda R. Cohen et al., *The Technology Pork Barrel* (Washington D.C.: Brookings Institutions, 1991), 365.

[63] Ibid., 71.

[64] Ibid., 53.

[65] See ibid, 392.

[66] See Lincicome and Zhu "Questioning Industrial Policy," 2.

[67] Ibid., 31-35.

[68] Ibid., 20-21.

[69] Ibid., 12-13, 18.

[70] Ibid., 19.

[71] Ibid., 18.

[72] Ibid., 17.

[73] Ibid., 37.

[74] Ibid., 9-12.

[75] See Lawrence Tabak, *Foxconned: Imaginary Jobs, Bulldozed Homes & and the Sacking of Local Government* (Chicago: University of Chicago Press, 2021), xiii.

[76] See ibid, 235-236.

[77] See David M. Hart, "Beyond the Technology Pork Barrel? An Assessment of the Obama Administration's Energy Demonstration Projects," *Energy Policy* 119 (2018): 367–376, accessed June 18, 2021, https://www.sciencedirect.com/science/article/pii/S0301421518302635?via%3Dihub.

[78] See Veronique de Rugy, Senior Research Fellow, Mercatus Center at George Mason University, "Testimony before the House Committee on Science, Space, and Technology, Subcommittee on Energy," 114th Cong., 1st sess., March 24, 2015, accessed June 18, 2021, https://www.mercatus.org/publications/government-spending/subsidies-are-problem-not-solution-innovation-energy.

[79] "Solyndra: Politics infused Obama energy program," *Washington Post*, December 11, 2011, accessed June 18, 2021, https://www.washingtonpost.com/solyndra-politics-infused-obama-energy-programs/2011/12/14/gIQA4HllHP_story.html.

Chapter 4: Business against the Market

[1] Business Roundtable, "Statement on the Purpose of a Corporation," August 19, 2019, accessed June 23, 2021, https://opportunity.businessroundtable.org/ourcommitment/.

[2] Milton Friedman, "The Social Responsibility of Business Is to Increase Its Profits," *New York Times Magazine*, September 13, 1970, accessed June 26, 2021, https://www.nytimes.com/1970/09/13/archives/a-friedman-doctrine-the-social-responsibility-of-business-is-to.html.

[3] See R. Edward Freedman, *Strategic Management: A Stakeholder Approach* (Cambridge: CUP, 1984/2010).

[4] See, for instance, Lynn Stout, *The Shareholder Value Myth: How Putting Shareholders First Harms Investors, Corporations, and the Public* (San Francisco, CA: Berrett-Koehler, Inc., 2012).

[5] See R. Edward Freedman et al., *Stakeholder Theory: The State of the Art* (Cambridge: CUP, 2010), 56.

[6] See Samantha Miles, "Stakeholder: Essentially Contested or Just Confused?" *Journal of Business Ethics* 108 (2012): 285–298.

[7] See Samantha Miles, "Stakeholder Theory Classification: A Theoretical and Empirical Evaluation of Definitions," *Journal of Business Ethics* 142 (3), 2017: 437-459.

[8] Freeman, *Strategic Management*, 25.

[9] See Lucian Bebchuk and Roberto Tallarita, "The Illusory Promise of Stakeholder Governance," *Cornell Law Review* 106 (2020): 91-178, accessed June 6, 2021, https://papers.ssrn.com/sol3/papers.cfm?abstract_id=3544978.

[10] See, for instance, "SASB Standards connect business and investors on the financial impacts of sustainability," accessed June 28, 2021, https://www.sasb.org/about/.

[11] See, for example, David Burton, "Nasdaq's Proposed Board-Diversity Rule Is Immoral and Has No Basis in Economics," Heritage Foundation Backgrounder no. 3591, March 9, 2021: 12-14.

[12] Ira Kay, Chris Brindisi and Blaine Martin, "The Stakeholder Model and ESG," Harvard Law School Forum on Corporate Governance, September 14, 2020, accessed October 26, 2021, https://corpgov.law.harvard.edu/2020/09/14/the-stakeholder-model-and-esg/.

[13] "Nasdaq to Advance Diversity through New Proposed Listing Requirements," accessed October 26, 2021, https://www.nasdaq.com/press-release/nasdaq-to-advance-diversity-through-new-proposed-listing-requirements-2020-12-01.

[14] See "Board Diversity Matrix Instructions," accessed October 26, 2021, https://listingcenter.nasdaq.com/assets/Board%20Diversity%20Disclosure%20Matrix.pdf.

[15] See Burton, "Nasdaq's Proposed Board-Diversity Rule Is Immoral and Has No Basis in Economics," 12.

[16] See ibid., 10.

[17] See Securities and Exchange Commission, (Release No. 34-92590; File Nos. SR-NASDAQ-2020-081; SR-NASDAQ-2020-082), accessed October 26, 2021, https://www.sec.gov/rules/sro/nasdaq/2021/34-92590.pdf.

[18] See Richard M. Reinsch II, "Larry Fink's Global Crusade to Advance Identity Politics," *Daily Signal*, January 28, 2022, accessed February 1, 2022, https://www.dailysignal.com/2022/01/28/larry-fink-esg-capitalism/

[19] Paul G. Mahoney and Julia D. Mahoney, "The New Separation of Ownership and Control: Institutional Investors and ESG," *Columbia Business Law Review* 2 (2021): 842-3.

[20] See Mark J. Roe, "Takeover Politics," in *The Deal Decade: What Takeovers and Leveraged Buyouts Mean for Corporate Governance*, ed. Margaret M. Blair (Washington, D.C.: Brookings Institution Press, 1993): 321, 338.

[21] See Stephen Bainbridge, "Four Answers to 'Why did the Business Roundtable Release its Statement on Corporate Purpose?'" August 19, 2019, accessed June 27, 2021, https://www.professorbainbridge.com/professorbainbridgecom/2019/08/three-answers-to-why-did-the-business-roundtable-release-its-statement-on-corporate-purpose.html.

[22] Paul G. Mahoney and Julia D. Mahoney, "'ESG' Disclosure and Securities Regulation," *Regulation* 44, no. 3 (2021): 12.

[23] See "Biden unveils economic plan, calls for end to shareholder capitalism," *Yahoo Finance*, July 10, 2020, accessed June 26, 2021, https://www.yahoo.com/lifestyle/biden-unveils-economic-plan-calls-153218779.html.

[24] Rebecca Henderson, *Reimagining Capitalism in a World of Fire* (New York, NY: Public Affairs, 2020), 11.

[25] See "Conservatives Should Ensure Workers a Seat at the Table," *American Compass*, September 6, 2020, accessed July 10, 2021, https://americancompass.org/essays/conservatives-should-ensure-workers-a-seat-at-the-table/.

26 See Klaus Schwab, "Why we need the 'Davos Manifesto' for a better kind of capitalism," December 1, 2019, accessed June 26, 2021, https://www.feelingeurope.eu/Pages/Klaus_Schwab_letter.pdf.

27 Klaus Schwab, "Davos Manifesto 2020: The Universal Purpose of a Company in the Fourth Industrial Revolution," accessed June 25, 2021, https://www.weforum.org/agenda/2019/12/davos-manifesto-2020-the-universal-purpose-of-a-company-in-the-fourth-industrial-revolution/.

28 Ibid.

29 Klaus Schwab with Peter Vanham, "What is stakeholder capitalism?" January 22, 2021, accessed June 27, 2021, https://www.weforum.org/agenda/2021/01/klaus-schwab-on-what-is-stakeholder-capitalism-history-relevance/.

30 See Samuel Gregg, *Becoming Europe* (New York: Encounter Books, 2013), 56-59.

31 See Wilhelm Röpke, "Fascist Economics," *Economica* 2, no. 5 (1935): 85-100.

32 See Constitution of the Italian Republic, Art. 41, accessed June 27, 2021, https://www.senato.it/documenti/repository/istituzione/costituzione_inglese.pdf.

33 See ibid., Art. 46.

34 See *Charter of the Fundamental Rights of the European Union*, Chapter IV, Article 27, December 18, 2000, accessed June 27, 2021, https://www.europarl.europa.eu/charter/pdf/text_en.pdf.

35 See Phelps, *Mass Flourishing*, 135-169.

36 See Nadia E. Nedzel, *The Rule of Law, Economic Development, and Corporate Governance* (Cheltenham: Edward Elgar, 2021), 213-217.

37 See Howard J. Wiarda, *Corporatism and Development* (Amherst: The University of Massachusetts Press, 1977).

38 See Mark Landler, "Volkswagen Corruption Trial Includes Seamy Testimony," *New York Times*, January 16, 2008, accessed June 27, 2021, https://www.nytimes.com/2008/01/16/business/16bribe.html.

39 Kate Connelly, "Bribery, Brothels, Free Viagra: VW trial Scandalises Germany," *The Guardian*, January 13, 2008, accessed June 27, 2008, https://www.theguardian.com/world/2008/jan/13/germany.automotive.

40 Stephen Bainbridge, *Corporate Law* 4th. ed. (St. Paul, MN: Foundation Press, 2020), 3.

41 Ibid., 98.

42 See Stephen R. Soukup, *The Dictatorship of Woke Capital: How Political Correctness Captured Big Business* (New York: Encounter Books, 2021), 35-48.

43 See Vivek Ramaswamy, *Woke, Inc.: Inside Corporate America's Social Justice Scam* (New York: Hachette Book Group, Inc., 2021), 56-81.

44 Jonathan Haidt and Greg Lukianoff, "How To Keep Your Corporation Out of the Culture War," *Persuasion*, December 3, 2021, accessed December 7, 2021, https://www.persuasion.community/p/haidt-and-lukianoff-how-to-end-corporate.

45 See Khadeeja Safdar and Andrew Beaton, "Nike Nixes 'Betsy Ross Flag' Sneaker after Colin Kaepernick Intervenes," *Wall Street Journal*, July 1, 2019, accessed June 27, 2021, https://www.wsj.com/articles/nike-nixes-betsy-ross-flag-sneaker-after-colin-kaepernick-intervenes-11562024126.

46 See Courtney Connley, "Jack Dorsey, Emily Weiss and 185 other CEOs sign letter calling abortion bans 'bad for business'," *CNBC*, June 10, 2019, accessed June 27, 2021, https://www.cnbc.com/2019/06/09/nearly-200-ceos-sign-letter-calling-abortion-bans-bad-for-business.html.

47 See Sarah Steimer, "Sell to Voters, Not Consumers," American Marketing Association, June 13, 2019, accessed June 27, 2021, https://www.ama.org/marketing-news/sell-to-voters-not-consumers/.

48 "#BrandsGetReal: Championing Change in the Age of Social Media," accessed June 27, 2021, https://sproutsocial.com/insights/data/championing-change-in-the-age-of-social-media/.

49 See "The Generation Gap in American Politics," Pew Research Center, March 1, 2018, accessed June 27, 2021, https://www.pewresearch.org/politics/2018/03/01/the-generation-gap-in-american-politics/.

50 See Richard Hanania, "Woke Institutions is Just Civil Rights Law," *Hanania Newsletter*, June 1, 2021, accessed October 7, 2021, https://richardhanania.substack.com/p/woke-institutions-is-just-civil-rights.

51 Richard Hanania, "The Weakness of Conservative Anti-Wokeness," *American Affairs* 5, no.4 (2021): 174, accessed January 30, 2022, https://americanaffairsjournal.org/2021/11/the-weakness-of-conservative-anti-wokeness/.

52 Ibid., 175.

[53] Friedman, "The Social Responsibility of Business Is to Increase Its Profits."

[54] Todd Zywicki, "Extending the Culture Wars," *Regulation* 44, no. 3 (2021), accessed October 25, 2021, https://www.cato.org/regulation/fall-2021/extending-culture-wars#.

[55] See Lucian A. Bebchuk and Roberto Tallarita, "Will Corporations Deliver Value to All Stakeholders?" August 5, 2021, accessed January 27, 2022, http://dx.doi.org/10.2139/ssrn.3899421.

[56] Stephen Bainbridge, "Making Sense of The Business Roundtable's Reversal on Corporate Purpose," *Journal of Corporation Law* 46, no. 2 (2021): 318, accessed September 17, 2021, https://ssrn.com/abstract=3664078.

[57] See Bebchuk and Tallarita, "Will Corporations Deliver Value to All Stakeholders?"

Chapter 5: Creative Nation

[1] See Charles L. Morris, *The Dawn of Innovation: The First American Industrial Revolution* (New York: Public Affairs, 2012).

[2] Alexis de Tocqueville, *Journey to America*, trans. George Lawrence (New Haven: Yale University, 1959), 271.

[3] See, for example, ibid., 75.

[4] Alexis de Tocqueville, *Democracy in America*, ed. Eduardo Nolla, trans. James T. Schleifer, A Bilingual French-English Edition, Vol. 3 (Indianapolis: Liberty Fund, 2010), 944.

[5] Ibid., Vol. 2, 516.

[6] Tocqueville, *Journey*, 269.

[7] See Janet Yellen, "Perspectives on Inequality and Opportunity from the Survey of Consumer Finances," Remarks at the Conference on Economic Opportunity and Inequality, Boston, Mass., October 17, 2014, accessed July 19, 2021, https://www.federalreserve.gov/newsevents/speech/yellen20141017a.pdf.

[8] See Daron Acemoglu et al., "Innovation, Reallocation, and Growth," *American Economic Review* 108, no. 11 (2018): 3450-3491, accessed July 7, 2021, https://www.aeaweb.org/articles?id=10.1257/aer.20130470.

[9] See John Haltiwanger et al., "High Growth Young Firms: Contribution to Job, Output, and Productivity Growth," in *Measuring Entrepreneurial Businesses: Current Knowledge and Challenges*, eds. John Haltiwanger et al. (Chicago: University of Chicago Press, September 2017), 11-62, accessed July 19, 2021, https://www.nber.org/books-and-chapters/measuring-entrepreneurial-businesses-current-knowledge-and-challenges/high-growth-young-firms-contribution-job-output-and-productivity-growth.

[10] See Ewing Marion Kauffman Foundation, "Who is the Entrepreneur? The Changing Diversity of New Entrepreneurs in the United States, 1996–2020," *Trends in Entrepreneurship* (Kansas City, Ms: Ewing Marion Kauffman Foundation, 2021), 3-5.

[11] See Ben Wilterdink, "Survey on American Attitudes—2021," *Archbridge Notes*, September 30, 2021, accessed October 1, 2021, https://medium.com/archbridge-notes/survey-on-american-attitudes-2021-ea65869a3670.

[12] See Congressional Budget Office, "Federal Policies in Response to Declining Entrepreneurship," December 2020, 1-3, accessed July 20, 2021, https://www.cbo.gov/system/files/2020-12/56906-entrepreneurship.pdf.

[13] See ibid.

[14] See Chris Edwards, "Entrepreneurs and Regulations: Removing State and Local Barriers to New Businesses," Policy Analysis no. 916, Cato Institute, Washington, DC, May 4, 2021: 3, accessed July 22, 2021, https://www.cato.org/sites/cato.org/files/2021-05/pa-916.pdf.

[15] See Frederic M. Scherer, *Industrial Market Structure and Economic Performance*, 2nd ed. (Boston, MA: Houghton Mifflin, 1980), 437–438.

[16] See CBO, "Federal Policies in Response to Declining Entrepreneurship," 1.

[17] See ibid.

[18] See ibid., 10.

[19] Harvey Leibenstein, *General X-Efficiency Theory and Economic Development* (Oxford: Oxford University Press, 1978), 9.

[20] Israel Kirzner, *Discovery and the Capitalist Process* (Chicago: University of Chicago Press, 1985), 3.

[21] Oswald von Nell-Breuning, S.J., "Socio-Economic Life," in *Commentary on the Documents of Vatican II*, ed. H. Vorgrimler, Vol.5 (New York: Herder and Herder, 1969): 291.

[22] Ibid., 299.

[23] See Wilhelm Röpke, *A Humane Economy* (Wilmington, DE: ISI Books, 2014), 30.

[24] Ludwig von Mises, *Human Action: A Treatise on Economics*, 3rd rev.ed. (Chicago: Henry Regnery, 1966), 255.

[25] See ibid, 2.

[26] Ibid., 13.

[27] Ibid., 255.

[28] See Antoinette Schoar, "The Divide Between Subsistence and Transformational Entrepreneurship," in *Innovation Policy and the Economy*, eds. Josh Lerner and Scott Stern (Washington D.C.: National Bureau of Economic Research, 2010), 57-81.

[29] Wolfgang Kasper and Manfred E. Streit, *Institutional Economics: Social Order and Public Policy* (Cheltenham: The Locke Institute/Edward Elgar, 1998), 243.

[30] See CBO, "Federal Policies in Response to Declining Entrepreneurship," 12.

[31] See Ryan Decker et al., "The Role of Entrepreneurship in US Job Creation and Economic Dynamism," *Journal of Economic Perspectives* 28, no.3 (2014): 7–8, accessed July 20, 2021, www.aeaweb.org/articles?id=10.1257/jep.28.3.3.

[32] See Daron Acemoglu et al., "Innovation, Reallocation, and Growth," *American Economic Review* 108, no. 11 (2018): 3468, 3471, accessed July 20, 2021, https://www.aeaweb.org/articles/pdf/doi/10.1257/aer.20130470.

[33] See Alfred D. Chandler Jr., *Scale and Scope: The Dynamics of Industrial Capitalism* (Cambridge, MA: Belknap Press, 1994).

[34] See Robert D. Atkinson and Michael Lind, *Big Is Beautiful: Debunking the Myth of Small Business* (Cambridge, MA: MIT Press, 2018).

[35] Some forms of R&D require companies with resources far larger than those possessed by small new businesses. See Ufuk Akcigit and Sina T. Ates, "Ten Facts on Declining Business Dynamism and Lessons from Endogenous Growth Theory," NBER Working Paper no. 25755, April 2019, accessed July 20, 2021, www.nber.org/papers/w25755.

[36] See Jorge Guzman and Scott Stern, "The State of American Entrepreneurship: New Estimates of the Quality and Quantity of Entrepreneurship for 32 US States, 1988-2014," NBER Working Paper no. 22095, March 2016, Revision Date July 2019, accessed July 20, 2021, https://www.nber.org/papers/w22095.

[37] See, for example, Hal Varian, "Automation versus Procreation (Aka Bots Versus Tots)," VoxEU, March 30, 2020, accessed July 22, 2021, https://voxeu.org/article/automation-versus-procreation-aka-bots-versus-tots.

[38] See Russell S. Sobel, "Missing: Entrepreneurship in Economic Education," *Library of Law and Economics*, August 20, 2020, accessed July 22, 2021, https://www.econlib.org/library/Columns/y2020/Sobelentrepreneurship.html.

[39] See Kasper and Streit, *Institutional Economics*, 243.

[40] See ibid., 242.

[41] See Richard Swedberg, *Tocqueville's Political Economy* (Princeton, NJ: Princeton University Press, 2009), 252-53.

[42] My emphasis.

[43] See, for example, Zoltán J. Ács et al., "The Global Entrepreneurship Index 2019," The Global Entrepreneurship and Development Institute, Washington, D.C., 2020, accessed July 20, 2021, https://thegedi.org/wp-content/uploads/2020/01/GEI_2019_Final-1.pdf.

[44] Heritage Foundation, "United States," *Index of Economic Freedom* (2022), accessed February 14, 2022, https://www.heritage.org/index/country/unitedstates.

[45] Edmund S. Phelps, "Economic Culture and Economic Performance: What Light Is Shed on the Continent's Problem?" *Perspectives on the Performance of the Continental Economies*, eds. Edmund S. Phelps et al. (Cambridge, MA: MIT Press, 2011), 447-8.

[46] Cited in Arnold Kling and Nick Schulz, *From Poverty to Prosperity: Intangible Assets, Hidden Liabilities and the Lasting Triumph over Scarcity* (New York: Encounter Books, 2009), 204.

[47] Edmund S. Phelps, "Macroeconomics for a Modern Economy," Prize Lecture to the Memory of Alfred Nobel, 8 December 2006, accessed July 21, 2021, http://nobelprize.org/nobel_prizes/economics/laureates/2006/phelps_lecture.pdf.

[48] Edmund S. Phelps, "Economic Culture and Economic Performance", 449.

[49] See Russ Roberts, "The Economist as Scapegoat," January 30, 2020, accessed July 22, 2021, https://russroberts.medium.com/the-economist-as-scapegoat-91b317a6823e.

[50] See Clyde Wayne Crews Jr., *Ten Thousand Commandments: An Annual Snapshot of the Federal Regulatory State, 2020 Edition* (Washington, D.C.: Competitive Enterprise Institute, 2020), 97.

[51] See Keith B. Belton and John D. Graham, "Deregulation under Trump," *Regulation* 43, no.2 (2020): 16-17.

[52] Ibid., 17.

[53] See U.S. Government, "Agencies: Partner Agencies," accessed July 22, 2021, www.regulations.gov/agencies.

[54] One effort to estimate how extensive state regulation extends throughout America may be found at the Mercatus Center's QuantGov website, "State RegData," accessed July 22, 2021, www.quantgov.org/state-regdata.

[55] See, for example, Germán Gutiérrez and Thomas Philippon, "The Failure of Free Entry," NBER Working Paper no. 26001 (2019), accessed July 22, 2021, http://www.nber.org/papers/w26001.

[56] See Michael Mandel and Diana G. Carew, "Regulatory Improvement Commission: A Politically-Viable Approach to U.S. Regulatory Reform," Progressive Policy Institute Policy Memo, May 2013: 3, accessed July 22, 2021, https://www.progressivepolicy.org/publication/regulatory-improvement-commission-a-politically-viable-approach-to-u-s-regulatory-reform/.

[57] See Edwards, "Entrepreneurs and Regulations," 7-8.

[58] See H. Beales et al., "Government Regulation: The Good, The Bad, & The Ugly," released by the Regulatory Transparency Project of the Federalist Society, June 12, 2017, accessed October 28, 2021, https://regproject.org/wp-content/uploads/RTP-Regulatory-Process-Working-Group-Paper.pdf.

[59] Department of the Treasury Office of Economic Policy, the Council of Economic Advisers, and the Department of Labor, "Occupational Licensing: A Framework for Policymakers," July 2015, accessed July 22, 2021, https://obamawhitehouse.archives.gov/sites/default/files/docs/licensing_report_final_nonembargo.pdf.

[60] See CBO, "Federal Policies in Response to Declining Entrepreneurship," 14.

[61] See Samuel Kortum and Josh Lerner, "Assessing the Contribution of Venture Capital to Innovation," *The RAND Journal of Economics* 31, no. 4 (2000): 674-692, accessed July 21, 2021, https://www.jstor.org/stable/2696354.

[62] See Samuel Gregg, "Founding Financial Father," *Law and Liberty*, April 23, 2018, accessed July 22, 2021, https://lawliberty.org/founding-financial-father/.

[63] See V. Hwang, S. Desai, and R. Baird, "Access to Capital for Entrepreneurs: Removing Barriers" (Kansas City: Ewing Marion Kauffman Foundation, 2019): 5, accessed July 25, 2021, https://www.kauffman.org/wp-content/uploads/2019/12/CapitalReport_042519.pdf.

[64] See Steven J. Davis and John C. Haltiwanger, "Dynamism Diminished: The Role of Housing Markets and Credit Conditions," NBER Working Paper no. 25466 (January 2019), accessed July 25, 2021, www.nber.org/papers/w25466.

[65] See Tad DeHaven, "Ten Problems with Small Business Administration Subsidies," *Discourse*, Mercatus Center, George Mason University, May 3, 2018, accessed October 1, 2021, https://www.mercatus.org/bridge/commentary/ten-problems-small-business-administration-subsidies.

[66] See Josh Lerner, "Government Incentives for Entrepreneurship," NBER Working Paper no. 26884, March 2020: 2-3, accessed July 25, 2021, https://www.nber.org/papers/w26884.

[67] See Jason Rowley, "Chinese Startups Net Smallest Share of Global VC Investment in Years," *Crunchbase News*, July 18, 2019, accessed July 25, 2021, https://news.crunchbase.com/news/chinese-startups-net-smallest-share-of-global-vc-investment-in-years/.

[68] See Lerner, "Government Incentives for Entrepreneurship," 11.

[69] See ibid., 16.

[70] See Ufuk Akcigit, Salomé Baslandze, and Francesca Lotti, "Connecting to Power: Political Connections, Innovation, and Firm Dynamics," NBER Working Paper no. 25136, April 2020, accessed July 25, 2021, https://www.nber.org/papers/w25136.

[71] See Sari P. Kerr and William R. Kerr, "Immigrant Entrepreneurship," in *Measuring Entrepreneurial Businesses: Current Knowledge and Challenges*, eds. John Haltiwanger et al. (Chicago, University of Chicago Press, 2017), 187-249.

[72] See Wil Schroter, "Top 10 Business Crowdfunding Campaigns Of All Time, *Forbes*, April 16, 2014, accessed

October 29, 2021, https://www.forbes.com/sites/wilschroter/2014/04/16/top-10-business-crowdfunding-campaigns-of-all-time/?sh=6e842ceb3e9f; and Emily Heaslip, "9 Wildly Successful Crowdfunded Startups," U.S. Chamber of Commerce, October 1, 2019, accessed October 29, 2021, https://www.uschamber.com/co/start/startup/successful-crowdfunded-startups.

[73] See J. Wallmeroth, P. Wirtz, and A. Groh, "Venture capital, angel financing, and crowdfunding of entrepreneurial ventures: A literature review," *Foundations and Trends in Entrepreneurship* 14, no. 1 (2017): 1-129.

[74] See Hwang et al., "Access to Capital for Entrepreneurs: Removing Barriers."

[75] See Samuel Gregg, *For God and Profit: How Banking and Finance Can Serve the Common Good* (New York: Crossroad Publishing, 2016), 39-66.

[76] See Julian L. Simon, *The State of Humanity* (Oxford: Blackwell, 1995).

[77] See Congressional Budget Office, "A Description of the Immigrant Population-2013 Update" (May 2013), accessed July 26, 2021, www.cbo.gov/publication/44134; and "The Foreign-Born Population and Its Effects on the U.S. Economy and the Federal Budget-An Overview," January 2020, accessed July 26, 2021, www.cbo.gov/publication/55967.

[78] See Sari P. Kerr and William R. Kerr, "Immigrant Entrepreneurship in America: Evidence From the Survey of Business Owners 2007 and 2012," *Research Policy* 49, no. 3 (April 2020), article 103918, accessed July 26, 2021, https://tinyurl.com/y2dqnan7; and Sari Pekkala Kerr and William Kerr, "Immigrants Play a Disproportionate Role in American Entrepreneurship," *Harvard Business Review*, October 3, 2016, accessed July 26, 2021, https://hbr.org/2016/10/immigrants-play-a-disproportionate-role-in-american-entrepreneurship.

[79] See William R. Kerr, "High-Skilled Immigration, Innovation, and Entrepreneurship: Empirical Approaches and Evidence," in *The International Mobility of Talent and Innovation: New Evidence and Policy Implications*, eds. Carsten Fink and Ernest Miguelez (Cambridge: Cambridge University Press, 2017), 193-221.

[80] Vivek Wadhwa et al., "America's New Immigrant Entrepreneurs: Part I", Duke Science, Technology & Innovation Paper no. 23 (January 4, 2007), accessed July 26, 2021, http://dx.doi.org/10.2139/ssrn.990152.

[81] See *Open for Business: Migrant Entrepreneurship in OECD Countries* (Paris: OECD, 2010).

[82] See Peter Vandor, "Why Immigrants are more likely to become entrepreneurs," *Harvard Business Review*, August 4, 2021, accessed October 21, 2021, https://hbr.org/2021/08/research-why-immigrants-are-more-likely-to-become-entrepreneurs.

[83] See Michael Walsh and Conor Peters, "Population Growth and Firm Dynamics," NBER Working Paper no. 29424, October 2021: 40, accessed November 2, 2021, http://www.nber.org/papers/w29424.

[84] See ibid., Abstract.

[85] See J. Liang, H. Wang, and E. P. Lazear, "Demographics and Entrepreneurship," *Journal of Political Economy* 126, s.1 (2018): S140–S196.

[86] See ibid.

[87] See Gideon Bornstein, "Entry and Profits in an Aging Economy: The Role of Consumer Inertia" (2020), accessed July 26, 2021, https://www.lse.ac.uk/economics/Assets/Documents/seminars/mcrw-seminar-papers/entry-and-profits-in-an-ageing-economy-the-role-of-consumer-inertia.pdf.

[88] See Andrew M. Baxter and Alex Nowrasteh, "A Brief History of U.S. Immigration Policy from the Colonial Period to the Present Day," Cato Policy Analysis no. 919, August 3, 2021: 3, accessed October 1, 2021, https://www.cato.org/policy-analysis/brief-history-us-immigration-policy-colonial-period-present-day#.

[89] See John Rawls, *The Law of Peoples, With "The Idea of Public Reason Revisited"* (Harvard: Harvard University Press, 2001); and John Finnis, "Migration Rights," in *Human Rights and Common Good*, Vol. III, *The Collected Essays of John Finnis* (Oxford: OUP, 2011), 116-124.

[90] See Thomas Aquinas, *Summa Theologiae*, ed. T. Gilby (Oxford: Blackfriars, 1963), q.66, a.2.

[91] See ibid., q.66, a.7.

[92] Baxter and Nowrasteh, "A Brief History of U.S. Immigration Policy from the Colonial Period to the Present Day," 3-4.

[93] See Samuel Gregg, "Shedding Light on Progressivism's Dark Side," *Public Discourse*, January 26, 2017, accessed October 1, 2021, https://www.thepublicdiscourse.com/2017/01/18550/.

[94] Baxter and Nowrasteh, "A Brief History of U.S. Immigration Policy from the Colonial Period to the Present Day," 1.

[95] Röpke, *A Humane Economy*, 30.

Chapter 6: Competitive Nation

[1] Tocqueville, *Democracy in America*, Vol. 3, 945.

[2] Phelps, *Mass Flourishing*, 166-167.

[3] Ibid.

[4] Robert D. Atkinson, "No, Monopoly has not grown," *National Review*, October 18, 2021, accessed October 27, 2021, https://www.nationalreview.com/2021/10/no-monopoly-has-not-grown/.

[5] See Jay Shambaugh et al., "The State of Competition and Dynamism: Facts about Concentration, Start-Ups, and Related Policies," The Hamilton Project, June 2018, accessed August 4, 2021, https://www.hamiltonproject.org/assets/files/CompetitionFacts_20180611.pdf.

[6] See ibid.

[7] Thomas Philippon, *The Great Reversal: How America Gave Up on Free Markets* (Cambridge, MA: Belknap Press, 2019), 205.

[8] Heritage Foundation, "United States," *Index of Economic Freedom* (2022).

[9] Council of Economic Advisors, "Labor Market Monopsony: Trends, Consequences, and Policy Responses," October 2016: 2, accessed August 3, 2021, https://obamawhitehouse.archives.gov/sites/default/files/page/files/20161025_labor_mrkt_monopsony_cea.pdf.

[10] Ibid., 4.

[11] Ibid., 10.

[12] "Executive Order on Promoting Competition in the American Economy," July 9, 2021, accessed August 3, 2021, https://www.whitehouse.gov/briefing-room/presidential-actions/2021/07/09/executive-order-on-promoting-competition-in-the-american-economy/.

[13] See Amy Klobuchar, *Antitrust: Taking on Monopoly Power from the Gilded Age to the Digital Age* (New York: Alfred A. Knopf, 2021), 175-214.

[14] See Josh Hawley, *The Tyranny of Big Tech* (Washington, D.C.: Regnery, 2021).

[15] Don Lavoie, *National Economic Planning: What's Left* (Arlington, VA: Mercatus Center, 2016), 38.

[16] James Pethokoukis, "5 questions for Thomas Philippon on the decline of free markets in the US," *AEI Ideas Blog*, February 11, 2020, accessed July 28, 2021, https://www.aei.org/economics/5-questions-for-thomas-philippon-on-the-decline-of-free-markets-in-the-us/.

[17] Wilhelm Röpke, *Economics of the Free Society* (Chicago: Henry Regnery Company, 1960), 237.

[18] This paragraph draws on Lavoie, *National Economic Planning*, 6.

[19] See Joseph A. Schumpeter, *Capitalism, Socialism, and Democracy* (New York: Harper & Brothers, 1942), 84.

[20] Simeon Alder, David Lagakos, and Lee Ohanian, "Competitive Pressure and the Decline of the Rust Belt: A Macroeconomic Analysis," NBER Working Paper no. 23583, October 2014: 2, accessed January 30, 2022, https://www.nber.org/system/files/working_papers/w20538/w20538.pdf.

[21] See "Executive Order: Steps to Increase Competition and Better Inform Consumers and Workers to Support Continued Growth of the American Economy," April 15, 2016, accessed August 3, 2021, https://obamawhitehouse.archives.gov/the-press-office/2016/04/15/executive-order-steps-increase-competition-and-better-inform-consumers.

[22] See ibid.

[23] See Clyde Wayne Crews Jr., "Why President Barack Obama's Executive Order on Competition Is Anti-Competitive," *Forbes*, April 15, 2016, accessed August 3, 2021, https://www.forbes.com/sites/waynecrews/2016/04/15/why-president-barack-obamas-executive-order-on-competition-is-anti-competitive/?sh=27590d5525ad.

[24] Heather Boushey and Helen Knudsen, "The Importance of Competition for the American Economy," July 7, 2021, accessed August 3, 2021, https://www.whitehouse.gov/cea/blog/2021/07/09/the-importance-of-competition-for-the-american-economy/.

[25] See "Executive Order on Promoting Competition in the American Economy," July 9, 2021.

[26] See ibid.

[27] Daren Bakst, Gabriella Beaumont-Smith, and Peter St. Onge, "Biden's 'Competition' Executive Order Realizes a Central Planner's Dream," *Daily Signal*, July 15, 2021, accessed August 3, 2021, https://www.dailysignal.com/2021/07/13/bidens-competition-executive-order-is-a-central-planners-dream/.

[28] See John McGinnis, "Abandoning the Consumer Welfare Standard," *Law and Liberty*, August 26, 2021, accessed September 23, 2021, https://lawliberty.org/abandoning-the-consumer-welfare-standard/.

[29] George J. Stigler, "Monopoly," accessed August 4, 2021, https://www.econlib.org/library/Enc/Monopoly.html.

[30] See Maureen K. Ohlhausen, "Does the U.S. Economy Lack Competition?" *The Criterion Journal on Innovation* 1 (2016): 51, accessed August 4, 2021, https://www.ftc.gov/system/files/documents/public_statements/982433/ohlhausen_-_does_the_us_economy_lack_competition_8-30-16.pdf.

[31] Ibid. See Harold Demsetz, "Industry Structure, Market Rivalry and Public Policy," *Journal of Law and Economics* 16, no.1 (1973): 1-9.

[32] Council of Economic Advisors, "Labor Market Monopsony: Trends, Consequences, and Policy Responses," 10.

[33] See Robert D. Atkinson and Filipe Lage de Sousa, "No, Monopoly had not Grown," Information Technology and Innovation Foundation, June 7, 2021, accessed September 21, 2021, https://itif.org/sites/default/files/2021-no-monopoly-has-not-grown.pdf.

[34] David Henderson, "The Decline of Competition?" *Defining Ideas*, August 20, 2020, accessed July 28, 2021, https://www.hoover.org/research/decline-competition.

[35] Ibid.

[36] See Atkinson, "No, Monopoly has not Grown."

[37] Pethokoukis, "5 questions for Thomas Philippon on the decline of free markets in the US."

[38] Ryan Bourne, "Is This Time Different? Schumpeter, The Tech Giants, and Monopoly Fatalism," Cato Institute Policy Analysis no. 872, June 17, 2019: 2, accessed August 4, 2021, https://www.cato.org/sites/cato.org/files/2019-09/Is%20This%20Time%20Different%3F.pdf.

[39] Pethokoukis, "5 questions for Thomas Philippon on the decline of free markets in the US."

[40] Lavoie, *National Economic Planning: What's Left*, 132.

[41] Röpke, *Economics of the Free Society*, 162-63.

[42] Wilhelm Röpke, *The Social Crisis of Our Time* (New Brunswick, NJ: Transaction Publishers, 1942/1992), 231.

[43] Stigler, "Monopoly."

[44] Ibid.

[45] Ibid.

[46] See Gordon Tullock "The welfare costs of tariffs, monopolies, and theft," *Economic Inquiry* 5, no.3 (1967): 224-232.

[47] For a comprehensive survey and analysis, see Marcus Olson, *The Rise and Decline of Nations: Economic Growth, Stagflation, and Economic Rigidities* (New Haven: Yale University Press, 1982).

[48] Germán Gutiérrez and Thomas Philippon, "Declining Competition and Investment in the US," NBER Working Paper no. 23583, July 2017: 56, accessed August 4, 2021, https://www.nber.org/system/files/working_papers/w23583/w23583.pdf.

[49] Ibid., 1.

[50] See James Bailey and Diana Thomas, "Regulating Away Competition: The Effect of Regulation on Entrepreneurship and Employment," Mercatus Working Paper (Arlington, VA: Mercatus Center at George Mason University, September 2015), accessed August 4, 2021, https://www.mercatus.org/publications/regulation/regulating-away-competition-effect-regulation-entrepreneurship-and.

[51] See ibid.

[52] Henderson, "The Decline of Competition?"

[53] Cited in Asher Schechter, "The Lack of Competition Has Deprived American Workers of $1.25 Trillion of Income," *Promarket: The Publication of the Stigler Center at the University of Chicago Booth School of Business*, December 9, 2019, accessed August 4, 2021, https://promarket.org/2019/12/09/the-lack-of-competition-has-deprived-american-workers-of-1-25-trillion-of-income/.

[54] See James E. Bessen, "Accounting for Rising Corporate Profits: Intangibles or Regulatory Rents?" June 19, 2016, accessed August 4, 2021, https://corpgov.law.harvard.edu/2016/06/10/accounting-for-rising-corporate-profits-intangibles-or-regulatory-rents/.

[55] Ibid.

[56] Ibid.

[57] See, for example, Mark Zuckerberg, "The Internet needs new rules. Let's start in these four areas," *Washington*

Post, March 30, 2019, accessed September 15, 2021, https://www.washingtonpost.com/opinions/mark-zuckerberg-the-internet-needs-new-rules-lets-start-in-these-four-areas/2019/03/29/9e6f0504-521a-11e9-a3f7-78b7525a8d5f_story.html.

[58] Pethokoukis, "5 questions for Thomas Philippon on the decline of free markets in the US."

[59] Stigler, "Monopoly."

[60] Mark Weinstein, "I Changed My Mind—Facebook is a Monopoly," *Wall Street Journal,* October 1, 2021, accessed October 7, 2021, https://www.wsj.com/articles/facebook-is-monopoly-metaverse-users-advertising-platforms-competition-mewe-big-tech-11633104247.

[61] Cited in Schechter, "The Lack of Competition Has Deprived American Workers of $1.25 Trillion of Income."

[62] See Ohlhausen, "Does the U.S. Economy Lack Competition?" 55.

[63] See ibid., 62.

[64] See ibid., 56.

[65] See ibid., 57.

[66] See Luigi Zingales, "Please Don't Feed the Businesses," *City Journal,* August 15, 2021, accessed August 17, 2021, https://www.city-journal.org/ending-crony-capitalism.

[67] See John G. Matsusaka, *Let the People Rule: How Direct Democracy Can Meet the Populist Challenge* (Princeton, NJ: Princeton University Press, 2020).

[68] Röpke, *Economics of the Free Society,* 25.

[69] Ryan Bourne, "Is This Time Different?" 1.

[70] Ibid., 6.

Chapter 7: Trading Nation

[1] See, for example, C.F. Goenner, "Uncertainty of the Liberal Peace," *Journal of Peace Research* 41, no. 5 (2004): 589-605; H.M Kim and D.L. Rousseau, "The Classical Liberals Were Half Right (or Half Wrong): New Tests of the 'Liberal Peace', 1960-88," *Journal of Peace Research* 42, no. 5 (2005): 523-543; and M.D. Ward, R.M. Siverson, and X. Cao, "Disputes, Democracies, and Dependencies: A Reexamination of the Kantian Peace," *American Journal of Political Science* 51, no. 3 (2007): 583-601.

[2] See David Hume, *Essays, Moral, Political, and Literary* (Indianapolis: Liberty Fund, 1752/1987), 85, 323-341.

[3] See ibid., 89, 92, 253-267, 308-31.

[4] George Washington, "From George Washington to Joseph Reed," May 28, 1780, accessed October 7, 2021, https://founders.archives.gov/documents/Washington/03-26-02-0150.

[5] Adam Smith, *The Theory of Moral Sentiments,* eds. D.D. Raphael and A.L. Macfie (Indianapolis: Liberty Fund, 1759/1982), VI.ii.2.4, 229.

[6] Ibid.

[7] Ibid., VI.ii.2.1-3, 227-9.

[8] See ibid.,VI.ii.2.3, 229.

[9] Smith, *Wealth of Nations,* Vol. I, IV.1.20, 440.

[10] See Maria Pia Paganelli and Reinhard Schumacher, "Do not take peace for granted: Adam Smith's warning on the relation between commerce and war," *Cambridge Journal of Economics* 43, no. 3 (2019): 785-797.

[11] Scott Lincicome, "Testing the 'China Shock': Was Normalizing Trade with China a Mistake?" Cato Institute Policy Analysis no. 895, July 8, 2020: 16, accessed August 16, 2021, https://www.cato.org/sites/cato.org/files/2020-07/PA-895-doi.pdf.

[12] "Full Text of Clinton's Speech on China Trade Bill," March 9, 2000, accessed August 16, 2021, https://www.iatp.org/sites/default/files/Full_Text_of_Clintons_Speech_on_China_Trade_Bi.htm.

[13] "Following are excerpts from prepared remarks by Governor George W. Bush of Texas today before Boeing workers, as provided by the Bush campaign," May 18, 2000, accessed August 16, 2021, https://www.nytimes.com/2000/05/18/world/in-bush-s-words-join-together-in-making-china-a-normal-trading-partner.html.

[14] Francis Fukuyama, *The End of History and the Last Man* (New York: Free Press, 1992/2006), xi.

[15] See Ezell, "False Promises II."

[16] National Security Strategy of the United States, December 2017, accessed August 16, 2021, https://trumpwhitehouse.archives.gov/wp-content/uploads/2017/12/NSS-Final-12-18-2017-0905-2.pdf.

[17] See Kurt M. Campbell and Ely Ratner, "The China Reckoning: How Beijing Defied American Expectations," *Foreign Affairs*, March/April 2018, accessed August 17, 2021, https://www.foreignaffairs.com/articles/china/2018-02-13/china-reckoning.

[18] See Jeffrey A. Bader and Ryan Hass, "Was pre-Trump U.S. policy towards China based on 'false' premises? China in Trump's National Security Strategy," Brookings Institution, December 22, 2017, accessed August 16, 2021, https://www.brookings.edu/blog/order-from-chaos/2017/12/22/was-pre-trump-u-s-policy-towards-china-based-on-false-premises/.

[19] See Steve Nelson, "Trump threatens to 'decouple' U.S. economy from China, accuses Biden of 'treachery'," *Market Watch*, September 8, 2020, accessed September 24, 2021, https://www.marketwatch.com/story/trump-threatens-to-decouple-u-s-economy-from-china-accuses-biden-of-treachery-11599553852.

[20] See Raj Varadarajan et al., "What's at Stake If the US and China Really Decouple," Boston Consulting Group, October 20, 2020, accessed September 24, 2021, https://www.bcg.com/publications/2020/high-stakes-of-decoupling-us-and-china.

[21] See Jeffrey D. Sachs, "Why the U.S. should pursue cooperation with China," *Project Syndicate*, February 25, 2021, accessed September 24, 2021, https://www.project-syndicate.org/commentary/biden-administration-should-pursue-cooperation-with-china-by-jeffrey-d-sachs-2021-02?barrier=accesspaylog.

[22] Lemieux, *What's Wrong with Protectionism*, 8.

[23] See Eric Nelson, "Global Supply Chain Explained . . . in One Graphic," US Chamber of Commerce, May 2, 2016, accessed August 17, 2021, https://www.uschamber.com/series/above-the-fold/global-supply-chains-explained-one-graphic.

[24] See Donald J. Boudreaux, "The Market Process Is Not an Intoxicated Ass," American Institute for Economic Research, accessed August 17, 2021, https://www.aier.org/article/the-market-process-is-not-an-intoxicated-ass/.

[25] See Lemieux, *What's Wrong with Protectionism?*, 70.

[26] See ibid.

[27] Romain Wacziarg and Karen Horn Welch, "Trade Liberalization and Growth: New Evidence," *World Bank Economic Review* 22, no.2 (2008): 212.

[28] International Monetary Fund, World Trade Organization, and the World Bank, *Making Trade an Engine of Growth for All: The Case for Trade and for Policies to Facilitate Adjustment* (Washington, D.C.: IMF, WTO, World Bank, 2017), 8.

[29] Ibid., 48.

[30] Ibid.

[31] See Lemieux, *What's Wrong with Protectionism?*, 67.

[32] See Lincicome, "Testing the 'China Shock': Was Normalizing Trade with China a Mistake?" 22-23.

[33] See Alan Berube and Cecile Murray, "Renewing America's economic promise through older industrial cities," Metropolitan Policy Program at Brookings Institution, April 2018, accessed October 14, 2021, https://www.brookings.edu/wp-content/uploads/2018/04/2018-04_brookings-metro_older-industrial-cities_full-report-berube_murray_-final-version_af4-18.pdf.

[34] Sait Akman et al., "Mitigating the Adjustment Costs of International Trade," *G20 Insights*, December 10, 2020, accessed August 17, 2021, https://www.g20-insights.org/policy_briefs/mitigating-the-adjustment-costs-of-international-trade/.

[35] See, for example, D.H. Autor et al., "The China Shock: Learning from labor-market adjustment to large changes in trade," *Annual Review of Economics* 8 (2016): 205-240.

[36] Sait Akman et al., "Mitigating the Adjustment Costs of International Trade."

[37] See Ilya Somin, "Voting with our Feet," *National Affairs* 49 (2021), accessed September 24, 2021, https://nationalaffairs.com/publications/detail/voting-with-our-feet.

[38] See Edward Glaeser and David Cutler, *Survival of the City: Living and Thriving in an Age of Isolation* (New York: Penguin Press, 2021), 243-318.

[39] See ibid.

[40] See, for example, Abraham S. Becker, "U.S.-Soviet Trade in the 1980s," *A RAND Note*, no.2682-RC, November 1987, accessed August 17, 2021, https://www.rand.org/content/dam/rand/pubs/notes/2009/N2682.pdf.

[41] See Wilhelm Röpke, *L'économie mondiale aux XIX et XX siècles* (Paris: Libraire Minard, 1959), 115-135.

[42] See Becker, "U.S.-Soviet Trade in the 1980s," v.

[43] See ibid.

[44] See Office of the United States Trade Representative, "The People's Republic of China: U.S.-China Trade Facts," accessed August 18, 2021, https://ustr.gov/countries-regions/china-mongolia-taiwan/peoples-republic-china.

[45] See ibid.

[46] See ibid.

[47] Smith, *Wealth of Nations*, Vol. I, IV.ii.30, 464-5.

[48] Ibid., Vol. I, IV.ii.24, 463.

[49] Ibid.

[50] See Oliver Morton Dickerson, *The Navigation Acts and the American Revolution* (Philadelphia, PA: University of Pennsylvania Press, 1951).

[51] See Smith, *Wealth of Nations*, Vol. I, IV.ii.30, 464.

[52] Ibid, Vol. I, IV.v.a.37, 523.

[53] Ibid, Vol. I, IV.v.a.36, 522.

[54] Ibid, Vol. II, IV.vii.b.44, 582.

[55] Milton and Rose D. Friedman, "The Case for Free Trade," *Hoover Digest*, no.4 (1997), accessed August 18, 2021, https://www.hoover.org/research/case-free-trade.

[56] Ibid.

[57] "Proclamation on Adjusting Imports of Derivative Aluminum Articles and Derivative Steel Articles into the United States," January 24, 2020, accessed October 14, 2021, https://trumpwhitehouse.archives.gov/presidential-actions/proclamation-adjusting-imports-derivative-aluminum-articles-derivative-steel-articles-united-states/.

[58] See Scott Lincicome and Inu Manak, "Protectionism or National Security? The Use and Abuse of Section 232," Cato Institute Policy Analysis no. 912, March 9, 2021: 4-5, accessed August 18, 2021, https://www.cato.org/policy-analysis/protectionism-or-national-security-use-abuse-section-232#.

[59] Department of Commerce, "The Effect of Imports of Automobiles and Automobile Parts on the National Security," February 17, 2019: 5, accessed August 18, 2021, https://www.bis.doc.gov/index.php/documents/section-232-investigations/2774-redacted-autos-232-final-and-appendix-a-july-2021/file. My emphasis.

[60] Ibid, 109.

[61] See Lincicome, "Manufactured Crisis," 35-36.

[62] Mike Watson, "Industrial Policy in the Real World," *National Affairs*, no. 41 (2021): 52.

[63] See World Trade Organization, "Report of the Working Party on the Accession of China" (WTO, November 10, 2001), Paragraph 203, accessed October 3, 2021, https://www.wto.org/english/thewto_e/acc_e/wp_acc_china_e.do; and Ezell, "False Promises II."

[64] See International Trade Commission, "U.S. Export Controls," accessed October 3, 3021, https://www.trade.gov/us-export-controls.

[65] See U.S. Department of Commerce, Bureau of Industry and Security, "United States Government Departments and Agencies with Export Control Responsibilities," accessed October 3, 2021, https://www.bis.doc.gov/index.php/about-bis/resource-links.

[66] See Emilia M. Jurzyk and Cian Ruane, "Resource Misallocation among Listed Firms in China: The Evolving Role of State-Owned Enterprises," IMF Working Paper no. 2021/075, March 12, 2021: 31, accessed January 30, 2021, https://www.imf.org/en/Publications/WP/Issues/2021/03/12/Resource-Misallocation-Among-Listed-Firms-in-China-The-Evolving-Role-of-State-Owned-50167.

[67] See Risk & Compliance Portal, "China Corruption Report," August 2020, accessed September 24, 2021, https://www.ganintegrity.com/portal/country-profiles/china-corruption-report/.

[68] Haas, *Stronger*, 26.

[69] See Jonathan Hillman, "How Big is China's Belt and Road Initiative?" Center for Strategic and International Studies, April 3, 2018, accessed December 7, 2021, https://www.csis.org/analysis/how-big-chinas-belt-and-road.

[70] See Tanner Green, "One Belt, One Road, One Big Mistake," *Foreign Policy*, December 6, 2018, accessed September 24, 2021, https://foreignpolicy.com/2018/12/06/bri-china-belt-road-initiative-blunder/.

[71] See, for example, Leo Lewis, "Companies prepare for a 'selective decoupling' with China," *Financial Times*, October 9, 2021, accessed October 10, 2021, https://www.ft.com/content/5ca525f7-cb40-468a-a294-5938d11af6a5; Liz Lin, "Yahoo Pulls Out of China, Ending Tumultuous Two-Decade Relationship," *Wall Street Journal*, November 2, 2021, accessed November 2, 2021, https://www.wsj.com/articles/yahoo-pulls-out-of-china-ending-tumultuous-two-decade-relationship-11635848926.

[72] See Josh Zumbrun and Stephanie Yang, "Chinese Tariffs Fuel Boom in U.S. Trade with Tech Exporter Taiwan," *Wall Street Journal*, December 5, 2021, accessed December 5, 2021, https://www.wsj.com/articles/us-china-taiwan-trade-11638663970?mod=hp_lead_pos4.

[73] See Nancy Hungerford, "Chinese theft of trade secrets on the rise, the US Justice Department warns," *CNBC*, September 22, 2019, accessed September 24, 2019, https://www.cnbc.com/2019/09/23/chinese-theft-of-trade-secrets-is-on-the-rise-us-doj-warns.html; and Dan Blumenthal and Linda Zhang, "China Is Stealing Our Technology and Intellectual Property. Congress Must Stop It," *National Review*, June 2, 2021, accessed September 30, 2021, https://www.nationalreview.com/2021/06/china-is-stealing-our-technology-and-intellectual-property-congress-must-stop-it/.

[74] See Christopher Balding and Donald C. Clarke, "Who Owns Huawei?" April 17, 2019, accessed September 23, 2021, https://ssrn.com/abstract=3372669.

[75] See Dan Strumpf, "Huawei Warns U.S. of Retaliation by Beijing; Profit Growth Slows," *Wall Street Journal*, March 31, 2020, accessed September 24, 2021, https://www.wsj.com/articles/huawei-warns-u-s-of-retaliation-by-beijing-profit-growth-slows-11585658329.

[76] See Corrine Ramey and Kate O'Keeffe, "China's Huawei Charged With Racketeering, Stealing Trade Secrets," *Wall Street Journal*, February 13, 2021, accessed September 24, 2021, https://www.wsj.com/articles/chinas-huawei-charged-with-racketeering-11581618336.

[77] See Danielle Cave et al., "Mapping more of China's tech giants: AI and surveillance," ASPI International Cyber Policy Centre, Issues Paper Report no. 24/2019, November, 2019, accessed September 24, 2021, https://www.aspi.org.au/report/mapping-more-chinas-tech-giants.

[78] See Joseph Marks, "The Cybersecurity 202: How Huawei helped extend China's repressive view of Internet freedom to African nations," *Washington Post*, August 15, 2019, accessed September 24, 2021, https://www.washingtonpost.com/news/powerpost/paloma/the-cybersecurity-202/2019/08/15/the-cybersecurity-202-how-huawei-helped-extend-china-s-repressive-view-of-internet-freedom-to-african-nations/5d547a72602ff15f906576c3/.

[79] See Jennifer Jacobs, "Biden Blocks 59 Chinese Companies in Amended Trump Order," *Bloomberg*, June 3, 2021, accessed December 7, 2021, https://www.bloomberg.com/news/articles/2021-06-03/biden-to-blacklist-59-chinese-companies-in-amended-trump-order.

[80] See Public Law No: 116-222 (12/18/2020), "Holding Foreign Companies Accountable Act," accessed October 13, 2021, https://www.congress.gov/bill/116th-congress/senate-bill/945/all-info.

[81] See Robert Olsen, "Trump Signs Bill That Could Delist Chinese Companies from U.S. Stock Exchanges," *Forbes*, December 18, 2020, accessed September 24, 2021, https://www.forbes.com/sites/robertolsen/2020/12/18/trump-signs-bill-that-could-delist-chinese-companies-from-us-stock-exchanges/?sh=d6d706c635c0.

[82] See, for example, Nathan Picarsic and Emily de La Bruyère (with contributions by Adrian Zenz), *Corporate Complicity Scorecard: An Assessment of U.S. Companies' Exposure to Military Modernization, Surveillance, and Human Rights Violations in the People's Republic of China* (Washington, D.C.: Victims of Communism/Horizon Advisory, 2022), accessed February 8, 2022, https://victimsofcommunism.org/wp-content/uploads/2022/02/Corporate-Complicity-Scorecard-2.3.22.pdf.

[83] See Jeffrey G. Richardson et al., "Recent Developments on U.S. Ban on American Investment in Chinese Military Companies," *National Law Review*, February 17, 2021, accessed February 8, 2022, https://www.natlawreview.com/article/recent-developments-us-ban-american-investment-chinese-military-companies.

[84] Irwin, *Clashing over Commerce*, 69.

[85] Gregory M. Collins, *Commerce and Manners in Edmund Burke's Political Economy* (Cambridge: Cambridge University Press, 2020), 209.

[86] Ibid., 211.

[87] Ibid.

[88] Ibid., 212.

[89] Nancy F. Koehn, *The Power of Commerce: Economy and Governance in the First British Empire* (Ithaca: Cornell University Press, 1994), 199.

[90] See Collins, *Commerce and Manners*, 239.

[91] See ibid, 238.

[92] Ibid., 241.

[93] Ibid., 240.

[94] See L. Stuart Sutherland, "Edmund Burke and the First Rockingham Ministry," *English Historical Review* 47 (1932): 66.

[95] Edmund Burke, "Letter to a Noble Lord," eds. Paul Langford et al., *The Writings and Speeches of Edmund Burke*, Vol. IX, Part 1 (Oxford: Clarendon Press, 1796/1991), 159.

[96] Collins, *Commerce and Manners*, 238.

[97] Edmund Burke, "A Short Account of a Late Short Administration," eds. Paul Langford et al., *The Writings and Speeches of Edmund Burke*, Vol. II. (Oxford: Clarendon Press, 1766/1981), 55.

[98] Collins, *Commerce and Manners*, 211.

[99] Ibid., 247.

Chapter 8: A Commercial Republic

[1] Thomas Jefferson, *Writings: Autobiography/Notes on the State of Virginia*, ed. Merrill D. Peterson (New York: Library of America, 1984), Query XIX, 290-1.

[2] George Washington, "From George Washington to Edward Newenham, 29 August 1788," National Archives, Founders Online, accessed August 24, 2021, https://founders.archives.gov/GEWN-04-06-02-0436.

[3] Henry Clay, "Speech of Henry Clay on American Industry, in the House of Representatives, March 30 and 31, 1824," in *State Papers and Speeches on the Tariff*, with an Introduction by F.W. Taussig (Cambridge, MA: Harvard University, 1892), 316.

[4] See Henry Clay, "The American System," February 2, 3, and 6, 1832 (In the Senate), ed. Wendy Wolff, *The Senate, 1789-1989: Classic Speeches, 1830-1993*, Vol. 3, Bicentennial Edition (Washington, D.C.: U.S. Government Printing Office, 1994), 91, accessed August 21, 2021, https://www.senate.gov/artandhistory/history/resources/pdf/AmericanSystem.pdf.

[5] Clay, "Speech of Henry Clay on American Industry," 316.

[6] See *Annals of Congress*, 4/2/1824, 2028.

[7] See Ibid, 4/30/1824, 649.

[8] See Watson, "Industrial Policy in the Real World," 47.

[9] John L. Larson, *Internal Improvement: National Public Works and the Promise of Popular Government in the Early United States* (Chapel Hill, NC: University of North Carolina Press, 2011), 165-166.

[10] See Irwin, *Clashing Over Commerce*, 158.

[11] "Rubio Delivers Lecture on How the Bipartisan Economic Consensus Is Destroying American Greatness," accessed December 9, 2021, https://www.rubio.senate.gov/public/index.cfm/2021/12/rubio-delivers-lecture-on-how-the-bipartisan-economic-consensus-is-destroying-american-greatness.

[12] Elizabeth Warren, "Defend and Create American Jobs," June 4, 2019, accessed August 22, 2021, https://elizabethwarren.com/plans/american-jobs.

[13] Ibid.

[14] Ibid.

[15] Elizabeth Warren, "A New Approach to Trade," July 29, 2019, accessed August 22, 2021, https://elizabethwarren.com/plans/new-approach-trade.

[16] See Elizabeth Warren, "Leading Green Manufacturing," June 4, 2019, accessed August 22, 2021, https://elizabethwarren.com/plans/american-jobs.

[17] Warren, "Defend and Create American Jobs."

[18] Elizabeth Warren, "End Wall Street's Stranglehold on our Economy," July 18, 2019, accessed August 22, 2021, https://elizabethwarren.com/plans/american-jobs.

[19] Warren, "Defend and Create American Jobs."

[20] For more on this point, see David L. Bahnsen, *Elizabeth Warren: How Her Presidency Would Destroy the Middle Class and the American Dream* (New York: Post Hill Press, 2020).

[21] See Samuel Gregg, "Free Trade Lessons from the British Empire," *Law and Liberty*, June 14, 2021, accessed August 23, 2021, https://lawliberty.org/free-trade-lessons-from-the-british-empire/.

[22] F.A. Hayek, "The Economic Conditions of Interstate Federalism" (1939), reprinted in *Individualism and Economic Order* (London: Routledge & Kegan Paul, 1949/1976), 269.

[23] F.A. Hayek, *The Road To Serfdom* (London: Routledge & Kegan Paul, 1944/1976), 175.

[24] F.A. Hayek, *The Constitution of Liberty: The Definitive Edition*, ed. Ronald Hamowy (Chicago: University of Chicago Press, 1960/2011), 38.

[25] See Michael Novak, *The Spirit of Democratic Capitalism* (New York: Lanham Books, 1982/1991), 19-21.

[26] See Jacques Maritain, *Reflections on America* (New York: Charles Scribner's Sons, 1958), 29-42, 101-120, 161-202.

[27] Novak, *The Spirit of Democratic Capitalism*, 116.

[28] Ibid., 117.

[29] See Ralph Lerner, "Commerce and Character: The Anglo-American as New-Model Man," *William and Mary Quarterly* 39 (January 1979): 3-26.

[30] See Federalist 49, *Federalist Papers: Primary Documents in American History*, accessed August 24, 2021, https://guides.loc.gov/federalist-papers/text-41-50#s-lg-box-wrapper-25493416.

[31] *The Papers of Alexander Hamilton*, eds. Harold C. Syrett et al. (New York: Columbia University Press, 1961-1987), Vol. 4, 140.

[32] Federalist 10.

[33] Anthony A. Peacock, *Vindicating the Commercial Republic* (Lanham, MD: Lexington Books, 2018), 139.

[34] Federalist 11, *Federalist Papers: Primary Documents in American History*, accessed August 24, 2021, https://guides.loc.gov/federalist-papers/text-11-20#s-lg-box-wrapper-25493283.

[35] Federalist 35, *Federalist Papers: Primary Documents in American History*, accessed August 24, 2021, https://guides.loc.gov/federalist-papers/text-31-40.

[36] Ibid.

[37] See D.R. McCoy, *The Elusive Republic: Political Economy in Jeffersonian America* (Chapel Hill: University of North Carolina Press, 1980), 86-87.

[38] See Robert E. Wright, "Rise of the Corporation Nation," in *Founding Choices*, 288.

[39] Federalist 62, *Federalist Papers: Primary Documents in American History*, accessed August 24, 2021, https://guides.loc.gov/federalist-papers/text-61-70#s-lg-box-wrapper-25493449.

[40] Federalist 11.

[41] Federalist 12, *Federalist Papers: Primary Documents in American History*, accessed August 24, 2021, https://guides.loc.gov/federalist-papers/text-11-20#s-lg-box-wrapper-25493283.

[42] Federalist 6, *Federalist Papers: Primary Documents in American History*, accessed August 24, 2021, https://guides.loc.gov/federalist-papers/text-1-10#s-lg-box-wrapper-25493269.

[43] Ibid.

[44] Ibid.

[45] Michael Novak, *Free Persons and the Common Good* (New York: Madison Books, 1989), 105.

[46] See Wood, *Power and Liberty*, 58.

[47] Federalist 11.

[48] Federalist 7, *Federalist Papers: Primary Documents in American History*, accessed August 24, 2021, https://guides.loc.gov/federalist-papers/text-1-10#s-lg-box-wrapper-25493269.

[49] Federalist 6.

50 Ibid.

51 See Hume, *Essays, Moral, Political, and Literary*, 273-4.

52 Federalist 55, *Federalist Papers: Primary Documents in American History*, accessed August 24, 2021, https://guides. loc.gov/federalist-papers/text-51-60#s-lg-box-wrapper-2549343.

53 See *Papers of Alexander Hamilton*, eds. Harold C. Syrett et al., December 1791-January 1792 (New York: Columbia University Press, 1966), Vol. 10, 262-263.

54 Irwin, *Clashing over Commerce*, 86.

55 Michael P. Federici, *The Political Philosophy of Alexander Hamilton* (Baltimore: John Hopkins University Press, 2012), 15.

56 See Irwin, *Clashing over Commerce*, 87.

57 See Douglas A. Irwin, "The Aftermath of Hamilton's 'Report on Manufactures'," *Journal of Economic History* 64, no. 3 (2004): 800-821.

58 See Matthew Spalding and Patrick J. Garrity, *A Sacred Union of Citizens: George Washington's Farewell Address and the American Character* (New York: Rowman & Littlefield, 1996), 46-55.

59 George Washington, "Farewell Address, September 17, 1796," The American Presidency Project, accessed August 24, 2021, https://www.presidency.ucsb.edu/documents/farewell-address.

60 Ibid.

61 Washington supported Hamilton's *Report on Manufactures* which proposed some limited proto-industrial policy, but doubted whether issuing bounties for such purposes was constitutional. See Spalding and Garrity, *A Sacred Union of Citizens*, 37.

62 Washington, "Farewell Address, September 17, 1796."

63 George Washington, "From George Washington to Lafayette, August 15, 1786," National Archives, Founders Online, accessed October 7, 2021, https://founders.archives.gov/documents/Washington/04-04-02-0200.

64 George Washington, "To Thomas Jefferson from George Washington, March 29, 1784," National Archives, Founders Online, accessed August 24, 2021, https://founders.archives.gov/documents/Jefferson/01-07-02-0052.

65 George Washington, "From George Washington to Benjamin Harrison, October 10, 1784," National Archives, Founders Online, accessed August 24, 2021, https://founders.archives.gov/documents/Washington/04-02-02-0082.

66 Guy de Montesquieu, *The Spirit of Laws* (New York: Prometheus Books, 2002), bk. 20.7, 321.

67 Federici, *The Political Philosophy of Alexander Hamilton*, 194-5, 238-9.

68 See Sir James Steuart, *An Inquiry into the Principles of Political Economy: Being an Essay on the Domestic Policy in Free Nations*, ed. A.S. Skinner (Edinburgh and Chicago: Oliver &Boyd, [1767] 1966), 196.

69 See Samuel Gregg, "George Washington's Constitutional Morality," *Public Discourse*, July 27, 2016, accessed August 24, 2021, https://www.thepublicdiscourse.com/2016/07/17081/.

70 George Washington, "Farewell Address, September 17, 1796."

INDEX